Jesus and the Politics of Mammon

Critical Theory and Biblical Studies

The Critical Theory and Biblical Studies Series (CTBS) publishes ground-breaking monographs that bring together critical theory and biblical studies. It publishes works in which past, present, and future innovations in critical theory shed light on the study of biblical texts. But CTBS also provides a crucial space for scholars to inform critically the themes and trends present in the broader field of critical theory. Far from "theory" being a fling of the 1980s in which biblical scholars could briefly dabble only to swiftly move on, it is increasingly clear that theoretical reflection on the frameworks, "foundations" and underpinnings of biblical interpretation are crucial for any scholarly enterprise, as well as impacting practices and ideologies that emerge from particular interpretations, relating for instance to race, class, and gender.

In the last decades, with the so-called "turn to religion," many prominent figures associated with critical theory are turning to the biblical archive, mining it for ideas and tropes to rethink European history and its philosophical heritage, to mobilize political thought and action, and to posit new directions for philosophical thought. Figures such as Jacques Derrida, Alain Badiou, Slavoj Žižek, and Giorgio Agamben are providing renewed stimulus to biblical studies in their fascination with this ancient archive. Critical engagement with their uses of the Bible, however, remains largely neglected among biblical scholars. At this juncture, it is necessary to provide a scholarly space for biblical scholars to become more prominent interlocutors in these debates, by contributing an expertise and knowledge of the Bible and its history of interpretation largely lacking in critical theory. Further, it is imperative for biblical scholars to analyze and reflect on what this turn to the Bible signifies, what assumptions are at play in these debates, and how scholars can build on this turn in critical and constructive ways.

Among the issues in critical theory that will be addressed in the series include: Gender studies, Marxist theory, postcolonialism, structuralism, post-structuralism, deconstruction, postmodernism, reconstructivism, psychoanalytic theory, queer theory, semiotics, cultural anthropology, theories of identity, linguistic theories of literature, animal studies, posthumanism, and eco-criticism.

Series Editorial Board:
Ward Blanton, *University of Kent, UK*
James Crossley, *St. Mary's University, Twickenham, London, UK*
Paul Middleton, *University of Chester, UK*
Robert Myles, *Murdoch University, AU*
Christina Petterson, *Australian National University, AU*
Hollis Phelps, *Mercer University, US*
Hannah M. Strømmen, *University of Chichester, UK*
Fatima Tofighi, *University of Religions, Qom, Iran*
J. Brian Tucker, *Moody Theological Seminary, US*

Forthcoming titles in the series:
Acts of Empire, Second Edition: The Acts of the Apostles and Imperial Ideology by Christina Petterson

Jesus and the Politics of Mammon

HOLLIS PHELPS

CASCADE *Books* • Eugene, Oregon

JESUS AND THE POLITICS OF MAMMON

Critical Theory and Biblical Studies

Copyright © 2019 Hollis Phelps. All rights reserved. Except for brief quotations in critical publications or reviews, no part of this book may be reproduced in any manner without prior written permission from the publisher. Write: Permissions, Wipf and Stock Publishers, 199 W. 8th Ave., Suite 3, Eugene, OR 97401.

Cascade Books
An Imprint of Wipf and Stock Publishers
199 W. 8th Ave., Suite 3
Eugene, OR 97401

www.wipfandstock.com

PAPERBACK ISBN: 978-1-5326-6447-2
HARDCOVER ISBN: 978-1-5326-6448-9
EBOOK ISBN: 978-1-5326-6449-6

Cataloguing-in-Publication data:

Names: Phelps, Hollis, author.

Title: Jesus and the politics of mammon. / Hollis Phelps.

Description: Eugene, OR: Cascade Books, 2019 | Series: Critical Theory and Biblical Studies | Includes bibliographical references and index.

Identifiers: ISBN 978-1-5326-6447-2 (paperback) | ISBN 978-1-5326-6448-9 (hardcover) | ISBN 978-1-5326-6449-6 (ebook)

Subjects: LCSH: Money—Biblical teaching. | Wealth—Biblical teaching. | Jesus Christ-Teachings. | Bible—Criticism, interpretation, etc.

Classification: BS2545.W37 P44 2019 (paperback) | BS2545.W37 (ebook)

Manufactured in the U.S.A.   10/18/19

For Paula

Contents

Acknowledgments | ix

INTRODUCTION
A Radical Christ: Jesus against Money, Work, and Family | 1

CHAPTER 1
Mammon and the Problem of Desire | 13

CHAPTER 2
Exchange, State, and Debt | 45

CHAPTER 3
Against Work and Family | 83

CHAPTER 4
Excess Against Asceticism | 125

Bibliography | 169
Index | 173

Acknowledgments

After a brief talk on the topic of Jesus and politics that I gave at the University of Mount Olive, my then colleague Christopher Skinner suggested I write a book on the subject. I laughed, telling him that I'd never write a book on Jesus. After thinking about it some more, I decided to give it a shot. I doubt that what follows is exactly what he had in mind, but here it is nonetheless (and it should go without saying that Chris bears no responsibility for any of the content).

Portions of this book were discussed at Loyola University Chicago, where in 2017 I had the pleasure of participating in a graduate theological colloquium held by Colby Dickinson. I am grateful to him and his students for the opportunity, incisive comments, and rigorous discussion. I also presented portions of this book at the University of Denver in 2017, where I was a Marsico Visiting Scholar. Thanks to Sarah Pessin, Carl Raschke, Thomas Nail, Ryne Beddard, Mason Davis, and Joshua Hanan for their hospitality and careful appreciation of my work.

While thinking about, writing, and editing this book, I have had numerous dialogue partners. I'd like to thank in particular Karen Bray, Jeffrey Robbins, Clayton Crockett, Will Schanbacher, Katy Scrogin, Bo Eberle, and Jordon Miller.

Finally, and on a more personal note, Alden, Sebastian, Jeronimo, and Luci deserve mention. They, individually and collectively, give me meaning in a world that otherwise often seems meaningless. As does Paula Del Rio, whose companionship is perhaps best described as a grace. I do not have enough words to express my gratitude to and for her. She knows why.

INTRODUCTION

A Radical Christ
Jesus against Money, Work, and Family

A REVOLUTIONARY JESUS?

In 2007 the well-known leftwing publisher Verso put out an edition of the Gospels in its *Revolutions* series.[1] The goal of the series is to resurrect the power of past revolutionary texts for our contemporary situation, with the hope that they may help "ignite new revolutions." Few would disagree with the revolutionary bona fides of many of the figures included in the series. Mao, Castro, Trotsky, Bolivar, Muntzer, Ho Chi Minh, Toussaint L'Ouverture, and even Thomas Jefferson all make an appearance. The status of Jesus Christ, however, seems less clear.

Terry Eagleton's introduction to the edition shares this initial skepticism. His essay begins with a simple question, "Was Jesus a revolutionary?" Eagleton's question is not rhetorical but genuine, and in the end he provides a somewhat ambivalent answer. If by "revolutionary" we have in mind a first-century version of a Lenin bent on overthrowing Rome, then we will be sorely disappointed. Jesus, to be sure, seems to have kept company with at least some Zealot insurrectionists, and often acted in ways that easily could have been interpreted by his disciples, the crowds that gathered around him, the religious establishment, and the Roman authorities as seditious.

1. Eagleton, *Terry Eagleton Presents*.

Nevertheless, even if Jesus considered his mission primarily in terms of a direct confrontation with the authorities, which is unlikely, Eagleton rightly notes that "the idea of a wandering charismatic with a largely unarmed, sizeable but not massive retinue could destroy the temple or overthrow the state was absurd, as the Jewish and Roman authorities must have recognized. There were thousands of temple guards, not to speak of the Roman garrison."[2] For Eagleton, the idea that Jesus was a revolutionary in that sense of the term is simply a non-starter, despite the occasional claims made otherwise.

Perhaps such ambivalence when it comes to the status of the relationship between Jesus and politics explains why some on the left have recently found an ally in Paul, rather than Jesus. Like Jesus, Paul certainly did not conceive of his gospel in terms of an antagonistic conflict with the state. Paul urges his compatriots in Rome to "be subject to the governing authorities; for there is no authority except from God, and those authorities that exist have been instituted by God" (Rom 13:1). Yet there remains a novelty in Paul's thought, a novelty that pries open sedimented structures and patterns of thought and pushes toward the revolutionary. Because Paul is basically the architect of much of what we now consider Christianity, the form and content of his thought contain a wealth of material that the insurrectionist may find useful. This is why major theological sea changes often find their impetus in a return to and reinvigoration of the apostle and his thought.[3] It also helps explain why many otherwise non-religious thinkers on the left have found it important to mine Paul's letters for philosophical and political insight. Thus, for Giorgio Agamben, Paul's letters are essential for dismantling and thinking beyond our current biopolitical predicaments, because his letters remain "the fundamental messianic text for the Western tradition."[4] Likewise, Alain Badiou's "reactivation" of the apostle reads him as "a poet-thinker of the event," even "a Lenin for whom Christ will have been the equivocal Marx."[5]

What follows is by no means an attempt to discredit these and other contemporary appropriations of Paul. Those who have turned to the apostle have, in their own ways, breathed new life into his thought, and in this sense such studies remain indispensable for philosophers and theorists, theologians proper and those who, like myself, find themselves situated in the spaces between these discourses. Yet the interest shown in Paul has almost

---

2. Eagleton, *Terry Eagleton Presents*, xi.
3. Robbins, "Politics of Paul," 89–94.
4. Agamben, *Time that Remains*, 1.
5. Badiou, *Saint Paul*, 3.

completely ignored or, to use Badiou's words, rendered "equivocal" the individual behind Paul's thought: Jesus of Nazareth.

That Jesus of Nazareth has not piqued similar interest is, on one level, not surprising. Paul himself in his letters shows little to no concern for what Jesus said and did, focusing instead on matters of what we could call theology. Paul must have been familiar with stories about what Jesus said and did, yet if we stick strictly to Paul's letters these appear to play no explicit role in his thought. Badiou makes much of this absence. For Badiou, the gospels are "obviously" meant to "emphasize Jesus' *exploits*, his life's exceptional singularity."[6] Badiou notes that, in the gospels, "All the trusted staples of religious thaumaturgy and charlatanism are abundantly mobilized: miraculous cures, walking on water, divinations and announcements, resuscitation of the dead, abnormal meteorological phenomena, laying on of hands, instantaneous multiplication of victuals.... Jesus' style, as recounted to us by the gospels, is in complete accordance with this itinerant magician's paraphernalia."[7] Paul ignores all of this, subtracting from the mythological shell that we find in the gospels an essential core: the resurrection of the crucified. Thus, on Badiou's reading of Paul, "there will be no parables, no learned obscurities, no subjective indecision, no veiling of truth. The paradox of faith must be brought out as it is, borne by prose into the light of its radical novelty."[8]

I suspect that others who have turned to Paul, sidestepping Jesus, feel similarly. However one feels about Paul, he is still, in a sense, removed from the center of Christianity, which is somewhat paradoxical given that he is its most recognizable and significant founder. One can thus appreciate his thought without making him an object of pious reflection or devotion. That is, one can, as Badiou does, understand him in formal terms, irrespective of theological content.

It is, however, more difficult to separate Jesus from mythology, much less theology. For the theological tradition, the church, and even still in much of the popular imaginary, Jesus is not so much a thinker as is Paul but, rather, an object of faith. What Jesus said and did, in other words, is completely wrapped up in who he putatively is, or at least claims to be. If and when Jesus is taken as a thinker in his own right, his thought is often reduced to a species of moralizing discourse. Loving our neighbor as ourselves, for instance, is all well and good, and may indeed make us "better"

---

6. Badiou, *Saint Paul*, 32.
7. Badiou, *Saint Paul*, 32–33.
8. Badiou, *Saint Paul*, 33.

people and ultimately benefit others, but it does not exactly constitute a radical trajectory.

The goal of what follows is an attempt to redress this situation. In the spirit of Badiou, I attempt to take Jesus out of the realm of piety, both in terms of expected piety toward him and of what he supposedly expects from us morally. I attempt to position him as a thinker in his own right, one whose discourse, embodied in his words and deeds, constitutes a form of disruption to the status quo. That disruption, which also offers glimmers of alternatives, does not, however, occur directly. Eagleton's apparent ambivalence is, I think, well placed in this sense. Jesus is not, on my account, a revolutionary in the strict sense of the term, meaning that he does not come out against the state directly in the form of insurrection. Rather, he focuses his attention on the institutions and social relationships that allow the state to function; that is, he focuses his attention on matters related to what Bruno Gulli calls a "social ontology."[9]

It is important to emphasize that this is not the same thing as saying that Jesus is a reformer, that his goal is merely to reshape existing institutions as a way to make them more equitable. Jesus may not be a state revolutionary, in the sense described above, but he is also no "liberal" reformer. Jesus' emphasis on social ontology rejects the false choice between these two options by rejecting the institutions and relationships themselves. He does not do this, I argue, as a means of withdrawing from the world, although there are moments in his thought that appear at first glance to move in this direction. Rather, he does so as a means of rethinking the world itself, which includes rethinking how human beings relate to each other through various media, broadly construed. The focus on social ontology, then, is a means of overthrowing the social, which indirectly foments insurrection against the state immanently, from within.

On my account, Jesus focuses his attention on three main institutions: money, work, and the family. He filters all of these, I argue, through one, primary disjunction: God or mammon. As I discuss in chapter 1, interpreters often rightly take mammon as referring directly to wealth or, more narrowly, money. Money and wealth, however, do not exist in isolation; they are irretrievably connected to the institutions of work and the family. We see this in Jesus' thought, as I suggest throughout, in the way in which the disjunction between God and mammon repeats itself in work and family. I use the term "mammon" throughout this book in a much broader sense, then: it certainly refers to wealth and money, but also to related institutions, such as work and the family. For this reason, the disjunction between God

---

9. Gulli, *Labor of Fire*.

and mammon becomes an organizing principle, or perhaps an incitement for refashioning the world, which for Jesus takes the name of the kingdom of heaven or God.

Jesus' critique of these social institutions and his suggestion of an alternative, however, do not constitute a program. Although we are, at times, given suggestions and glimmers of hope, these do not constitute a blueprint that would indicate how such a refashioning is possible. This is an important point to emphasize, and it fits with the shape of Jesus' discourse itself. In what follows, I provide very strong readings of Jesus' attack on money, work, and family. As I discuss in chapters 1 and 2, for instance, Jesus' critique of mammon is not merely about our dispositions with respect to money and wealth but, rather, money and wealth *as such*. The disjunction between God and mammon, that is, is real, and if anything is to be taken literally in the Bible, this should be it. The immediate objection to such a reading, which I also mark similarly in relation to work and family, is that the upshot is not only impractical but impossible. It certainly is, but that is really the whole point: the apparent impossibility of what Jesus suggests is the very means through which he incites us to think otherwise. Attenuating the force of Jesus' words and deeds to make them more palatable is, really, a means of denying them. By doing so, we miss out on the possibilities that they contain for a radical re-envisioning of thought, practice, and relationality. It is left up to us to put the disjunction to use, but to do that, we must take the full force of it seriously, no matter how inconceivable it might first appear.

A WORD ABOUT METHOD, THEOLOGY, AND LANGUAGE

What follows is, in a way, a book about Jesus, but not in the traditional sense. Although I provide a reading of Jesus—or, rather, certain portions of the texts that constitute our knowledge of him—my goal is not to produce an authoritative portrait of him, theologically or historically. In terms of theology, I largely bracket traditional theological concerns about who the church claims Jesus is. Otherwise put, if for Badiou Paul is not an apostle, for me in what follows, Jesus is not the Son of God, at least in the sense that the theological traditional has given that title. I do not argue against such a claim but, rather, largely ignore it as a thematic concern.

My reasons for doing so are twofold. First, bracketing the theological claims made for Jesus, bracketing, that is, the so-called religious sense of the gospels, opens the latter up to new and different readings and uses, ones unconstrained by the weight of theological reception. That reception, I routinely suggest throughout, tends to blunt the force of much of what Jesus says, in the name of theological and social respectability. Second, bracketing theological claims about Jesus also allows us to reconsider the apparent impossibility of what he says and does. The theological tradition has, again, tended to associate much of the latter with Jesus' supposed uniqueness, his divine status. So-called miracles—say the feeding of the five thousand—serve primarily to indicate something *about* Jesus. If and when they are interpreted as broader in scope, as indicative of a possible alternative, that scope is limited due to our finitude. They are, in other words, proleptic in nature, signs of the *future* coming of God's kingdom. Bracketing theological claims about Jesus, however, allows us to reconsider his words and deeds as incitements to the here and now, indicating what is possible in the present, even if the form may seem impossible.

Even though I for the most part bracket theological claims about Jesus, I still use theological, quasi-theological, and popular religious language throughout. Part of this has to do with the nature of Jesus' discourse. It is obviously saturated with the language of God and God's kingdom. But rather than attempt to reword what he says into a more general philosophical lexicon, to "secularize" it, I repeat it and use it, putting it into direct dialogue with other, non-theological lexicons. I want to be clear that this is not out of any covert, pious desire to restate traditional theological tropes, or out of any expressed "belief" in the object to which Jesus refers. My point, in other words, is not to reposition theology and its God over against the world, in simplistic, metaphysical fashion. Rather, I use such terminology because the force of Jesus' pronouncements is contained in the language he uses. The problem with sacrificing theological language at the altar of philosophical conceptuality and consistency is that something is lost in the process. I put Jesus' theological language in direct relationship to the language of other thinkers throughout, in the hope that the sense of both will emerge immanently, through that interaction. Generally speaking—and it is a principle that I think extends beyond the confines of this book—my repetition of theological language is about using that language and various tropes without regard to their proper sense, as a means of creating something new. Ultimately, on my reading, the name of God and its cognates signify an alternative, an opening of possibilities within sedimented systems, and so I use that name freely, as does Jesus, without regard to provenance. The language of theology is not proprietary.

If what follows, then, is not theology in the traditional sense of the term, it is also not one more critical attempt to provide a historically and contextually accurate portrait of Jesus, or even of how he is portrayed in one particular gospel. As valuable as such studies are, mine should not—and would not—be included among them. Indeed, although I draw on historical-critical materials when it is absolutely necessary, my overall approach is to read Jesus as a contemporary, as Badiou does with Paul. I read him, in other words, with contemporary concerns in mind, concerns related to the neoliberal organization of the world along the lines of money, work, and family. Rather than situating his discourse in light of his contemporaries, as a biblical scholar would, I situate it in light of some of ours. Indeed, although what follows is in some way informed by contemporary critical discourses within the realm of biblical studies, I on the whole ignore conventions associated with the latter.

For example, it is a scholarly commonplace that Jesus is presented differently in each of the four gospels. A "responsible" reading would respect those differences, teasing out the overt and sometimes subtle differences among those portrayals. I instead draw freely from among the gospels, without much regard to provenance. This is not because of any disagreement, necessarily, or worse laziness. As with my treatment of theology, it is again about bracketing sedimented discourses to hopefully produce new readings. Ignoring the lines that divide the gospels from each other allows me to isolate and draw out what Deleuze and Guattari might call certain "lines of flight" that occur among the gospels, without any concern for authorial or editorial intent.

I am fully aware that such an approach opens me to the charge of anachronism and irresponsibility, of "reading in" to the texts at issue what I want to find in and among them. It is worth saying that no matter how careful one is, a certain amount of "reading in" is usually inevitable, especially in constructive work. This is not necessarily out of any sort of nefarious desire but simply a facet of the fact that we always approach texts from our own situation and with our own concerns in mind, which do not often line up with those present in and behind the materials under consideration. So much seems especially the case with readings of Jesus, as others have emphasized.[10]

Nevertheless, there are different ways of being anachronistic and irresponsible. On the one hand, anachronism can creep in through simple ignorance, whether it is intentional or not. Again, a certain amount of ignorance is, it seems, unavoidable, which is why all reading is at least to some extent interpretation. But one can also practice a deliberate anachronism and ignorance, suspending the conditions that produced the materials under consideration as a means of making them available for new uses. Such an

---

10. Albert Schweitzer's point concerning the way in which historical reconstructions of Jesus mirror the concerns of the author still stands. See his *Quest of the Historical Jesus*.

approach may produce what we might call a "short circuit" in our received assumptions and the texts themselves, which opens them up for reconsideration and, more importantly, novel appropriations for both thought and practice.[11]

My attempt to read Jesus as our contemporary can be understood along these lines, but the "short circuit" runs in both directions. That is, it is not merely the case that I read Jesus in light of certain strands of contemporary critical theory and philosophy related to money, work, and family. Nor is it the case that I do the opposite, reading contemporary theory and philosophy in light of Jesus. Either approach risks devaluing one side of the conversation, giving the impression of some sort of inadequacy. The goal is, rather, to read them together, to read them vis-a-vis one another simultaneously, without necessarily privileging one over the other. Another way to put the matter is that I read Jesus as a thinker whose thought demands that it be read with and among other thinkers.

At the end of the day, it is about thinking with Jesus today, in the present, rather than simply about him and his context. My goal in what follows, then, is not to think what Jesus thinks, to conceptualize his thought into a coherent whole. Given the nature of the source material, I doubt that that is even possible. Rather than a systematic approach, my approach, then, is to grasp certain moments in his thought, to pull at certain threads and trace various lines so as to use him as a resource for the development of a social ontology focused on money, work, and family. To borrow the language of Badiou, it is about releasing or resurrecting certain eventual components contained in Jesus' words and deeds.

OUTLINE OF THE BOOK

In order to work through the disjunction between God and mammon and the way in which it cuts through the social field for Jesus, it is obviously necessary to understand Jesus' expressed attitudes toward wealth and money. Indeed, the disjunction between the two, which Jesus presents in terms of an antagonism, is the guiding thematic through which Jesus filters his critique of money and wealth and, by extension, work and family. Accordingly, in chapter 1, I begin by drawing attention to the real, that is, material, distinction Jesus marks between God and mammon. Filling out the sense of the disjunction requires understanding what mammon actually is and how it functions, a task that is fundamental to the book as a whole. Nevertheless, as

---

11. I borrow the use of the term "short circuit" here from the MIT Press Series *Short Circuits*. See https://mitpress.mit.edu/books/series/short-circuits.

a way into its sense, I briefly provide a broad statement of the way in which mammon becomes personified as a force set over against God. If mammon is understood in this way, it is not primarily because it is ascribed certain abstract qualities that cohere with deity but, rather, because it functions as a competing locus of value. Jesus' attitudes toward mammon, or here more particularly qua money and wealth, are by no means unique in the ancient world and later Christian traditions. I thus provide a brief survey of such attitudes to help situate the disjunction within a broader narrative. The discussion of various attitudes toward money and wealth, read through mammon in the Christian theological tradition, allows me in addition to add another layer to its personification. Mammon competes with God, but this is because, once established, mammon acts with a force that is opposed to God but that also resists subjective motivations.

Mammon's autonomy from the subject, to individual desires, is crucial to the argument of the chapter and book as a whole. The mainstream of the Christian theological tradition has as a whole taken the disjunction between God and mammon in primarily subjective terms. That is, when Jesus critiques money and wealth, he is not critiquing them as such but, rather, our attitudes toward them. The question of money and wealth is, in this sense, usually treated as a question of desire and its reorientation away from the material world and toward God. Although such an emphasis has some utility, I ultimately argue that it misunderstands the way in which mammon operates over against subjects and thus ultimately blunts the force of Jesus' distinction between God and mammon. Mammon certainly captures desire, but it does so in a material way, which means that the choice between God and mammon is, to a large extent, a forced one. Mammon, that is, does not just operate as a source of value internally but more importantly externally, in the mere fact of its use. I situate this discussion, which rests on an understanding of the way in which ideology functions materially, around two well-known episodes in Jesus' teachings and deeds: the Parable of the Rich Man and Lazarus and the story of the Rich Young Ruler. The material force of mammon, which I draw out of these parables, helps explain why Jesus recommends not just an internal reorientation of desire but a material reorientation of one's life. The latter takes the form of a radical choice for God against mammon, which involves what looks like an almost impossible subjective destitution.

The opposition between God and mammon is a material one, in the sense that both compete for complete allegiance. That allegiance is not only internal, however, but external as well, in the way that each concretely organizes time, attention, and devotion, to borrow from the work of Philip

Goodchild.[12] If we are accustomed, on the far side of Nietzsche, to saying that "God is dead," this is not because we lack an ultimate source of value but, rather, because mammon has taken that place.

Nevertheless, part of the reason that the Christian theological tradition has understood our relationship to mammon in primarily subjective rather than material terms has to do with a particular, and incomplete, understanding of money and, by extension, wealth. In short, the Christian theological tradition, and much of the popular imaginary, tends to understand money as a neutral object that arises naturally out of exchange. Chapter 2 works through this understanding of money and, drawing on Marx, shows how money can be understood to emerge out of exchange. Even if we understand money in such terms, however, it cannot be understood as a neutral object, since the process of exchange allows money to emerge as a transcendent object with a force all its own set over against subjects. That force expresses itself effectively but also materially, in the ubiquity of the exchange relationship. Nevertheless, in order to fully grasp the disjunction between God and mammon, we cannot limit ourselves to a commodity theory of money. Thus, in chapter 2 I also discuss how money can be understood as constituted through relationships of credit and debt, which means that it is also tied to sovereignty. The relationship between credit and debt constitutes money but also the social sphere itself, creating debtors through the threat of scarcity.

This fuller understanding of money helps provide another lens through which to view Jesus' own teachings and activity. It is not accidental, in this sense, that one of the ways in which Jesus marks the disjunction between God and mammon concretely is in his emphasis on debt and the importance of its forgiveness or dissolution. Jesus' emphasis on the release of debt becomes a means through which the coercive power of mammon may be undercut, but it also challenges the sovereignty on which mammon rests. Jesus' claim that we "Give to the emperor the things that are the emperor's and to God the things that are God's" (Matt 22:21) is not in this sense a call to divided allegiance but, rather, a critique of state power, one based on the disjunction between God and mammon. Devotion to God, that is, cannot take the form of mammon, and vice versa.

Chapter 3 continues this line of thought, but extends the disjunction between God and mammon to work and family. The coercive nature of money via exchange, differentiating wealth, debt, and sovereignty outlined in chapter 2 implies that money mediates life to and for us. It does so, however, through other institutions as well. Any critique of mammon, in this

12. Goodchild, *Theology of Money*.

sense, must also focus on the way in which money intersects the realms of work and the family. Chapter 3 thus discusses various ways in which work and family find themselves entangled in money, and money in work and family. If that is the case, then the disjunction between God and mammon should be understood to extend to those spheres of social organization as well. Combined with Jesus' critique of money and wealth, then, is a denial of work and family as forms of practice and social organization guided by mammon.

Just as the Christian theological tradition has attenuated Jesus' critique of money, so too has it done so with Jesus' claims about work and family. Rather than tracing a more subversive trajectory found within his teachings and actions in this respect, the theological tradition has tended to sanctify work and family along more just lines. Although seeking justice when it comes to such matters is certainly a worthy endeavor given the alternatives, Jesus' own position, I argue, is anti-work and anti-family. This is not because Jesus advocates for an other-worldly asceticism, which would constitute itself through passivity and relational detachment; it is, rather, because of the way in which both work and family as constituted under mammon function to support mammon. If one must choose between God and mammon, one must also, it seems, leave one's work and one's family, not because these are evils in and of themselves but, rather, because without doing so one remains on the side of mammon.

The first three chapters are largely negative in scope, in that they carve out the way in which Jesus' discourse is against mammon, is against money, work, and family. The negative emphasis here, which is experienced by the subject as destitution, may lead to the assumption that, as mentioned above, Jesus advocates for a certain type of asceticism over against the world. Indeed, although the theological tradition has, I suggest, attenuated Jesus' attitudes toward money, work, and family, it has largely read him in ascetic terms. Such asceticism manifests itself variously, but in current discussions that position Christianity as an alternative to capitalism, it often takes the form of a critique of consumption.

I argue instead in chapter 4, the conclusion, that Jesus is not so much against consumption as accumulation and possession. Accumulation and possession assume scarcity as their horizon and, in this sense, go hand in hand with mammon. When detached from mammon, however, consumption relates to a fundamental excess at the heart of the organization of the world. I draw on Bataille's distinction between a general economy and a restricted economy to make this point. Jesus' discourse and actions can be read in terms of the former, as a means of prying open sedimented structures and hinting at an alternative organization of the world. Jesus often accomplishes this in grand, so-called miraculous gestures, but he also advocates using mammon against mammon, as his parables related to the shrewd use of dishonest wealth suggest. Thus, although Jesus takes the disjunction between God and mammon as absolute, it is not pure: sometimes one must work to undermine mammon from within.

CHAPTER 1

Mammon and the Problem of Desire

The most obvious, yet also the best, place to begin when discussing how Jesus understands money, wealth, and related matters is the well-known opposition between God and mammon. In Matt 6:24, the opposition comes to us as part of a series of sometimes-disparate sayings lumped together in the so-called Sermon on the Mount (Matt 5–7):

> No one can serve two masters; for a slave will either hate the one and love the other, or be devoted to the one and despise the other. You cannot serve God and wealth [mammon].

In Luke, the opposition appears in the midst of a series of parables. Specifically, the claim occurs immediately after The Parable of the Dishonest Manager, although on the surface the link between the two is not immediately clear:

> No slave can serve two masters; for a slave will either hate the one and love the other, or be devoted to the one and despise the other. You cannot serve God and wealth [mammon]. (Luke 16:13)

Save for context, the sayings in Matthew and Luke are virtually identical.[1] In both cases, and irrespective of context, Jesus institutes a clear opposition: that one cannot serve two masters simultaneously means that one must, it seems, side with either God or mammon.

---

1. Many biblical scholars would claim that this is, of course, the result of it coming from a common source.

Despite the clear either/or logic that governs Jesus' statement, the overwhelming tendency of the theological and ecclesiastical traditions has been to blunt its force, as an idea but also when it comes to practical matters. Because of its apparent harshness, especially in a world governed by money, the statement goes through all manner of qualifications so as to avoid the dichotomy it introduces. It is common, for instance, to claim that the opposition has more to do with primacy than competition, with the priority we give to one over against the other. To use temporal and spatial metaphors, what Jesus really means, so this line of thinking goes, is that we should serve God *before* or *above* mammon. Doing so usually involves a two-pronged approach, at the very least. On the one hand, it is necessary to shift the locus of one's desire away from mammon and toward God. To continue using the spatial metaphor, the idea is that one should detach from the things of this world, as a means of reorienting desire upwards, toward God and what God desires. On the other hand, this reorientation of desire frees up mammon itself, making it available for beneficent ends. Combined with a reconstituted desire, mammon can be used *for* God and what God desires, rather than for the sort of self-serving motives with which it is normally associated. The opposition between God and mammon, then, is not *necessarily* antagonistic. Any antagonism is the result of subjective orientation and misuse, rather than any essential quality of mammon as such and its operation in the world.

Understanding the opposition in such terms is certainly a more congenial way to parse what Jesus is saying, but it tends to reduce the force of the opposition to a rhetorical ploy. Jesus himself doesn't qualify the opposition but simply states it, without any apparent ambivalence: one can choose to serve God or mammon, but not both. Moreover, even if we grant some amount of rhetorical license to the opposition, when lined up with similar distinctions, statements, and actions, it is clear that the opposition cannot be reduced to a simple figure of speech. This is not to say that how the disjunction between God and mammon plays out in practice is straightforward or one-dimensional. It is just to say that the choice itself as presented represents a clear decision on the distinction between the two. That decision is, of course, severe, but severity should not function as an excuse for downplaying the opposition between God and mammon. It should, rather, lead us to ask why Jesus institutes this disjunction in the first place. The opposition represents an opportunity for thought, an opportunity that is obviated once it is approached as qualified in advance. What is it about mammon, then, that makes it God's antagonist and, by implication, God's competitor?

WHO, OR WHAT, IS MAMMON?

The Greek term *mamōnas* is usually translated as "money" or "wealth." The exact etymology of the term is uncertain, although it may come from the root *amn*, which means "that in which one trusts"; or from the root *mon*, which means "food, maintenance, provisions."[2] There has sometimes been speculation that *mamōnas* was a Syrian deity, but there is little credible evidence to support that idea. Nevertheless, the etymology of the term, although telling in its own right, is less important than its use. The Aramaic term *māmōn* does not appear in the Hebrew Bible, although it and related terms do occur elsewhere in later rabbinic literature. Its use in the New Testament is confined solely to Jesus, specifically in and around the passages discussed in the previous section. When Jesus does use the term, moreover, he does so negatively and, ultimately, personifies it: Mammon is set over against God as a substantive force.

In what follows, I use the term mammon broadly to refer to money, wealth, and related notions, such as the market and finance; it also, in my usage, extends to matters related to work and family, as these are inseparable from economic matters. Such terms are, of course, not exactly synonymous, and in certain contexts it is important to draw distinctions between them. Nevertheless, the terms and their related concepts do overlap considerably in practice and, taken together, carve out a specific sphere of influence, or economy. Indeed, as we will see throughout what follows, mammon for Jesus names a broad problematic, the sense of which is lost if we confine the term narrowly to money or wealth. Given its etymology and use, then, using mammon in this expansive sense seems warranted: it does not just designate money or wealth individually but names an entire economy, one that Jesus opposes to God. Using the term in this sense also helps to avoid the pitfall of interiorizing mammon as greed or avarice, which ultimately limits the analytical and political potential of what Jesus says about it.

Understanding in what sense mammon is opposed to God is the task of all that follows. Nevertheless, on a side note it is worth pointing out that certain streams in later Christian theological and literary traditions continue this line of thought, that is, conceiving mammon as a substantive force. Mammon is set over against God, and often equated with the devil. In a commentary on Jesus' statement in the Sermon on the Mount, Augustine, for instance, states:

---

2. Kittel, *TDNT*, 388–90; Danker, *Greek-English Lexicon*, 614–15. *TDNT* notes numerous other possibilities as well, though all have related senses.

> But he who serves mammon certainly serves him who, as being set over those earthly things in virtue of his perversity, is called by our Lord the prince of this world. . . . For whoever serves mammon submits to a hard and ruinous master: for, being entangled by his own lust, he becomes a subject of the devil, and he does not love him; for who is there who loves the devil? But yet he submits to him; as in any large house he who is connected with another man's maid-servant submits to hard bondage on account of his passion, even though he does not love him whose maid-servant he loves.[3]

Similar identifications can be found throughout the medieval period up to the present, though one of the most literarily striking is Milton's in *Paradise Lost*, where mammon is personified as a fallen angel:

> Mammon led them on—
> Mammon, the least erected Spirit that fell
> From Heaven; for even in Heaven his looks and thoughts
> Were always downward bent, admiring more
> The riches of heaven's pavement, trodden gold,
> Than aught divine or holy else enjoyed
> In vision beatific. By him first
> Men also, and by his suggestion taught,
> Ransacked the centre, and with impious hands
> Rifled the bowels of their mother Earth
> For treasures better hid. Soon had his crew
> Opened into the hill a spacious wound,
> And digged out ribs of gold. Let none admire
> That riches grow in Hell; that soil may best
> Deserve the precious bane. And here let those
> Who boast in mortal things, and wondering tell
> Of Babel, and the works of Memphian kings,
> Learn how their greatest monuments of fame
> And strength, and art, are easily outdone
> By Spirits reprobate, and in an hour
> What in an age they, with incessant toil
> And hands innumerable, scarce perform.[4]

It is all too easy to downplay such personifications as mere subjective metaphors with limited utility. The equation of mammon with a substantive force, with the devil himself, has theological, rhetorical, and moral effect, in this sense, but only because it represents a subjective disposition. Mammon

---

3. Augustine, *On the Sermon on the Mount*, Book II, XIV.
4. Milton, *Paradise Lost*, I.678–99.

may be pictured as evil itself, but we should remember that it is really "the love of money [that] is the root of all evil" (1 Tim 6:10, KJV). Exaggerated representations of mammon, Jesus' included, are in this line of thinking really just stand-ins for the nature of unbridled, disordered desire. Hence, although Augustine attributes to it a particular power, he also emphasizes in the quotation above that it is through our "own lust" that we submit to mammon as master, through which we become a "subject of the devil."

I discuss the notion of individual desire in relation to mammon in more detail below, but it is worth pausing for a moment to consider the notion of personification, specifically as it relates to mammon. Campbell Jones has recently called attention to the function of prosopopoeia, the attribution of speech to otherwise non-speaking things and abstractions, and personification more generally, in relation to the market. Drawing on numerous examples, Jones argues that we personify the market—ascribing to it an interior life with a reason, will, and emotions—in numerous ways and for different purposes. Jones seems to think that prosopopoeia and personification go hand in hand with language itself, so it is not a question of if we should or should not ascribe human characteristics and qualities to non-human realities. Doing so is simply an innate feature of the symbolic and representational activities of human beings. The question is, instead, a matter of what purposes such attributions serve and how they function. From a psychoanalytic perspective, one important function of prosopopoeia and personification is to externalize desire, to locate desire in and have it recognized by and through the symbolic order. In the case of the market, Jones notes that there is "a raising up of market relationships into that of an imagined external agent with special powers. Along with this projection comes the frustrating unattainability of that object of desire, the delusion that strengthens with the idea of the supersensual nature of that object."[5] So understood, the market serves as an external placeholder for individual and collective desire but, because of this, also causes desire itself, as it structures it symbolically. To use Lacanian terminology, the market functions as *objet petit a*, as the object-cause of desire that itself is never attainable.[6] Desire, in other words, is located in the other, meaning that desire is always the other's desire: "It is not me who wants these things. I am merely giving voice to the desires of an external other."[7]

---

5. Jones, *Can the Market Speak?*, 17–18.

6. For a concise discussion of Lacan's use of this term throughout his career, see Evans, *Introductory Dictionary*, 124–26.

7. Jones, *Can the Market Speak?*, 18.

The externalization of desire in the other, its materialization in inanimate objects and abstractions, can also, however, serve to concretize that which appears as outside our control. To the extent that something like the market, as Jones rightly notes, is something that no one person—or even collective body—can contain and control with absolute precision, prosopopeia and personification function strategically to provide knowledge of and access to the apparently unknowable and unattainable, albeit in a limited way. Such projections, however, are self-reinforcing: although prosopopeia and personification serve to anchor desire in the other, giving it a definable body, externalization further reinforces its opacity. In the case of the market, for instance, we may affirm that the market "speaks," as a means to get a handle on its workings, but the "intent" behind its "speech" is not altogether clear. The market "mumbles," as Jones puts it.[8]

Prosopopeia and personification, and anthropomorphism more generally, often conceal a religious impulse as well. In making this claim, I am not suggesting that the externalization of desire in the other and the forms that it takes are necessarily religious, that we can reduce all such processes to a so-called religious motivation. From a theological perspective, such a reduction may serve apologetic purposes, but it often conceals important differences and the interplay of other motivations. Still, anthropomorphism—the attribution of human characteristics to nonhuman things, events, and abstractions—is often part and parcel of what we call religion, meaning that it is a matter of seeing how it functions in context to determine its sense.[9]

In the case of mammon, its personification does contain what we could call a religious impulse, at least when thought according to the vocabulary and architecture of Christian belief. It is hard not to come to that conclusion, given the way that mammon has been used, identified, and personified throughout the Christian theological and literary traditions and culture more broadly. Indeed, the choice for God or mammon, as Jesus articulates it, is a "religious" decision, but one that involves in addition to an impulse the option for a total perspective on life. If mammon is opposed to God, that is not merely because the former shares certain abstract qualities with the latter. More substantially, mammon competes with God for the position of the source of all value, as Philip Goodchild has recognized,[10] and that is why one cannot, in the end, serve both.

---

8. Jones, *Can the Market Speak?*, 37–44.

9. Stewart Guthrie grounds religion itself in anthropomorphism. For his theory of religion, see Guthrie, *Faces in the Clouds*.

10. Goodchild, *Theology of Money*.

A SUSPICION OF MAMMON

Jesus' suspicion of money, wealth, and related matters is far from unique, at least at a basic level. The identification of mammon with the devil and the forces of evil more generally in Christian-influenced thought and culture proves the point, even if the latter tradition undoubtedly finds much of its inspiration in Jesus himself.

But some amount of suspicion of what I, following Jesus, am referring to as mammon, is endemic in one way or another to many religious and philosophical traditions, at least in their initial form. Plato's well-known animosity toward the Sophists, for instance, correlates with a more general suspicion of money, trade, and exchange. It is not just that, on Plato's account, the Sophists are charlatans who profit from their reduction of philosophy to an instrumental rationality, one that values expediency over virtue. More to the point, the problem is, as Marcel Hénaff has detailed,[11] that reduction assumes that philosophical knowledge is something that can be bought and sold, traded in the marketplace like any other good. Philosophy, so understood, becomes little more than an object of economic exchange, meaning that it is possible to put a price on wisdom, virtue, and knowledge.

Plato's criticism of the Sophists along these lines only makes sense, of course, if philosophical knowledge, in terms of both form and content, is not ultimately subject to monetary value and, thus, cannot really be gained through financial transaction. Hence the contrast that the figure of Socrates provokes. Unlike the Sophists, Socrates does not accept payment for his wisdom, because what he has to offer is public and in no way subject to a price. Plato has him say in the *Apology*, "Nor do I discuss for a fee and not otherwise. To rich and poor alike I offer myself as a questioner, and if anyone wishes to answer, he may then hear what I have to say."[12] This suspicion of the relationship between money and philosophy also helps explain more fully, as Hénaff suggests, the ironic identification of wisdom and self-conscious ignorance: knowledge is easy to sell, but it is much harder to sell something that one claims, in the end, to know little about.[13]

---

11. Hénaff, *Price of Truth*, 27–58.

12. Quoted in Hénaff, *Price of Truth*, 49.

13. Indeed, one could argue, as Richard Seaford has, that the widespread use of coinage among the Greeks to facilitate trade and represent value is a precondition for the emergence of pre-Socratic and, later, Socratic philosophy. The impetus to metaphysics can be understood as an unconscious projection of the universal power and exchange value of money onto the cosmos itself, which is then used retroactively to critique the supposed vagaries of economic rationality. See Seaford, *Money and the Early Greek Mind*. Philip Goodchild adopts a similar view, but extends it throughout a range of philosophical materials, up to the present. See Philip Goodchild, *Capitalism*

It is important to emphasize here what is really at stake. Philosophy, for the Greeks, was not just an isolated intellectual exercise, as it is often viewed today. Philosophy constitutes an entire way of life, in that its practice shapes the philosopher to see, be, and act in the world in a particular way, a way that ultimately coincides with some form of happiness or flourishing. Although the various Greek philosophical schools articulated and adopted different forms of life with regard to this goal, the practice of philosophy itself was understood as so many "spiritual exercises," and thus can be understood as a discipline for living well in the world.[14] So, when Plato criticizes the Sophists for apparently reducing philosophy to a financial transaction, more is at stake than a simple disagreement. For Plato an entire way of life is at issue, which also means that philosophy for him has, at the very least, an ambivalent relationship to money, trade, and exchange.

We see a similar concern in Aristotle, even if he is "more pragmatic" about the function of money than Plato.[15] For Aristotle, the "natural" domain of wealth is the household, meaning that production and exchange is properly focused on "household management." This sort of "wealth-getting" is, on Aristotle's account, "necessary and honorable," and serves an important function. When understood in these limited terms, gaining wealth may serve to solidify and, indeed, enhance social cohesion, since interactions in and between households always presuppose and find their end in the good of the *polis*.

The widespread "use of coin" as a medium of exchange and a store of value, however, presents a problem. On the one hand, the use of coinage certainly helps ease the procurement of the basic necessities of life, which is why, Aristotle says, money was invented in the first place. Aristotle has no qualms about money and wealth, in this respect, since it is limited to its "natural" function. On the other hand, the development of coinage qua money enables "retail trade," which allows the function of money to become detached from its limited, natural end in household management, in the process becoming an end in its own right. "Retail trade," in other words, abstracts goods and their exchange from their household use-value and, in so doing, allows "wealth-getting" to become its own principle, one which knows no end.

---

and Religion.

14. I am drawing here, of course, on Pierre Hadot's work. See Hadot, *Philosophy as a Way of Life*; and Hadot, *What is Ancient Philosophy?* For a contemporary exploration of philosophy as a "spiritual exercise," see Goodchild, *On Philosophy*.

15. Hénaff, *Price of Truth*, 79. The discussion of Aristotle is informed by Hénaff's own discussion, but is also based on my own reading of Aristotle, *Politics*, I, 8–10.

Another way to put the difference is to mark it as one between quality and quantity, and Aristotle makes clear that what is at issue in these two understandings of wealth is life itself. He writes:

> Hence some persons are led to believe that getting wealth is the object of household management, and the whole idea of their lives is that they ought either to increase their money without limit, or at any rate not to lose it. The origin of this disposition in men is that they are intent upon living only, and not upon living well; and, as their desires are unlimited, they also desire that the means of gratifying them should be without limit. Those who do aim at a good life seek the means of obtaining bodily pleasures; and, since the enjoyment of these appears to depend on property, they are absorbed in getting wealth; and so there arises the second species of wealth-getting. For, as their enjoyment is in excess, they seek an art which produces the excess of enjoyment; and, if they are not able to supply their pleasures by the art of getting wealth, they try other arts, using in turn every faculty in a manner contrary to nature.[16]

This subjective unnaturalness, however, applies to money itself when it becomes its own principle. Such is the case, especially, with usury, which seeks increase through "interest." Aristotle says, "And this term interest [*tokos*], which means the birth of money from money, is applied to the breeding of money because the offspring resembles the parent. Wherefore of all modes of getting wealth this is the most unnatural."[17]

Such unnatural generation also helps to explain the medieval church's official condemnation of usury as a sin, one whose deserved punishment is, in certain instances, eternal damnation. There are, of course, numerous biblical injunctions against the practice of usury: Exod 22:25; Levi 25:27; and Deut 23:20 all put limitations on usury, including prohibiting it in relation to the poor, in which case it is considered as akin to extortion, and to one's fellow Israelites; Ps 15 excludes those who "lend money at interest" from dwelling in the "tent" of YHWH (v. 5); and in Luke's gospel, followers of Jesus are expected to lend without expecting anything in return (Luke 6:34–35). As Jacques le Goff has detailed, medieval theologians largely took such injunctions as equating usury with injustice, a type of "unlawful surplus" or "illegitimate excess" that, in the end, is really theft. So, says Thomas Aquinas, "Making a charge for lending money is *unjust* in itself, for one

---

16. Aristotle, *Politics*, I, 9.
17. Aristotle, *Politics*, I, 10.

party sells the other something non-existent, and this obviously sets up an *inequality* which is contrary to justice."[18]

In addition to this concern for justice, usury is seen as naturally or metaphysically suspect, as it was for Aristotle. Thus, on the one hand, we find the same concern with birth or generation in respect to money. The usurer, in other words, lends money in the hope of begetting money from money, but money is not the type of thing that is or should be subject to its own reproduction. Lending money at interest is thus not only unjust but also unnatural, at least within the presupposed metaphysical framework.

On the other hand, and more interestingly, the theft involved in usury, as le Goff shows, is not ultimately a theft from others, of their property. It is, of course, that too, but more seriously the usurer steals what belongs to God alone: time itself. The usurer, that is, steals and exploits the temporal interval between lending and repayment, turning time into interest and, subsequently, individual profit. Hence the medieval English theologian Thomas of Chobham expresses a view shared among many at the time, when he writes, "The usurer sells nothing to the borrower that belongs to him. He sells only time, which belongs to God. He cannot, therefore, make a profit from selling someone else's property."[19] The usurer's appropriation of time also explains in part the reason for descriptions of him as an indolent opportunist. The usurer's theft of time enables him to profit at all times, but without actually working: "The usurer wants to make a profit without doing any work, even while he is sleeping, which goes against the precepts of the Lord, who said, 'By the sweat of your face shall you get bread to eat' [Gen 3:19]."[20]

Such suspicions of money, trade, exchange, and usury—of what I am calling mammon—obviously contain a moral component, one that paints those on the "wrong side" of the issue as in some way deviant from the good life and, in the case of Christian thinkers, God's law. But it is also important not to reduce these broad suspicions to morality, as if the issue were only one of individual comportment with respect to an otherwise benign instrument or object. In each of the examples discussed above and elsewhere, the problem with mammon is not just with the subject's relationship to it but the thing itself or, perhaps better put, the way that mammon determines the subject's relationship to it and, in addition, others. Mammon, that is, is not inert: once it's established as mammon, as a source of value set in

---

18. Quoted in le Goff, *Your Money*, 27–28.
19. Quoted in le Goff, *Your Money*, 39.
20. Quoted in le Goff, *Your Money*, 42.

competition to other values (e.g., truth, philosophy, God), it exercises an autonomous agency over against the subject and, indeed, the world.

This is in part the significance of the metaphysical criticisms mentioned above. In the case of profiting from interest, for example, the subject certainly acts "unnaturally" or as a "thief of time," but that activity is only possible to the extent that the object itself enables it. Aristotle and the medieval theologians who follow him, such as Thomas Aquinas, may bemoan that money is not subject to self-generation, but it does actually generate itself, taking unto itself qualities that for them do not "naturally" belong to it. Likewise, the medieval theologians may criticize the usurer for "stealing time," which belongs to God, but the usurer is only able to steal time because interest allows him to do so. The moral criticism of such activity, we might say, is only possible to the extent that mammon actually has power, an agency of its own that allows it to "act" on subjects and the world itself and against opposing powers, such as God, in particular ways. Hence its personification, as we discussed in the last section. This applies, moreover, even if we don't adopt the specific metaphysical framework that informed the Aristotelian and medieval worldviews. The basic point, which still holds, is that mammon has a power that cannot be reduced to subjective motivations.

PARABLES ABOUT MAMMON

The disjunction between God and mammon is, for Jesus, absolute, which also means that it is objective in addition to subjective, external in addition to internal. The problem with mammon, in other words, cannot be reduced to an assumed self-directed will or properly determined desire, to the "inner life" of the subject. Otherwise put in more colloquial language, the problem of mammon cannot be reduced to a matter of the heart. To say that the disjunction between God and mammon is absolute is to say that each competes with the other as the value of values, over against the stated motivations of any particular individual. That may seem like an obvious point. Indeed, I have already briefly noted a long theological, literary, and cultural tradition that identifies mammon as an agent set antagonistically against the subject, an agent that is at times even associated with evil itself.

Nevertheless, the implications of that identification have often been dissolved into the internal dispositions of the subject. When it comes to thought and practice, that is, the disjunction has often been understood in moral terms: what matters is not so much mammon itself but how one relates to it, actually and in the recesses of one's thoughts and desires. Such a moral emphasis is important as far as it goes, and we should by no means dismiss it, but it tends to elide mammon's power, which is directly related to its unicity opposite God. A moral understanding of the problem of mammon, in other words, turns a problem with mammon into a problem with individuals and their desires.

To understand how this is the case, we can begin by returning to the context of Jesus' claim that one cannot serve God and mammon. In Luke's gospel it occurs immediately after the Parable of the Dishonest Manager (Luke 16:1–13). The parable tells of a manager who had been squandering the property of his master, a rich man. The rich man calls his manager to account and, apparently not satisfied, threatens to release the manager from his service. Either unwilling or unable to do much else and likely fearing for his own livelihood ("I am not strong enough to dig, and I am ashamed to beg," he says [16:3]), he devises what looks like a personal welfare scheme to win favor with his master's debtors, in the hope that the latter will "welcome [him] into their homes" (16:4). Seemingly without the knowledge of his master, he calls the debtors to him, offering a cut-rate on what they owe if paid on the spot. "'How much do you owe my master?' He answered, 'A hundred jugs of olive oil.' He said to him, 'Take your bill, sit down quickly, and make it fifty.' Then he asked another, 'And how much do you owe?' He replied, 'A hundred containers of wheat.' He said to him, 'Take your bill and make it eighty'" (16:5–7). The manager's acumen with respect to debt collection, however, impresses his master. After finding out about the manager's activities, he commends him for acting "shrewdly" because, as he goes on to say, "the children of this age are more shrewd in dealing with their own generation than are the children of light. And I tell you, make friends for yourselves by means of dishonest wealth so that when it is gone, they may welcome you into the eternal homes" (16:8–9).

It is an extremely odd and difficult parable, one that on the surface appears to extol dealing shrewdly, even dishonestly, with wealth. So understood, such praise would seem to conflict directly with the impossibility of simultaneously serving God and mammon, which is stated just after. I will suggest in chapter 4 another way to read this parable, one that emphasizes debt forgiveness and resistance, putting it more in line with the overall thrust of Jesus' claims regarding mammon. For now, however, we can focus on two related scenes that occur in proximity to and deal directly with the disjunction between God and mammon.

The first is the parable of "The Rich Man and Lazarus," which follows closely on the heels of The Parable of the Dishonest Manager in Luke's gospel. The parable illustrates Jesus' opposition between God and mammon by contrasting Lazarus, a poor man, with a rich man. The rich man, as

Jesus tells the story, dwells comfortably in his abode day in and day out, extravagantly dressed ("in purple and fine linen" [Luke 16:19]) and stomach more than full (he "feasted sumptuously every day" [Luke 16:19]). All of this while a poor man named Lazarus sits sick and hungry outside his gate. Both eventually die, but after they are buried their respective post-death destinations invert their earthly lots: Lazarus is "carried away by the angels to be with Abraham" while the rich man finds himself tormented in Hades (Luke 16:23). Looking up and seeing Abraham with Lazarus by his side, the rich man cries out, "Father Abraham, have mercy on me, and send Lazarus to dip the tip of his finger in water and cool my tongue, for I am in agony in these flames" (Luke 16:24). Abraham responds definitively, "Child, remember that during your lifetime you received your good things, and Lazarus in like manner evil things; but now he is comforted here, and you are in agony. Besides all this, between you and us a great chasm has been fixed, so that those who might want to pass from here to you cannot do so, and no one can cross from there to us" (Luke 16:27). Accepting his fate, the rich man asks that Lazarus at least be allowed to go to his brothers, to warn them about the consequences of their actions, presumably with respect to wealth and how they treat the poor. Abraham refuses this request, however, since they have, in effect, already been warned: "They have Moses and the prophets; they should listen to them" (Luke 16:29). If that is not enough, nothing is, not even "if someone rises from the dead" (Luke 16:30).

With a nod to the resurrection, the parable quite obviously illustrates the reversal of values that Jesus institutes in his famous Sermon on the Mount (Matt 5:1–11) or Sermon on the Plain (Luke 6:20–26). In that sermon, we are told that the kingdom of God is for the poor (or, for Matthew, the "poor in spirit"), who, although hungry and distressed, will find relief and be full; having already received their consolation, the rich can only look forward to hunger, mourning, and weeping, which is illustrated in The Parable of the Rich Man and Lazarus in the rich man's torment. It also, however, shows the disjunction between God and mammon: wealth ultimately and, if the parable is to be believed, eternally separates one from God and God's kingdom. Wealth not only divides the rich man from Lazarus before death: it also, and more seriously in such a worldview, reverses and fixes that division after death, hence the great, unbridgeable chasm that separates them.

The same sentiment is expressed in the story about the rich young ruler who comes to Jesus asking what he must do to gain eternal life. Jesus responds to the rich young ruler in similar fashion, citing the importance of keeping "the commandments" (Luke 18:20; cf. Matt 19:16–22; Mark 10:17–27). In other words, the rich young ruler, like the rich man in the parable above, already knows very well what is required of him, and he does not hesitate to say that he has "kept all these since [his] youth" (18:20). Jesus then says to him, "There is still one thing lacking. Sell all that you own and distribute the money to the poor, and you will have treasure in heaven; then, come follow me" (18:22). At this command, the rich young ruler "became sad; for he was very rich" (18:23). Jesus then looks at him, and says, "How hard it is for those who have wealth to enter the kingdom of God! Indeed, it is easier for a camel to go through the eye of a needle than for someone who is rich to enter the kingdom of God" (18:24–5).

I will return to some of the narrative features of these parables in more detail in what follows. For now I call attention to how the severity of Jesus' teachings about mammon, condensed in the stated opposition between God and mammon and illustrated in the passages just mentioned, has often been interpreted in largely individualistic moral terms. The problem in these and other instances is not with money, wealth, or possessions as such. The problem, rather, lies in one's relationship to mammon, in one's particular disposition with respect to money, wealth, and possessions. Otherwise put, such readings displace the opposition between God and mammon onto the subject, where it is understood primarily as a dramatization of individual, internalized desire directed toward an otherwise inert object.

This is how Clement of Alexandria, who provides one of the first systematic treatments of the relationship between faith and wealth, interprets the opposition, for instance.[21] Commenting on the story of the rich young ruler, Clement notes that when Jesus bids the man to sell all he has and redistribute it to the poor, he does not urge him to "throw away the substance he possessed, and abandon his property; but bids him banish from his soul his notions about wealth, his excitement and morbid feeling about it, his anxieties, which are the thorns of existence, which choke the seed of life."[22] In more general terms, Jesus' command to the rich young ruler is about his passions, about the disposition of his soul toward material things. The problem lies, in other words, in one's attachment to or desire for wealth or, for that matter, anything else, and not in the object so desired.[23]

For Clement, whose position in its basic points is fairly representative of the mainstream of the theological tradition as a whole, money and wealth cannot be a problem in and of themselves. Indeed, when in the right hands, that is, the hands of those who have had their desire reoriented toward God, money and wealth enables much good. The possession of money and wealth, on this view, provides opportunities for giving, for charity, which

---

21. See Gonzalez, *Faith & Wealth*, 112–18.
22. Clement of Alexandria, "Who Is the Rich Man?"
23. Clement of Alexandria, "Who Is the Rich Man?" xii.

simultaneously benefits giver and recipient. Clement says, "For if no one had anything, what room would be left among men for giving! ... Riches, then, which benefit also our neighbors, are not to be thrown away. For they are possessions, inasmuch as they are possessed, and goods, inasmuch as they are useful and provided by God for the use of men; and they lie to our hand, and are put under our power, as material and instruments which are for good use to those who know the instrument."[24] Wealth, on this account, is merely a passive object, pliable toward good or ill according to the disposition of the individual.

What matters, then, is not that one has money, wealth, or possessions, but how one uses them. Ultimately, mammon, for Clement and the mainstream of the tradition, is not a problem in and of itself, as long as one controls it and is not controlled by it. Indeed, since wealth is, for Clement, merely an instrument, one that can be used for good or ill but is neither good nor ill in and of itself, its nature is to be subservient to us, rather than us to it. Clement thus writes:

> If you use it skillfully, it is skillful; if you are deficient in skill, it is affected by your want of skill, being itself destitute of blame. Such an instrument is wealth. Are you able to make a right use of it? It is subservient to righteousness. Does one make a wrong use of it? It is, on the other hand, a minister of wrong. For its nature is to be subservient, not to rule. That than which of itself has neither good nor evil, being blameless, ought not to be blamed; but that which has the power of using it well and ill, by reason of its possessing voluntary choice. And this is the mind and judgment of man, which has freedom in itself and self-determination in the treatment of what is assigned to it.[25]

Such a view of wealth enables Clement to interpret Luke 16:9 ("make friends for yourself by means of dishonest wealth") rather easily: being a friend of wealth, dishonest or not, provides one with the resources to "give food to the hungry, and drink to the thirsty, clothe the naked, and shelter the houseless."[26]

This subjective understanding of money, wealth, and possessions certainly has broad support, and is so commonplace that it passes virtually unquestioned in the theological tradition and, indeed, the popular imagination more generally. There is, however, much to take issue with in such a view, not the least of which is that, taken on its own terms, it reduces the

---

24. Clement of Alexandria, "Who Is the Rich Man?" xiii, xiv.
25. Clement of Alexandria, "Who Is the Rich Man?" xiv.
26. Clement of Alexandria, "Who Is the Rich Man?" xiii.

problem of mammon to little more than an appeal to individual or collective moral sentiment. The problem with money, wealth, and possession is one's relationship to them. Rather than investing in them as a means of finding happiness or fulfillment, one's relationship to money, wealth, and possessions should be one of lightness and restraint, because they are mere objects.[27] What is required, in other words, is a reorientation of desire, through which one directs one's attention away from lower, material things and toward higher, immaterial things, and ultimately toward God, the source of all that is. According to Augustine, the things of this world are not sinful in and of themselves; they rather become occasions for sin to the extent that we focus our desire on them rather than on God. As he puts it in his *Confessions*, "All these [material] things and their like can be occasions for sin because, good though they are, they are of the lowest order of good, and if we are too much tempted by them we abandon those higher and better things, your truth, your law, and you yourself."[28] Hence the need to reshape desire, in which alone we find true freedom. Commenting on Augustine's understanding of desire, William T. Cavanaugh notes that the "key to true freedom is not just following whatever desires we happen to have, but cultivating the right desires. This means that the internal movement of the will is not a sufficient condition for freedom; we must consider the end toward which the will is moved."[29]

It is this reorientation of desire that ultimately enables charity, since it detaches us from what we have, thereby enabling us to give freely out of our excess. For those who have mammon, then, one's relationship to those who have less or nothing at all is mediated in part through charity, which binds both parties together. Again, as Clement reminds us, at issue are "the passions of the soul" and not money and material wealth as such.[30] Hence, to reiterate what the author of 1 Timothy states, it is the *love* of money that is the root of all kinds of evil and not money itself (6:10).[31]

Indeed, beyond the ostensible benefits that those in need receive from such charitable action, early church theologians viewed charity as eschatologically and sacramentally beneficial for the giver. As Gary A. Anderson emphasizes, almsgiving was understood to fund "a treasury in heaven, a

---

27. For a modern statement of this view, which emphasizes "joyful and light-hearted generosity" as subversive to the money economy, see Gay, *Cash Values*, 96

28. Augustine, *Confessions*, 48/II.5.

29. Cavanaugh, *Being Consumed*, 14–15.

30. Clement of Alexandria, "Who Is the Rich Man?" xiv.

31. An exemplary reiteration of this point can be found in Augustine, *Sermons*, III/5, Sermon 177.

treasury that can pay down the debt owed on one's sin."[32] We see this understanding expressed in nascent form, for instance, in the story of the rich young ruler, mentioned above (Luke 18:22, "Sell all that you own and distribute the money to the poor, and you will have treasure in heaven").[33]

Anderson notes that understanding charity in terms of benefits might on the surface smack of self-interest (one could, for instance, say that it appears as the theological equivalent of the current practice of giving for the sake of a tax break). Nevertheless, although one might give in full awareness of the gains that such giving entails for the giver, the giving itself, understood in terms of lending to God, has more to do with the faith one professes, in "putting [one's] money where [one's] mouth is," as Anderson puts it.[34] Faith without works is, of course, dead, as James reminds us (Jas 2:14–26). Moreover, and perhaps more importantly, in addition to what charity says about the individual doing the giving, almsgiving is "a declaration of belief about the world and the God who created it."[35] That is, it says that the world, although marred by sin, is ultimately good, a manifestation of God and God's goodness in and for creation.

It is in this sense that charity, too, can be understood as sacramental, as a means of being open to the mercy and grace of God. The crucial text for the early church in this respect is in Matt 25, where Jesus tells his disciples that their heavenly inheritance is bound up with how they have treated Jesus and those in need, which are one and the same.

> Then the king will say to those at his right hand, "Come, you that are blessed by my father, inherit the kingdom prepared for you from the foundation of the world; for I was hungry and you gave me food, I was thirsty and you gave me something to drink, I was a stranger and you welcomed me, I was naked and you gave me clothing, I was sick and you took care of me, I was in prison and you visited me." Then the righteous will answer him, "Lord, when was it that we saw you hungry and gave you food, or thirsty and gave you something to drink? And when was it that we saw you a stranger and welcomed you, or naked and gave you clothing? And when was it that we saw you sick or in prison and visited you?" And the king will answer them, "Truly

---

32. Anderson, *Charity*, 3. For more on the notion of sin as debt, see also Anderson, *Sin*.

33. Anderson's discussion of this story in these terms can be found in *Charity*, 152–55.

34. Anderson, *Charity*, 4.

35. Anderson, *Charity*, 4.

I tell you, just as you did it to one of the least of these who are members of my family, you did it to me." (25:34–40)[36]

"Eternal punishment" (25:46) awaits those at the left hand, those who did not give to those in need. As in the case of the rich man in The Parable of the Rich Man and Lazarus, the idea expressed here is that one's eschatological fate is wrapped up with one's actions toward others, especially those in need. For those with means, such actions, more often than not, involve some sort of use of one's material resources for the benefit of others. As Anderson rightly emphasizes, moreover, the theological tradition has in addition taken this passage on the whole to mean that we encounter the presence of God in the poor—and not just metaphorically but literally or, rather, sacramentally: scripture, along with the theological tradition, promises that we "meet God in the face of the poor."[37] The poor, in this sense, become a point of contact between the believer and God, a sacrament made real through the act of giving from out of one's wealth to those in need.

Although Anderson is sympathetic to this overall line of thought, he does rightly point out that it fails to grasp the nature of poverty as a structural problem, one that might be better addressed through political, rather than moral and theological, means. The emphasis on charity throughout the theological and ecclesiastical traditions as a means of expressing faithfulness—indeed, as a means for meeting God—could, in this sense, be understood to perpetuate poverty through its paternalism rather than alleviate it. That is, at least, the Marxist-liberationist critique, an element of which we will return to momentarily. Nevertheless, here we focus on what this line of thought assumes about mammon by juxtaposing it with Jesus' own statements, which, when read without the normal theological baggage, come across as more pointed and potent.

To begin with, one of the problems with understanding one's relationship to mammon in primarily subjective terms is that it tends to dissolve the way in which money and wealth more generally appear as specific targets of Jesus' teachings. That is, when individual and collective relationships to mammon are treated largely in terms of subjective dispositions, the unicity of mammon itself and its field of influence can be, and usually is, ignored. When thinking about money, the problem, in other words, is with the subject of money rather than money itself, which the latter is, as stated above, nothing more than an instrument or, as mainstream economic theory holds, a neutral medium of exchange. It is this view of money that lies behind the possibility of charity as a mode of faithfulness and means

36. Also quoted in Anderson, *Charity*, 6.
37. Anderson, *Charity*, 7.

of grace but also, it is important to emphasize, contemporary popular and, at times, political discussions of the economy. For instance, from this perspective, the 2007–2008 financial crisis, the effects of which we will likely deal with for the foreseeable future, had more to do with a culture of greed than anything else. The problem, in other words, is not in the end social, political, economic, or financial, that is, something to do with the structure of capitalism itself, but unrestrained desire, the moral failings of some bad actors. A former hedge fund manager has recently referred to the problem that plagues Wall Street as "wealth addiction."[38] Hence, President Obama's insistence in the aftermath of the crisis that the "American people will not excuse or tolerate" Wall Street's "arrogance and greed."[39]

No doubt that Wall Street, along with its counterparts, is full of "arrogance and greed," and it is not overstating the matter to say that money can function as a drug on par with any other. Witness, for instance, the analogical slippage between money and actual drug addiction in a movie like *The Wolf of Wall Street*, an adaptation of infamous stock trader Jordan Belfort's memoir.[40] But to conceive of such problems in primarily moral terms is already, in the end, to tolerate such behavior, for it fails to account for the fact that the problem lies just as much, perhaps more, on the side of the object, in money itself qua mammon. Moreover, by locating the problem on the side of the subject, in his or her desire, virtually anything can take the place of money as an object of desire, given the right circumstances. The addiction metaphor, in this respect, is telling. One can, really, be addicted to anything: heroin, shopping, sex, and money, for instance, certainly have different properties and vary with regard to legality, social acceptability, and potential for harm, but at the level of desire, each can be understood as analogically on par with the other. That is why, for instance, in addition to Alcoholics Anonymous and Narcotics Anonymous, we have groups such as Overeaters Anonymous, Online Gamers Anonymous, Sex Addicts Anonymous, and countless others, all of which adopt the same basic principles.

To use more contemporary theological language, any object can function as an object of faith or devotion, as an "ultimate concern," as Paul Tillich would say. For Tillich, faith is not particular to the so-called religious dimension of human experience but is an existential feature of human experience itself, to the extent that we are concerned about our existence.[41] Faith,

38. Polk, "For the Love of Money."
39. Hendren, "Obama."
40. Scorcese, *Wolf of Wall Street*.
41. Such concern or care is also central to Heidegger's articulation of the existential posture of Dasein in Heidegger, *Being and Time*.

in this sense, is "the state of being ultimately concerned" and the object of that faith is that which concerns us ultimately, that is, that which promises "ultimate fulfillment."[42] The object of faith, what we have faith in, determines how we take and organize the various other concerns that shape our lives, whether these are significant or mundane. So-called religious faith, on this account, is simply one species of faith or concern or, conversely, all faith or concern is ultimately "religious." When faith is understood in general existential terms, virtually any object can occupy the position of "that which concerns us ultimately." Tillich often uses the nation, money, and success as examples. Just because almost anything *can* occupy that position for us does not mean, however, that it *should*. Tillich is clear that only faith in God, the ground of being, is authentic, since all other concerns are finite and, thus, idolatrous.[43]

Despite his analysis of faith as a general existential condition, it is important to emphasize that Tillich does not lapse into an overly subjective view when discussing the content of ultimate concern. He does, of course, conceive of faith as an expression of the subject that seeks recognition in an outward movement toward its object of concern, but the object of faith, too, is not entirely passive, a blank screen on which the subject merely projects his or her desires. Rather, in Tillich's thought, the object of ultimate concern seems to possess some amount of agency in that it can and does make claims on the subject, compelling it toward corresponding ends: "If it claims ultimacy it demands the total surrender of him who accepts this claim, and it promises total fulfillment even if all other claims have to be subjected to it or rejected in its name."[44] It still remains the case, however, that the object of faith itself can and does take a variety of forms, forms that for Tillich compete with God for ultimacy.

Jesus, in contrast, tends to speak of what Tillich calls "ultimate concern" not as a general, existential category, but as divided in two, subject to either God or mammon. For Jesus, it seems, these two options determine penultimate and subordinate concerns, and either does so in diametrical opposition to the other. Mammon, in this sense, is not a metaphor, a stand in for whatever might capture and orient desire and life entirely away from God and God's kingdom, but rather *mammon is the thing itself*.

Recall the story of the rich young ruler, mentioned above. Clearly his wealth is the issue, in a very real sense, and it is his inability to part with it materially that, Jesus says, hinders him from entering the kingdom of God.

---

42. Tillich, *Dynamics of Faith*, 1, 2.
43. Tillich also develops this theme at length in Tillich, *Systematic Theology*.
44. Tillich, *Dynamics of Faith*, 1.

The rich young ruler is, in other words, divided between two masters rather than metaphors, and when pushed to make a decision for one or the other, he sides with his wealth. That wealth and not a generic, subjective desire is at issue is clear from Peter's response to the apparent harshness of Jesus' claims and the latter's response to him and the other disciples:

> Then Peter said, "Look, we have left our homes and followed you." And he said to them, "Truly I tell you, there is no one who has left house or wife or brothers or parents or children, for the sake of the kingdom of God, who will not get back very much more in this age, and in the age to come eternal life." (Luke 18:28–30)

Clearly, Jesus' disciples seem to have understood the sense of Jesus' claims, and it is hard to turn Peter's declaration about leaving all behind for the sake of the kingdom of God into a pious metaphor for the "passions of the soul" and the like, at least if one takes seriously the immediate and overall context (cf. Matt 4:18–22; Mark 1:16–20; Luke 5:1–11).

Jesus does not, then, as Clement and much of the theological tradition would have it, bid the rich man to get rid of his notions about wealth only, as if he could keep his material possessions while simultaneously discharging his desire for them.[45] Clement's reading is a generally representative example of the type of Platonic, allegorizing exegesis that has shaped the reception of many of Jesus' more difficult teachings, especially when they refer to money and wealth.[46] But it fails to grapple adequately with the material power of mammon over the rich young ruler, a power that resides in mammon uniquely and in itself. The rich young ruler's wealth, in other words, is not an inert object that can merely be repurposed through a shift in his disposition, through a certain rehabilitation and reorientation of his desire. It is his wealth as such that is the problem, the very possession of which seems to necessitate that he serve it and not God. That is why, Jesus says, it is "hard . . . for those who have wealth to enter the kingdom of God" (Luke 18:24). Mammon has a power all its own, a power different in kind than other so-called ultimate concerns, concerns which are, under mammon, relegated to the penultimate. The only real rival is God, which is why, Jesus says, we cannot serve God and mammon.

The opposition between God and mammon, then, is a material opposition. If pressed most would, of course, align themselves with God over mammon, or at least with something else besides mammon. Save for the

---

45. See Clement of Alexandria, "Who is the Rich Man?" xi.

46. For overviews of allegory as an interpretative method, see Hanson, *Allegory & Event*; and de Lubac, *Medieval Exegesis*.

unapologetically greedy and cynicism aside, most people do not really want to be seen as ultimately serving money and wealth, as opposed to other, so-called higher values. The alignment with God over mammon is, in this sense, a moral concern, but it is also an ideational one as well: we simply do not believe that mammon has a power in its own right, because we view it merely as a passive object, a neutral but useful medium that can be manipulated at will. To understand mammon and our relationship to it in these terms, however, reduces its objective status, rendering its opposition to God into an internal, subjective drama.

However, as I have emphasized, for Jesus the opposition is, in fact, real, and can in no way be reduced to the subject. Moreover, once we shift attention away from the putative internality of subjective desire, we can treat mammon as a real force, which is felt in what we actually do, despite the claims we may make to the contrary. To make sense of this, we can reference Slavoj Žižek's claims about ideology. Drawing on the work of Peter Sloterdijk, Žižek argues convincingly that ideology no longer functions primarily through some sort of naïve or false consciousness, if it ever really did. It functions, rather, through cynical distance: we are, for the most part, fully aware of the fetishistic components of our beliefs and actions, and yet we continue to invest in them and, thus, the ideological structure that supports them. Cynical consciousness, in this sense, is not a knowledge that is transparent to itself, as if it were simply the case that we choose to ignore the ideological sense of our beliefs and actions and act otherwise through a perverse act of will. So-called false consciousness is still there, but it is transposed onto the material realm and reflected in our actual actions. Belief is thus not an internal phenomenon, theoretically separate from what we actually do, but a material phenomenon that takes shape through habit and practice, which help shape desire.

Such is how the Marxian notion of commodity fetishism works for Žižek, and he uses the example of money in particular. I will return to a fuller discussion of the relationship between commodity fetishism and the supposed origins of money out of exchange in the next chapter, but suffice it here to note that Žižek emphasizes that when we use money, we at some level know that there is nothing "magical" about it, that it is merely a reflection of social relations and a useful tool for exchange. In actual practice, however, the opposite is the case. "The problem is that in their social activity itself, in what they are *doing*, they are *acting* as if money, in its material reality, is the immediate embodiment of wealth as such. They are fetishists in practice, not in theory. What they 'do not know,' what they misrecognize, is the fact that in their social reality itself, in their social activity—in the act of commodity exchange—they are guided by the fetishistic illusion."[47] Belief, then—in money or in anything else—is a radically external phenomenon: it cannot be equated with the internal disposition of the believer but is "embodied in the practical, effective procedures of people."[48] So understood, belief qua cynical takes the form of a structural gap between what we do (i.e., what we "actually believe") and what we think or say we are doing (i.e., what we claim we believe). The important point, here, is that the maintenance of this gap is necessary for ideology and its mechanisms to function. Ideology depends, in other words, on the non-coincidence of, or even contradiction between, our claimed beliefs and the material practices that manifest their truth.

We see, I think, the structure of cynical consciousness at work in the Parable of the Rich Man and Lazurus and the story of the rich young ruler. In the case of the rich man in the parable, he apparently knows very well the dangers of wealth and his responsibility to the poor and to those generally in need, represented in the person of Lazarus. Like his five brothers, for whom he fears a similar fate as his, he has heard "Moses and the prophets" (Luke 16:29), yet during his life he ignored the responsibilities outlined therein, dressing lavishly and feasting sumptuously which, in the parable, goes hand in hand with turning a blind eye to Lazarus and his plight. Similarly, the rich young ruler knows well what is required of him—he must sell all that he has and give the money to the poor. He opts instead to keep his wealth, even if that apparently means going against his stated desires and, consequently, forfeiting eternal life. In both cases, there is a gap between "belief," or what one claims to know to be the case, and what one does, and it is this gap which, in both instances, constitutes individual subjectivity. To act otherwise, which here means acting in accordance with stated belief or knowledge, would entail immediate subjective and material destitution. "Truly I tell you, there is no one who has left house or wife or brothers or parents or children, for the sake of the kingdom of God, who will not get back very much more in this age, and in the age to come eternal life" (Luke 18:29–30).

Now, it is tempting to read these and similar stories and parables primarily as examples of hypocrisy, of momentary or, in some cases, extended instances of acting inauthentically with respect to stated beliefs. Otherwise put, it is all-too-easy to moralize these instances, to read them in terms of individual or collective failing and, in turn, force a metaphor out of the presented problems. Such a hermeneutic, however, often conveniently

---

47. Žižek, *Sublime Object of Ideology*, 31; original emphasis.
48. Žižek, *Sublime Object of Ideology*, 34.

functions to displace the point of identification in the pericope and the latter's overall sense. Through such a lens we read the story of the rich young ruler, for instance, as indicative of his personal flaws, of his inability to put aside his base desires to become a disciple. He functions, in this sense, as a paradigm of what not to do: we may, if we are honest, sympathize with his situation but we ultimately do not identify with him, since that would entail putting ourselves on the wrong side of faith and eternal life.

In order to accomplish this displacement, moreover, we also have to insist that the story is not really about money, that it only uses money as a vehicle for indicating the nature of desire in general. The rich young ruler's wealth, in other words, could be anything, anything, that is, that hinders us from gaining what both the rich young ruler and Jesus refer to in the story as eternal life. If we took it literally, then we would have to identify with the rich young ruler and the consequences of his failure to let go of and disperse his wealth. Moralization and metaphorization allow us to establish and maintain distance through claiming the ostensible high ground. With respect to Jesus and his teachings, however, that often results in irony or—ironically—hypocrisy: "God, I thank you that I am not like other people: thieves, rogues, adulterers, or even like this tax collector" (Luke 18:11). And, we could add, like this rich person, even if the reader is rich, relatively speaking.

We should not dismiss such readings out of hand. The charge of hypocrisy and all that it entails can, in certain instances, remain a powerful moral and political tool, although it can always be turned back on the one making the charge. This is what Jesus seems to be getting at, when he states:

> Do not judge, so that you may not be judged. For with the judgment you make you will be judged, and the measure you give will be the measure you get. Why do you see the speck in your neighbor's eye, but do not notice the log in your own eye? Or how can you say to your neighbor, "Let me take the speck out of your eye," while the log is in your own eye? You hypocrite, first take the log out of your own eye, and then you will see clearly to take the speck out of your neighbor's eye. (Matt 7:1–4)

Nevertheless, the problem with hypocrisy as a diagnosis is that it is of limited value when it comes to the way in which our beliefs and practices take place within a broader symbolic framework. That is, hypocrisy conceives of belief idealistically, as a primarily "internal" matter: the issue is with the practice or action rather than the belief, meaning that even though one may act contrary to it, the belief itself remains unproblematically intact. Although no one likes to be called a hypocrite, the charge is less severe than is often assumed, because it fails to identify our actual practices *as* our beliefs, as the form that what we "really believe" takes.

Jesus does often charge his opponents with hypocrisy, especially in Matthew (see, for instance, Matt 7:4; 15:7–9; 23:13–33; cf. Luke 12:1), but he also pushes the logic involved further. It is telling, in this respect, that in both instances mentioned above, judgment is rendered according to what the individual involved does or has done, irrespective of what each might claim to believe. The problem with both the rich man and the rich young ruler is not hypocrisy but their actions as such, which shows what they truly believe. That is, both the rich man and the rich young ruler show that they "really" believe in their wealth and, conversely, disbelieve in "Moses and the prophets" and Jesus' own command, because this is what their actions indicate. In both cases, money and wealth are obviously involved, which means that they are not so much hypocrites as unbelievers or, rather, believers in a competing deity, in mammon. This is why the rich man is barred from "mercy" and the rich young ruler seemingly from "eternal life": such notions play no structuring role in their respective actions, that is, in their material existence, even if acknowledged at the level of the idea.

At his most radical, then, Jesus parses matters not merely along the lines of authentic and inauthentic belief, which tends to conceive of belief as an internal phenomenon theoretically separable from practice, but along the lines of belief and unbelief. Thus when a father brings his young son to Jesus to have him healed of a "convulsing spirit," Jesus assures the father that "All things can be done for the one who believes" (Mark 9:23). The father cries out to Jesus, "I believe; help my unbelief!" (Mark 9:24). We can read the interplay of belief and unbelief, then, as radicalizing the notion of hypocrisy. Whereas hypocrisy is usually understood as a moral failing, it is, rather, structural, in the sense that it is a component of belief itself. Or, said otherwise, belief lies in practice, in what we actually do.

We should not, then, overly moralize the problem here, in the sense that one's actions on behalf of mammon rather than God could be reduced to individual failing, a failing that could be fixed through a relatively straightforward, though not necessarily pleasant, reordering of desire. Sure, we can all point to isolated, and apparently conscious, instances of enormous greed, and go on to identify these at the extreme end with the antagonists in Jesus' sayings, parables, and interactions. But doing so often results in an all-too-convenient diversionary tactic, consciously undertaken or not, that gets us off the hook by displacing and, thereby, eliding the point of identification. The rich man, the rich young ruler, and the "hypocritical" Pharisee are not exceptions but the rule: they are screens that simultaneously project "normal" practices but also, in so doing, reflect back to us our pious attempts to label them as abnormal.

If there is an exception, it lies with Jesus and his disciples, and this is because they have left everything, including work and family (Luke 18:28–30), which, as I will discuss in more detail in chapter 3, are two of the spheres through which mammon exerts its authority. The exception that marks Jesus' inner circle, as I will develop later on, is not merely a simple exception, one that results in an otherworldly and destructive asceticism. It is, rather, one that disavows these spheres and mammon itself as a means of envisioning a new world. In order for that to be possible, however, a radical break—such as the one Jesus urges the rich young ruler to take—is, at first, necessary. That break cannot merely be chalked up to a so-called internal change in one's desire, one that keeps the objects of one's desire relatively intact; that change, rather, can only result through a material reorientation, an actual change in practices and, consequently, the objects themselves. Such is, perhaps, how we should initially make sense of Jesus' claim, "If any want to become my followers, let them deny themselves and take up their cross daily and follow me. For those that want to save their life will lose it, and those who lose their life for my sake will gain it" (Luke 9:23–4; cf. Matt 16:24–5).

But such material reorientation, which takes the form of a decision for God and against mammon, cannot be reduced to a unilateral act of the will. At times it may come across that way, at least on the surface. Such is the case, for instance, when Jesus calls his first disciples:

> As Jesus passed along the Sea of Galilee, he saw Simon and his brother Andrew casting a net into the sea—for they were fishermen. And Jesus said to them, "Follow me and I will make you fish for people." And immediately they left their nets and followed him. As he went a little farther, he saw James son of Zebedee and his brother John, who were in their boats mending their nets. Immediately he called them; and they left their father Zebedee in the boat with the hired men, and followed him. (Mark 1:16–20; cf. Matt 4:18–22)

Although here following Jesus is reduced to the immediacy of the act, it is important to emphasize the consequences of that act. The decision to follow Jesus is, in one sense, an act of will, but it is also an act that destroys and reconstitutes the individual as a subject, precisely because of the destitutions that it involves. The decision, that is, should be understood not piously but economically, as a decision for God against mammon. Thus, in order to follow Jesus, the first disciples leave behind their livelihood, that is, their work, but also the sphere of the family—and it seems safe to assume that their act bears consequences for the latter, as well. We will return to this in more detail in chapter 3, but it is a literal and, perhaps, extreme example of what Dietrich Bonhoeffer famously called "costly grace" in contrast to "cheap grace": costly grace is costly because it "costs a man his life, and it is grace because it gives a man the only true life."[49]

Nevertheless, elsewhere Jesus implies that even this decision is not up to the subject, and is de-centered from the will, meaning that the will is not sufficient in and of itself. This is because that decision involves abasement, the dissolution of one's life, in the form of the material means by and through which one lives in the world. Indeed, equating the decision to follow Jesus with an assumed self-sufficient will is one of the ways that the force of the distinction between God and mammon gets blunted, since it reads the decision in moral terms. In the case of the rich young ruler, in contrast, although Jesus rebukes him ("How hard it is for those who have wealth to enter the kingdom of God! Indeed, it is easier for a camel to go through the eye of a needle than for someone who is rich to enter the kingdom of God" [Luke 18:24–25]), he immediately labels the decision as "impossible," in effect shifting its ground away from the rich young ruler and to God: "What is impossible for mortals is possible for God" (Luke 18:27).

One way to read this "impossibility," which shifts the locus of decision outside the subject and thus outside the realm of morality, is along the lines of what Jacques Lacan calls a "forced choice." For Lacan, the forced choice signifies the symbolic alienation of the subject, the subject's exposure to the "lethal factor" through which it and its supposed freedom are constituted. To illustrate this, Lacan uses an example that dovetails well with the story of the rich young ruler and the general distinction between God and mammon: the command, "Your money or your life!" As Lacan comments, "If I choose money, I lose both. If I choose life, I have life without the money, namely, a life deprived of something."[50] Both options presented in the command involve some form of deprivation, although the actual loss of life if one were to choose to hold on to one's money would clearly seem the worse of the two.

The choice, in other words, is really no choice at all, at least in any real sense: one is "forced" to choose life over money, in that the option is already chosen in advance in the form of the command. One could always commit a radical act of freedom and choose otherwise, but the result of that choice would, of course, entail the loss of life itself, which renders one's so-called

49. Bonhoeffer, *Cost of Discipleship*, 45.
50. Lacan, *Four Fundamental Concepts*, 212.

freedom meaningless. As Lacan says in reference to another forced choice, that between freedom or death, "You choose freedom. Well! You've got freedom to die. Curiously enough, in the conditions in which someone says to you, *freedom or death!*, the only proof of freedom that you have in the conditions laid out before you is precisely to choose death, for there, you show that you have freedom of choice."[51]

So understood, the forced choice appears as one form of what Žižek, following Lacan, calls an empty gesture.[52] As a forced choice, an empty gesture is, simply put, an offer made to be rejected. Although it offers the appearance of choice at the literal level, that is, at the level of the gesture, its real sense, that is, how it is to be taken, relies on an unwritten, sociosymbolic framework that structures the choice itself. If, for instance, when passing one of my colleagues in the hall I say, "How's it going?," we all know, as Žižek points out, that I'm for the most part not asking a real question in search of an honest response. I'm merely being polite, doing what is socially expected of me, and it would be a violation of those expectations if either I or my colleague took my question as real, that is, if my colleague were to respond in any other way than with, "Well. And you?" But, as Žižek also points out, we cannot simply chalk up the empty gesture—in this case, the question to my colleague—to hypocrisy, "since in another way, I *do* mean it: the polite exchange does establish a kind of pact between the two of us."[53] To not make the gesture is, in a way, unthinkable, because it, like taking the gesture literally, would be a violation of social norms. We should not take such a violation too lightly, since, for Žižek, such symbolic gestures and their formally determined responses contribute to the maintenance of social cohesion. This is why, Žižek says, taking the empty gesture literally is a means of "traversing the fantasy" that structures the sociosymbolic order: "[T]he act of taking the empty gesture (the offer to be rejected) literally—to treat the forced choice as a true choice—is, perhaps, one of the ways to put into practice what Lacan calls 'traversing the fantasy': in accomplishing this act, the subject suspends the phantasmatic frame of unwritten rules which tell him how to choose freely—no wonder the consequences of this act are so catastrophic."[54] Indeed, since one only recognizes oneself as subject within this "phantasmatic frame," taking the gesture literally, as a real offer or choice, may involve no less subjective destitution, the loss of life itself.

51. Lacan, *Four Fundamental Concepts*, 213.

52. Žižek discusses this notion throughout his writings in numerous ways, as it is essential to how ideology functions. The discussion that follows draws specifically on Žižek, *Plague of Fantasies*, 109–11.

53. Žižek, *Plague of Fantasies*, 111.

54. Žižek, *Plague of Fantasies*, 29.

Returning to the rich young ruler, we see something similar at work, though the position of "money" and "life" are reversed. In commanding the rich young ruler, "sell all that you own and distribute the money to the poor, and you will have treasure in heaven; then come follow me" (Luke 18:22), Jesus offers the rich ruler a version of the command: "Your money or your life!" The rich young ruler, in other words, can certainly choose to sell all he has—he can choose, that is, God over mammon—but that involves total subjective destitution, because "he was very rich" (Luke 18:23). It is a question, then, of losing his life, his means of security, in order to save it (see Luke 17:33). Because of the severity of Jesus' command in light of the rich young ruler's great wealth, we can read that command as a sort of empty gesture: Jesus well knows that, at one level, the choice is forced, that is, no choice at all, which is why he later goes on to refer to its impossibility (Luke 18:27). It is not at all shocking, then, that the rich young ruler goes away sad, since his response is determined by the very structure of the command. In a way, we could say that Jesus uses the rich young ruler's question against him to expose him and, of course, the hearers/readers of the story to the "lethal factor" that structures his, their, and our subjectivity.

The rich young ruler, to his credit, appears to understand the severity of the apparent dilemma, and is appropriately shaken by it. The disciples, too, understand matters, though they find themselves on the other side of the decision. Later readers of the story, including contemporary readers, tend to elide the choice's severity by projecting it inward. That is, the choice appears unreal or, more properly, immaterial rather than material, because we do not take it as a real choice: in what we actually do, we act is if we can serve God and mammon, and this dual servitude is justified by an appeal to existential categories. Using the language of popular theology and spirituality—which is, in its own way, deeply rooted in the mainstream of the Christian theological and ecclesiastical traditions—so long as we "put God first," so long as our "heart is in the right place," there is no problem with pursuing mammon as well as God. Indeed, as mentioned above, within such a framework mammon can even be considered a good, since having it allows for an expression of faithfulness through charity. By eliding the severity of Jesus' claims, however, we allow mammon to rule because, as discussed above, belief is in the first instance a material phenomenon.

It is important to stress, however, that this way of understanding the problem (i.e., internalizing it) often appears to us as the only way, to the extent that mammon actually functions in opposition to God as the source of value and, indeed, life, for the world. Since we must live in the world, since the majority do not and never have had the luxury of monasticism, even if the latter were desired, how could we ever think that things could be otherwise? Internalizing the disjunction between God and mammon, which transposes the opposition between the two into a piously constructed hierarchy, then, allows us to live in the world, allows us to provide for the basic needs, wants, and desires that sustain our lives in the world. It also, of course, allows for abuse, for rampant greed and exploitation. That Jesus intends something else, however, is apparent in his harsh words for this line of thinking as well. Jesus is against mammon, but he also seemingly has no time for a more practical disposition in regard to it: "Therefore I tell you, do not worry about your life, what you will eat, or about your body, what you will wear" (Luke 12:22).

Thus the problem, although it can take the form of individual greed or desire, cannot be reduced to them. The issue is, in other words, primarily structural and symbolic rather than moral: Mammon, because it facilitates access to our needs, wants, and desires, functions by default as the source of our values, indeed, our very being in the world. This is the case, moreover and generally speaking, even if our stated desire is otherwise. The rich young ruler, for instance, actually comes to Jesus desiring "eternal life" but walks away "sad" when he cannot meet the conditions for it, that is, sell and redistribute all that he has. The point is not that the rich young ruler is somehow unique in his apparent inability to part with his wealth. He is, rather, a stand in, the real point of identification in the narrative, not in some metaphorical sense but materially, in his wealth.

That Jesus' command to the rich young ruler is universal in scope and material in orientation (i.e., really concerned with money or wealth) is clear from the disciples themselves, who do not hesitate to remind Jesus that they have left everything to follow him (Luke 18:28–30). The universality involved does not necessarily entail a singular straightforward approach, as I will discuss in chapter 4 in regard to the use of "dishonest wealth." Nevertheless, Jesus elsewhere makes the point even more explicit, where its scope is unquestionable. Thus in Luke 14, for instance, we read of Jesus addressing the "large crowds traveling with him" as follows:

> Whoever comes to me and does not hate father and mother, wife and children, brothers and sisters, yes, and even life itself, cannot be my disciple. Whoever does not carry his cross and follow me cannot be my disciple. For which of you, intending to build a tower, does not first sit down and estimate the cost, to see whether he has enough to complete it. Otherwise, when he has laid a foundation and is not able to finish, all who see it will begin to ridicule him, saying, "This fellow began to build and was not able to finish." Or what king, going out to wage war against another king, will not sit down first and consider whether he is

able with ten thousand to oppose the one who comes against him with twenty thousand? If he cannot, then, while the other is still far away, he sends a delegation and asks for the terms of peace. So, therefore, none of you can become my disciple if you do not give up all your possessions. (Luke 14: 25–34)

Rather than sweeping the difficulties away under the metaphorical rug, we should, rather, take seriously their implications. One such implication, as I have been emphasizing, is that the choice to follow Jesus—the choice for God against mammon—appears as forced. To borrow a phrase from Philip Goodchild,[55] we direct our time, attention, and devotion to mammon not necessarily because of some moral weakness or fault but, rather, because we have to. If the world runs on and under mammon, how else can one actually live in the world, except through it? Hence, as Jesus says, with human beings, matters look impossible.

But only for human beings, for, as Jesus says, "What is impossible for mortals is possible for God" (Luke 18:27). We should not understand Jesus' appeal to God, here, in an overly pious way, which would lead us back into the problem we have been discussing in regard to the internalization of one's relationship to God. We should, rather, understand Jesus' appeal to God as making the impossible possible in terms of Jesus' own life. However, to claim that the meaning of Jesus' appeal is found in Jesus himself, in his thought, words, and deeds, is not the same thing as making a traditional theological claim that insists on his uniqueness, on his divine status. It is, rather, to claim that Jesus enacts what he says and, in so doing, offers a glimpse of what an alternative to mammon might look like, even if he does not offer a program. Jesus invites others to enact this alternative as well—and they can, because, as I will discuss in the following chapters, that alternative is already present, as Jesus' actions make clear.

---

55. Goodchild, *Theology of Money*, 201: "For the alternative between God and wealth (personified as mammon) is that between two masters. In either case, it is a question of service. Wealth attracts time, attention, and devotion; it constructs a perspective from which the world is to be seen."

CHAPTER 2

Exchange, State, and Debt

In the last chapter, I argued that how we relate to either God or mammon cannot be reduced to subjective desire, that it is, in fact, marked materially, in how we actually act with respect to either. To borrow Philip Goodchild's words again, it is a matter of time, attention, and devotion: where these lie determines one's fidelity. Moreover, I also suggested toward the end of the chapter that if that is the case, then most of us, by default, serve mammon. That fact has nothing to do with our desire per se, if, that is, we understand desire in terms of the subject. Rather, it has to do with the fact that mammon organizes the world materially, which means that it is the God of this world, in a very real sense. Otherwise put, it is mammon, not God, that is the source of value in the world, meaning that access to life is always mediated through mammon.

Philip Goodchild reads the ascendancy of mammon as the source or value of values as coinciding with what Nietzsche diagnosed as "the death of God," or, as Goodchild more correctly refers to it, "the murder of God." As Goodchild points out, Nietzsche's recognition of God's death has to do with the loss of God's foundational role in human activity. To say that "God is dead" is not to make a metaphysical claim regarding God's existence. Rather, it is to say that "God" no longer orders existence, our relationships to ourselves, others, institutions, and even reality itself. This death or murder—as Nietzsche says, "we have done it ourselves"—does not simply result in a void, in a complete loss of value. Although Nietzsche's madman, at least on one reading, does appear to interpret it in just this way, Goodchild emphasizes that what we are dealing with is more of a shift in the locus of value and, moreover, the piety that goes along with it. Specifically, it is a shift from

God to mammon. Thus Goodchild says that the "murder of God reflects a shift in pieties. God has stopped paying us our ordered existence; or rather, there is another God who pays us, who responds more immediately, directly, and tangibly to our prayers: mammon."[1] He continues:

> This conversion is accompanied by a progressive reorganization of daily life. Where the activities of daily life had been ordered by the expectations of the community or obligations to a deity, economic rationality brings an abstract symbolization of space and time. Enclosure of the commons, the replacement of communal resources with private property, changes the function of work for producing for one's community to producing for the market; similarly, market relations enact an "enclosure" of time, whereby the quantity of labour takes on more significance than the lived experience of work. Once subjected to the abstract determinations of private property and the market, daily life can become regulated by economic rationality, which had formerly been limited by a consensus on the limitation of needs.[2]

It is in this sense that God's murder coincides with the emergence of the self-regulating market and the invasion of most social relationships by its rationality.

Although the emergence of capitalism as an ever-expanding political-economic system over against other forms of organization marks a clear difference, it is important not to overplay the difference that this "great transformation," to use Polyani's phrase, institutes.[3] Indeed, overplaying that difference all-too-often results in an unhelpful nostalgia for times past, a longing for a time when human relationships were supposedly more organic and reciprocal and, for some theologians, ordered analogically toward God.[4] Goodchild himself, I should stress, does not fall into this trap, rightly refusing to ground his theology of money in this sort of theological difference.[5] Nevertheless, in order to avoid the pitfalls of nostalgia, we should conceive of this difference as one of degree, not kind. The power of abstraction, although accelerated in capitalist forms of socioeconomic organization, resides in money itself, historically and conceptually. That is, money

---

1. Goodchild, *Capitalism and Religion*, 27.
2. Goodchild, *Capitalism and Religion*, 28.
3. See Polyani, *Great Transformation*.
4. This is, of course, the general position of the theological movement known as radical orthodoxy. See, for instance, Milbank, *Theology and Social Theory*.
5. Specifically, Goodchild argues for a rethinking of credit in terms of evaluation. See *Theology of Money*, 241–55.

can and does take the place of God because of the type of object that money is, not physically, of course, but in its power of abstraction and its function.[6]

It is on this point, then—that is, money as the power of abstraction—that we can understand the death of God not only in temporal terms, where the death of God names an event in history at which point money ascends to its position as the highest value, as the source of all values. God's death is, rather, a feature of money itself, even if the news takes a while to get around. Otherwise put, God's death is implied in the disjunction that Jesus institutes between God and mammon. Because it is mammon, and not God, that rules the world, God can be understood, then, as always-already dying—or always-already dead.

There is, of course, a tradition of theologically inflected literature that makes a similar claim, which runs from Hegel and Nietzsche, to Altizer and, now, Žižek. That strand of thought is interesting in its own right, and it has heavily influenced my own thinking. Nevertheless, the claim I am making is slightly different and, I would suggest, more material: it's not a metaphysical claim about the being of God or transcendence and its loss per se but, rather, the way in which mammon qua source of value structurally limits alternatives to its rule as it gradually gains ascendency.[7] Although the latter process can, of course, be understood in historical terms, that history is only possible based on what money is and can do. Money, that is, contains within itself the notion of God's death, the propensity toward God's murder. God or mammon, Jesus says, and that disjunction perhaps means even more today than it did then, but it did actually mean something then as well.

EXCHANGE

I said above that money can rival God, to the extent that it can take God's place after God's murder, because of the type of thing that money is and how it functions: in other words, what money does. Perhaps the best place to start in understanding money in more detail is with a discussion of the so-called commodity theory of money, which understands money as arising out of exchange. To be clear ahead of time, the goal in what follows is not

---

6. Although the development and spread of coinage certainly facilitates this power. For a discussion of money's development as a form of abstraction in relation to coinage in ancient Greece, see Seaford, *Money and the Early Greek Mind*.

7. Contra Mark C. Taylor's equation of the death of God with the abandonment of the gold standard. See Taylor, *After God*, 222: "Going off the gold standard was the economic equivalent of the death of God. Gold functions in the economic system just as God functions in religious schemata: gold is a sign constructed its status as sign and thereby ground the value of other monetary signs." See also Taylor, *Confidence Games*.

to develop a full-fledged theory of money, or even a theology of money, as Goodchild has recently done. Readers familiar with Goodchild's work will clearly see the influence it has had on my own thinking, particularly when it comes to understanding the ways in which money functions theologically as the value of values. That said, the goal is not simply to repeat his and other analyses but, rather, to use them to understand more fully the distinction between God and mammon as Jesus articulates it and the consequences of this distinction.

Mainstream economics for the most part understands money in terms of a set of linked, though analytically distinct, functions. Money functions, variously yet simultaneously, as a medium of exchange, a store of value, a means of payment, and a measure of value. Money is, in other words, a commodity, though a peculiar one: in its functions it is a commodity that is not a commodity, one that provides a neutral medium for the circulation of all other commodities.

In this respect, commodity theories of money consider money as originating out of exchange, as a means of alleviating the difficulties that supposedly attend so-called barter economies. Although in general terms we find such an understanding of the function of money as far back as Aristotle, the theory contains little to no anthropological and historical data to support it.[8] The origination narrative that sees money as the logical outcome of barter, in this sense, is more of a retroactive justification of money as a neutral and passive medium. Nevertheless, attending to that narrative and to the features of exchange itself, at least in a general sense, is crucial for understanding the power of money, since, whatever one's theory of money, there is no doubt that it functions in and through exchange.

In focusing on exchange, then, the point is not to reduce money to exchange, and in the next section I draw on other theories of money to add more depth to the arguments presented here. Ultimately, it seems to me that money is overdetermined as an object, both in origin, history, and in terms of function.[9] Practically speaking, one's perspective on it shifts according to how one understands it, and each perspective is productive of some sort of useful knowledge. Focusing on exchange, then, is one means among others of grasping Jesus' opposition to mammon. Drawing on Marx's well-known discussion of the commodity form and the money form in volume 1 of *Capital* is helpful, in this respect. Although Marx in many ways gives a fairly standard account of the emergence of money out of exchange, he

---

8. See Graeber, *Debt*, who emphasizes this point in particular.

9. I borrow the term "overdetermined," of course, from Louis Althusser. See his essay "Contradiction and Overdetermination."

is also tuned in to certain theological sensibilities that attach to money so understood and more generally.

Commodities, the accumulation and distribution of which is essential to wealth in general but also specifically to the wealth of capitalist economies, are in the simplest terms external objects that satisfy various human needs, either directly through consumption or indirectly through production. How a commodity satisfies a need has no bearing on its status as a commodity, and Marx is clear that the same object simultaneously can and usually does serve multiple functions in regard to its overall usefulness. Marx refers to the usefulness of a commodity as its use-value, but this value does not "dangle in mid-air," he says.[10] That is, the use-value of a commodity is directly related to what it is apart from its use, what it is in its material existence. Marx says that the use-value of an object is "the physical body of the commodity itself" and, as such, is a property that is "independent of the amount of labor required to appropriate its useful qualities."[11] I will discuss labor in more detail in chapter 3, but it is important to point out that although use-value is a more or less objective property independent of the subject, that value only becomes actual or realized "in use or in consumption."[12] Thus, although we can speak in abstract terms of the material properties of commodities that account for their eventual use-value, use-value itself is determined dialectically. Commodities only become commodities through actual use, which requires production to mediate the usefulness of the otherwise inert materiality of objects.

Marx contrasts use-value with exchange-value, which appears initially as a purely quantitative determination of the object in relation to other commodities. That is, whereas use-value inheres in the object as qualities to be exploited through production and consumption, exchange-value abstracts itself from use-value and becomes actual in its relationship to the exchange-value of other objects. In exchange, the use-value of an object is thus of no real consequence, at least generally speaking. Sure, certain commodities appear to have more value relative to the labor that produced them than other commodities, but it is precisely the apparent inequality of value that exchange mediates and dissolves: x amount of commodity a can be exchanged for y amount of quantity b. Marx thus says that in "the exchange relation, one use-value is worth just as much as another, provided only that it is present in the appropriate quantity."[13]

10. Marx, *Capital*, 126.
11. Marx, *Capital*, 126.
12. Marx, *Capital*, 126.
13. Marx, *Capital*, 127.

At this basic level, however, exchange is cumbersome, and taken on its own terms essentially amounts to a "barter" economy, in which individuals utilize the exchange-value of their own commodities to attain other commodities for their use-value. Whether or not a pure barter economy has ever existed is beside the point, here. The point is, rather, that an economy based on exchange logically and practically entails the development of money, that is, an independent and universal form of value to represent the value of all commodities in relation to it rather than each other. Aristotle, as we said above, knew as much, and it is central to Adam Smith's argument in *The Wealth of Nations*, which still informs contemporary discussions of money.[14] But as Marx notes, so long as that medium is lacking, we technically do not have commodities at all. That is, without a universal, abstract equivalent, each person will count his or her own commodity as an equivalent which, all things being equal, amounts to no equivalent at all: "there is in fact no commodity acting as a universal equivalent, and the commodities possess no general relative form of value under which they can be equated as values and have the magnitude of their values compared. Therefore they definitely do not confront each other as commodities, but as products or use-value only."[15] What is needed, in other words, is a money-form to act as a basic standard of value for commodities and their circulation.

Money arises, according to Marx, when one particular commodity is transformed into a medium of universal exchange and is socially recognized as such. Gold, along with other precious metals, is the classic example of such a transformed commodity. Indeed, gold itself remains in the social imaginary the very image of "moneyness," even if gold no longer plays the role it once did in the economy.[16] Nevertheless, for Marx the reason that gold and other precious metals emerge out of exchange and take up their position as money is partly due to their use-values but also, and perhaps more importantly, because of the ease with which they are capable of precise quantitative differentiation and transport.

According to this commodity theory of money, then, "money" originally appears as one commodity among others but, through the development of exchange, takes the form of a general equivalent. Money is, in this

---

14. Smith, *Wealth of Nations*, 24–32.
15. Marx, *Capital*, 180.
16. President Richard Nixon severed the relationship of the US dollar to the gold standard on August 15, 1971, which served to shift international currency to a floating system of fiat money. Debates over the relationship between money and gold, which are ultimately debates about what constitutes money as money, are nothing new. See, for instance, Shell, *Money, Language, and Thought*. Chapter 1 is especially relevant, in that it discusses debates over paper money in the United States in the nineteenth century.

sense, a commodity that is the exception to commodities and, as exception, transcends the world of commodities through its power of abstraction. Although, to emphasize again, money cannot be reduced to exchange, the way that Marx articulates money as emerging out of exchange is helpful, since he draws attention to the theological qualities that money gains and then maintains in its abstraction. That is to say, once a particular object is excepted from the world of commodities and established as money, it tends to take on almost God-like qualities.

To understand how this is the case, it is important to emphasize that a commodity, which includes money as a universal equivalent in the form of an exception, is, according to Marx, "a very strange thing, abounding in metaphysical subtleties and theological niceties."[17] The peculiar nature of commodities does not arise out of their use-value and the labor expended to extract it but out of the commodity-form itself, that is, out of the process of exchange. The commodity qua commodity, that is, appears in exchange to have a set of objective characteristics apart from its specific use-value, characteristics that account for its value, whether in and of itself or in relation to money. The world of commodities, then, seems to exist independently of the subjects who enter that world through exchange, through the actual process that creates commodities. However, for Marx, such a view is an abstraction, a reification of the social processes of production. There is nothing "natural" about commodities: they are, rather, reflections of the labor of, and social relations among, those who produced them. One could say that commodities arise through misrecognition, through mistaking the social for the physical or natural or, put differently, displacing the processes of production onto the material relations among external objects. Marx says that "the commodity-form, and the value-relation of the products of labor within which it appears, have absolutely no connection with the physical nature of the commodity and the material [*dinglich*] relations arising out of this. It is nothing but the definite social relation between men themselves which assumes here, for them, the fantastic form of a relation between things."[18]

The best analogy for understanding this is, Marx suggests, religion. Although elsewhere critical of Feuerbach, Marx here relies on Feuerbach's suggestion that religion is really anthropology: God, the gods, and all other so-called religious objects are, in substance, external projections of human characteristics.[19] Marx thus says in "the misty realm of religion" the "prod-

---

17. Marx, *Capital*, 163.
18. Marx, *Capital*, 165.
19. See Feuerbach, *Essence of Christianity*. Marx's critique of Feuerbach can be

ucts of the human brain appear as autonomous figures endowed with a life of their own, which enter into relations both with each other and with the human race. So it is in the world of commodities with the products of men's hands."[20]

Marx refers to this substantialization and separation of labor in its objects as the "fetishism of the world of commodities." It is important to note, however, that commodity fetishism does not necessarily depend on an expressed belief in the "misty realm" of objects, that is, in the independence of the world of commodities. The misrecognition that occurs in the substitution of an external and, thereby, self-legitimating sphere of exchange for the social production of commodities, rather, takes place materially, in how we actually relate to commodities and, especially, money. As I pointed out in the last chapter in reference to Žižek's discussion of cynical consciousness, belief is embodied, marked in what we actually do. To the extent that we act "as if" commodities, and money in particular, exercise an independence with respect to the social realities out of which they emerge, then we actually believe as much. Moreover, it is this misrecognition that, at least in part, accounts for their power, and again money in particular. Once money is fetishized, it takes on a power in its own right, a power that no one individual can subvert. It does not matter if one, as an individual, cuts through money's ideological underpinnings, in both theory and practice; most everyone else believes otherwise, acting "as if" money were an object endowed with its own unique power and sense.

We act "as if" because, in a way, it really does have its own power and sense, at least once it has attained transcendence from its immanent, social production. It is this power that, of course, makes it attractive, but also constitutes money as desirable, because of its utility in exchange (the more money, the more one can get) but also in and of itself. Although in our current system, money is for the most part necessary in order to gain access to basic goods and services, that is, to those things needed to sustain life and a degree of comfort, the allure of money also engages us in activities above and beyond the latter, in practices focused on maintaining, gaining, and increasing wealth. Many of these practices, such as building equity and saving for retirement are, of course, considered commonplace, a basic aspect of life in a capitalist economic system, even if many do not have the basic resources to participate in them.

Nevertheless, even at the extreme end, such practices are not considered abnormal or pathological but are, instead, normalized as a sign of

---

found in his "Theses on Feurbach," in Tucker, *Marx-Engels Reader*.

20. Marx, *Capital*, 165.

success. We can see this anecdotally, for instance, by contrasting how we treat the accumulation of wealth with other commodities. I noted in the last chapter that, although it is common to collapse desire for money into a generalized desire that can, abstractly, be applied to any object whatsoever, in practice we actually do treat money differently. Noam Yuran uses the example of Imelda Marcos, former first lady of the Philippines, who in 1986 was reported to own 3,000 pairs of shoes, to illustrate this point. Noting that it is all too easy to chalk up such behavior as an instance of the "quirkiness of the rich" or, more seriously, as an instance of "pathological desire," Yuran questions why we do not treat collecting money in the same way. He writes:

> [W]ithout implying that anything is out of the ordinary, the media inundates us with a stream of information about people who acquire enormous amounts of money. It is considered a sign of craziness to collect shoes in excess of a certain number, whereas it is considered perfectly normal to amass an unlimited amount of money. Moreover, in these media stories, it goes without saying that a person with three thousand pairs of shoes in obsessed with that particular item. The mere possession of the collection attests to a somewhat pathological desire. However, in the same media space, rarely is it automatically assumed that a person in possession of millions or billions of dollars is obsessed with money.[21]

A more contemporary example might be the phenomenon of hoarding. Although we gaze with disgusted fascination at those who hoard,[22] at those who express a seemingly unlimited desire to collect and store the most mundane, useless objects, even labeling it a "mental illness," in contrast we treat those who "hoard" money as examples to be emulated, so long as the means through which it is acquired is at a surface-level on the up and up. Someone like Bill Gates is, in our minds, not a hoarder but a model citizen: his monopolistic accumulation of wealth simultaneously enables him to enact generosity through philanthropic means. The structure, here, is similar to that discussed in chapter 1, where the principle of charity coincides with a view of money as a neutral object.[23]

21. Yuran, *What Money Wants*, 13.

22. Hence the popularity of the television show *Hoarders*, which turns struggles and treatment of those who suffer from compulsive hoarding disorder into viewer spectacle. http://www.aetv.com/shows/hoarders.

23. In Žižek, *Violence*, Žižek points out this contradiction in someone like Bill Gates, whom he labels a "liberal communist": "Bill Gates is already the single greatest benefactor in the history of humanity, displaying his love for neighbors with hundreds of millions freely given to education, and the battles against hunger and malaria. The

We treat money differently than other commodities at least in part because of its relationship to the latter. The relationship between money and other commodities, that is, is asymmetrical, in the sense that money can always be exchanged for commodities but commodities cannot always be exchanged for money. Some commodities of course are, all things considered, more exchangeable than others because of the way in which they store value (e.g., real estate, art, gold, etc.), which may even out some of the asymmetry involved, at least in practice. Structurally, however, it always remains the case that the relationship of a given commodity to money is indirect: even if the commodity is considered valuable, its value is only such according to its potential or actual liquidity. Simply put, a commodity is only worth what someone will pay for it. Money, and the person who possesses it, thus always has the upper hand in exchange, and it is because of this that money—and not commodities—can be considered the real source of wealth. As Kojin Karatani puts it, "The person who has money can always exchange it for commodities: it carries the right of direct exchangeability. To own money is to possess a 'social pledge' that can be directly exchanged at any time and any place for any commodity."[24]

The role that money plays here, along with the subject's relation to it, cannot simply be chalked up to psychological factors or, more simply, greed. Although money can and certainly often is leveraged in just this manner, its power is worked into the role that it plays in exchange. It is this that, Marx says, constitutes money as "the *object* of eminent possession."[25] Because it provides and secures access to commodities, money is that commodity which, under normal circumstances, we seek out above all else. Such seeking, moreover, cannot be reduced to a moral concern, as if one consistently had a choice; it is, rather, forced, to the extent that we actually need money in order to enter the sphere of exchange, which is constitutive of life itself.

Borrowing the Tillichian language I referred to in the last chapter, to say that our relationship to money as "ultimate concern" is forced is not to say that money exercises its power over us only or primarily as a sovereign, coercive entity. In the next section I will discuss money in relationship to sovereignty, specifically the state, but since Foucault we have become accustomed to understanding the functioning of power through more subtle,

---

catch, of course, is that in order to give, first you have to take—or, as some would put it—create. The justification of liberal communists is that in order to really help people, you must have the means to do it" (20). Gates' charity is, in a sense, "the humanitarian mask hiding the face of economic exploitation" (22).

24. Karatani, *Structure of World History*, 93.

25. Marx, "The Power of Money," in *Economic and Philosophic Manuscripts*, 119; original emphasis.

disciplinary means.[26] Power, in other words, is not concentrated but dispersed in the social-symbolic field, acting through a variety of institutions, measures, and practices. Power is, to a large extent, biopower, meaning that it works in, through, and on life itself: power is produced and reproduced through systems of control, systems that form our bodies and desires.

It is no different with money, and numerous theorists have recently called attention to the affective dimensions of our relationship to money under neoliberalism.[27] But whereas we often recognize, at least intellectually, the various disciplinary techniques that constitute the social-symbolic field in which we live, move, and have our being, to borrow language from Saint Paul (Acts 17:28), we often fail to grasp how money works similarly. Money is effective as a disciplinary instrument *because* it works affectively on us. As Martin Konings points out, "Money is not just an abstract symbol, an empty universal, but a sign that is capable of speaking to our most intensely felt individual needs. Even when we subscribe to discourses that depict money as soulless and destructive, our practical conduct remains fully organized around the awareness that money gives life, will provide us access to whatever complex experiences we are after. We experience no trade-off in life."[28] Nevertheless, we experience no trade-off because there actually is no trade-off, at least if one assumes the current organization of the economy and its world. The affectivity of money, then, although palpable, is always correlated to its necessity: we cannot get away from it, no matter how we feel.[29] Even Jesus and his disciples carried money, though in the form of a "common purse" (John 12:6; 13:29).

Nevertheless, to say that money is unique among all other commodities in the sense described above is also to make a theological claim: its role in exchange constitutes "the omnipotence of its being." Money is, as Marx says, the great mediator: "Money is the *procurer* between man's need and the object, between his life and his means of life. But *that which* mediates my

---

26. For Foucault, power in the modern era morphs from a sovereign, top-down model to a disciplinary one, where power is dispersed throughout institutions and internalized by subjects. Power is, in other words, biopower. As Foucault puts it in *History of Sexuality*, 140: "During the classical period, there was a rapid development of various disciplines—universities, secondary schools, barracks, workshops; there was also the emergence, in the field of political practices and economic observation, of the problems of birthrate, longevity, public health, housing, and migration. Hence there was an explosion of numerous and diverse techniques for achieving the subjugation of bodies and the control of populations, marking the beginning of an era of 'biopower.'"

27. See, for instance, Massumi, *Power at the End*; Lazzarato, *Signs and Machines*; Konings, *Emotional Logic*.

28. Konings, *Emotional Logic*, 19.

29. Konigns notes, for instance, that the solution to money problems is more money.

life for me, also *mediates* the existence of other people for me. For me it is the *other* person."[30]

The power of money, however, also transcends the sphere of exchange proper or, said otherwise, turns the seemingly unexchangeable into a commodity. This is, of course, a common feature of neoliberalism, in which we see the extension of a market logic into aspects of life that, presumably, used to be relatively free from such calculation.[31] But money does not just buy access to an ever-increasing world of commodities but to desire itself, which means that money is, again, of all commodities the most desirable, the highest good. Marx puts it this way:

> That which is for me through the medium of *money*—that for which I can pay (i.e., which money can buy)—that am *I myself*, the possessor of the money. Money's properties are my—the possessor's—properties and essential powers. The extent of the power of money is the extent of my power. Money's properties are my—the possessor's—properties and essential powers. Thus, what I *am* and *am capable of* is by no means determined by my individuality. I *am* ugly, but I can buy for myself the *most beautiful* of women. Therefore I am not *ugly*, for the effect of *ugliness* – its deterrent power—is nullified by money. I, according to my individual characteristics, am *lame*, but money furnishes me with twenty-four feet. Therefore I am not lame. I am bad, dishonest, unscrupulous, stupid; but money is honoured, and hence its possessor. Money is the supreme good, therefore its possessor is good. Money, besides, saves me the trouble of being dishonest: I am therefore presumed honest. I am *brainless*, but money is the *real brain* of all things and how then should its possessor be brainless? Besides, he can buy clever people for himself, and is he who has power over the clever not more clever than the clever? Do not I, who thanks to money am capable of *all* that the human heart longs for, possess all human capacities? Does not my money, therefore, transform all my incapacities into their contrary?[32]

30. Marx, "The Power of Money," in *Economic and Philosophic Manuscripts*, 119.

31. As Connolly puts it in his *Fragility of Things*, 22: "Perhaps the quickest way, then, to dramatize the difference between classical market liberalism and contemporary neoliberalism is to say that the former wanted the state to minimize interference with 'natural' market processes as it purported to leave other parts of civil society to their own devices, while the latter campaigns to make the state, the media, schools, families, science, churches, unions, and the corporate estate be ordered around neoliberal principles of being." See also Brown, *Undoing the Demos*.

32. Marx, "The Power of Money," in *Economic and Philosophic Manuscripts*, 121; original emphasis.

Money does not merely respond to or reflect the world as it is, acting on and facilitating relationships between otherwise already-existing, passive objects. Money actually transforms the world, turning the seemingly impossible into the possible: like the biblical God, it creates the world in its own image.

But the world it creates is a divided world. Money shapes who we are and mediates social relationships, that is, the other, for us (and, we could add, non-human relationships as well),[33] but it does not do so evenly. In abstraction, exchange is often assumed to be a neutral medium that rests on a basic equality between and among actors, because it relies on money. Indeed, that assumption is crucial to the mythology of the market, which stipulates that legally amassed wealth is, generally speak, fair game: it is the natural result of competition for scarce resources. We never come to the market in abstraction, however, but as embodied, laden with particularities and histories, which to a large extent determine in advance one's position in exchange, at least initially. Exchange, in this sense, entails inequality which, when combined with the power of money results in differentiating wealth.

I draw this notion of differentiating wealth from Jose Porfirio Miranda's short polemical book *Communism in the Bible*. For Miranda, Jesus' numerous and varied condemnations of money, wealth, and the wealthy should not be understood as a condemnation of wealth as such. Nor should Jesus' converse exaltation of the poor through his reversal of values (e.g., "the last shall be first, and the first shall be last") be understood as an exhortation to poverty, as if lacking wealth were somehow good in and of itself. To assume as much would be to assign an otherworldly asceticism to Jesus, a withdrawal from the world that is completely foreign to his words and deeds. "Jesus has," Miranda says, "no horror of wealth, neither in itself nor in its use and enjoyment."[34] When Jesus condemns the rich and wealth more generally, he is doing so not absolutely but in relation to the poor. What Jesus is against, Miranda argues, is "*differentiating*, or relative, wealth," and it is this he condemns "implacably—so intransigently and unexceptionably that official Western theology is too traumatized to take a really close look at the condemnation for fear the whole meaning of the Bible may depend on it."[35]

Whereas, as I have discussed above, the mainstream of the theological tradition and the church have tended to deal with poverty ultimately

---

33. For a discussion of the way in which capitalism organizes our relationship to nature, see Moore, *Capitalism in the Web of Life*.

34. Miranda, *Communism in the Bible*, 21.

35. Miranda, *Communism in the Bible*, 21, 22.

in moral terms, the practical results of which amount to charity, Miranda's notion of differentiating wealth conceives of it as a structural issue.[36] That is, the differentiating wealth that marks and divides rich and poor is a moral problem because its gain is illicit, at the expense of the poor. Surveying numerous biblical passages—which he does more copiously in his *Marx and the Bible*—Miranda concludes that "it is inescapable that according to the Bible there is no legitimate fashion of acquiring differentiating wealth."[37] Legitimacy is, of course, a relative notion, but Miranda's claim here is not legal but theological. One can and often does, of course, acquire differentiating wealth through means that are more or less in accordance with established laws, but Miranda stresses that the latter by no means function as the ultimate horizon of the biblical traditions. For the biblical traditions, differentiating wealth is, on Miranda's account, evil: the biblical authors "know that *all* differentiating wealth is ill-gotten, that it has necessarily been obtained by despoiling and oppressing the rest of the population, and that therefore to be rich is to be unjust."[38] This is why, Miranda says, that when the rich man in the Parable of the Rich Man and Lazarus is punished, it is simply because he is wealthy opposite Lazarus.

CREDIT AND DEBT

I have been discussing money, as an aspect of mammon, primarily in terms of commodities and exchange, that is, as emerging out of exchange as a particular commodity that functions as a universal medium. As part of this discussion, I also pointed out the way in which exchange, taken as a whole, tends toward differentiating wealth, which for Miranda makes it unjust. This is basically Marx's view, and, with the exception of the notion of differentiating wealth, mainstream economics, and a sort of common sense grasp of matters, all seem to understand money in these terms. Understanding money in these terms, moreover, is helpful for my own purposes, since through it we can get a sense of the theological workings of money through exchange, the inequality that such exchange assumes and fosters, and the basic limitations of the subject to act otherwise. Nevertheless, understanding money solely through exchange has limited value and, in the end, presents

---

36. This is, of course, not to say that the theological tradition ignores structural issues. Catholic social teaching and liberal Protestantism have repeatedly emphasized the importance of addressing these. Nevertheless, so long as money is not the real issue, these ultimately run aground.

37. Miranda, *Communism in the Bible*, 24.

38. Miranda, *Communism in the Bible*, 32.

a one-sided picture of what money is and does. The commodity theory of money, although compelling in certain respects, lacks full explanatory force, and in a very elementary sense: it assumes what it wants to explain, that is, the emergence of money out of exchange. It cannot on its own terms explain the leap from commodity to money, along with the subjective agreement that would make it possible, and tends to confuse money with the object that represents it.

Along with other functions, money certainly facilitates exchange, but it is important not to confuse the material instantiation of money with money itself. According to Geoffrey Ingham, discussions of money as a medium of exchange tend to confuse the particular form that money takes, its physical or, today, virtual appearance, with "moneyness," that is, the abstract measure of value behind its material embodiment. The latter, of course, can vary widely, and there is no dearth of commentary on the peculiar forms that money has taken through its historical development.[39] But, according to Ingham, the existence of money qua commodity implies an independent standard, or money of account, the value of which is represented in and through various and differentiated media. Indeed, the emergence of stable markets requires this money of account and cannot be explained solely through the concept of exchange alone. Ingham writes, "The market model of the spontaneous emergence of a common medium of exchange fails to explain how myriad bilateral exchange ratios of barter trades could produce a stable price for any commodity standard. Rather, it is the money of account, regardless of the existence of any media of exchange or means of payment, which makes an orderly market possible. Money of account is logically anterior to the market."[40]

If we really want to understand money, then, Ingham argues that we must focus on the money of account that lies behind, so to speak, the money used in transactions, the physical stuff that we normally take for money. For Ingham, this means understanding money as "*a measure of abstract value* (money of account) . . . and as a *means of storing* and *transporting* this abstract value."[41] This entails, for Ingham, that money is first and foremost a social mechanism, which means that it is constituted through credit-debt relations backed by some authority that grants these legitimacy.

As a way into understanding this, note that something like barter ostensibly relies on a certain amount of interpersonal trust. Because of this, barter is not only clumsy in an economic sense, as commodity theorists

---

39. See, for instance, Davies' massive *History of Money*.
40. Ingham, *Nature of Money*, 34.
41. Ingham, *Nature of Money*, 70; original emphasis.

have long recognized; it is also limiting in an interpersonal sense, since barter exchange so understood would rely on determinations of individual trustworthiness. In contrast, as Ingham points out, a "money transaction differs from barter in that the burden of trust is removed from the participants in the actual transaction and placed on a third party—the issuer of money."[42] Money is impersonal, and it is this impersonality that allows it to function as money. Money, one could say, inserts itself in the midst of so-called natural relationships, neutralizing and/or ignoring them for the purpose of exchange. To borrow language made popular by the Jewish existentialist philosopher Martin Buber, money has the power to transform exchange from I-Thou relationships to I-It relationships—and it is extremely adept at doing so.[43]

This does not mean that historically and conceptually all exchange relationships are, in the end, reducible to money, even if neoliberalism pushes them in this direction. The extensive literature on the gift and gift economies proves otherwise and, indeed, even in highly developed money economies not all exchanges can be chalked up to money, at least in actual practice.[44] David Graeber has rightly drawn attention to this, referring to a sort of base-level "communism" that subtends social relations.[45] Money does, however, have the power to transform these relationships, which is why money appears as a virtual necessity for complex market economies, in which the responsibility for labor, production, goods, and services is dispersed throughout the social realm, albeit unevenly. Money thus allows for the expansion of the social realm, allowing for a degree of interaction beyond normal, communally based ties. That interaction is, of course, to a large extent impersonal, constituted and governed as it is by money, but the necessary impersonal element also may enable more substantive, interpersonal interactions.

At the same time, however, the impersonal character of exchange relationships when mediated through money may also allow individuals to limit, if not avoid altogether, interpersonal interactions, because of the non- or extra-monetary obligations these often entail. Lacan makes this point in Seminar II, when he notes, "Everyone knows that money doesn't just buy things, but that the prices which, in our culture, are calculated at rock-bottom, have the function of neutralizing something infinitely more dangerous

---

42. Ingham, *Nature of Money*, 72.
43. Buber, *I and Thou*.
44. The classic discussion of the notion of "the gift" is, of course, Mauss's *The Gift*.
45. See Graeber, *Debt*, 89–126.

than paying in money, namely owing somebody something."[46] The immediate context of Lacan's comment is the relationship between the analyst and the analysand. The analysand must pay, and the analyst must accept payment, for analysis because the monetary exchange for services renders treatment impersonal and clinical. It assures, in other words, that analysis cannot be confused with something else, however we might conceive the latter. Commenting on the role of money in analysis, Bruce Fink notes that the "money we give analysts means that they are not playing this role as a favour for which we must be eternally grateful, as we often feel we must to our parents, whom we can never adequately thank for having brought us into the world. Payment means they are not doing it out of charity, because they love us, or because they think we are good-looking or charming or might turn out to be useful to them in some way. Payment means they are doing it because it is their job to do so."[47] Otherwise put, the impersonality of the analysand-analyst relationship makes analysis impersonal too, which also makes it more effective—and it is money that guarantees this impersonality. Monetary exchange bars the relationship from the interpersonal dynamics that contribute to psychic disturbances in the first place, thus allowing the analysand to confront his or her dis-ease. Although the analysand will likely project onto the analyst the unconscious *jouissance* that structures his or her subjectivity, that projection is not, strictly speaking, interpersonal, since the analyst is only playing a part, paid to take on a role. Thus, as Fink says, "Payment means they are doing it because it is their job to do so."[48]

What applies in analysis has, as is often the case, a more general, social purview. That is, just as the impersonal nature of the analysand-analyst relationship makes analysis possible, so too does the impersonal character of exchange relationships make the market possible. Indeed, it is hard to see how there would be a market, at least as we normally understand it, without a degree of anonymous neutrality. Some may bemoan that fact, pining nostalgically for some sort of lost community of face-to-face interactions, the kind that involve the intra- and interpersonal relationships ostensibly absent, seemingly absent as a general principle in monetary exchange. Hence the attraction of something like "the gift" or, in more recent theological thought, neo-communitarian forms of thought and organization.[49] There is

---

46. Lacan, *Ego in Freud's Theory*, 204.
47. Fink, "Analysand and Analyst," 32.
48. Fink, "Analysand and Analyst," 32.
49. The latter is more of a general trend within certain theological and ecclesiastical circles. Stanley Hauerwas's work is extremely influential to this line of thinking. Since, for instance, his collaboration with Will Willimon, *Resident Aliens*, for a more popular account that has seen a broad readership over the past few decades. The so-called

something to that impulse, of course, though it often gets expressed nostalgically or, conversely, exploited in something like the "sharing economy," as supposedly personal interactions become the means through which market dominance is gained.[50] Nevertheless, few of us would want all of our interactions, all of the time, to be organized as such, especially with the sense of psychological and moral indebtedness that goes along with it. It would, in other words, amount to psychic and material overload, inhibiting our subjectivity from the other direction. To borrow again from Buber, I-It relationships, although they always run the risk of depersonalization, allow us to function as a subject in the world at all. Money helps make this possible.

One criticism of the sort of impersonal anonymity that money makes possible is that it results in a self-interested individualism. The logic of the market, so this line goes, uproots individuals from "natural" relationships, obligations, and shared ends. Individuals may be allowed to pursue their interests, which is a positive, even if it can result in certain myopia; but without any grounding or sense of the common good, the individual is, to put it bluntly, doomed, utterly depersonalized for the sake of economic gain.[51] As with the critique of anonymity, there is certainly something to this line of thought, and it would not be hard to come up with numerous examples of the negative aspects of capitalist deterritorialization, to use Deleuze and Guattari's term.[52] Nevertheless, what the critique misses is the productive component at work in deterritorialization or, to borrow from Deleuze and Guatarri again, the various movements of reterritorialization that money makes possible. Said differently, while money displaces some social relationships, it replaces these with others.[53] Capitalism, in this sense, is not so much a-social but manifests another sociality, one that cannot be reduced simply to a depersonalized individualism.

So understood, the latter, if and when it does occur—and it does occur—is more of a by-product of the expanding social logic of current political-economic arrangements rather than the goal. Indeed, the un-rooted individualism that critics bemoan is, from another perspective, the very thing that promotes the social good: so long as all others are acting in their own interests as well, being self-interested in one's actions miraculously promotes the good of all, as if an "invisible hand" were guiding the market and

---

new-monasticism is one such expression of Hauerwas's vision. See, for instance, Wilson-Hartgrove, *New Monasticism*.

50. See Sundararajan, *Sharing Economy*.
51. This is Bell's criticism in Bell, *Economy of Desire*, 81–122.
52. Deleuze and Guattari, *Anti-Oedipus*.
53. See Konings, *Emotional Logic*; and Joseph, *Debt to Society*.

its actors, as Adam Smith famously said.⁵⁴ Moreover, this expanding social logic does not take place for its own sake, but for money's, for mammon's. Money, and the exchange it makes possible, is not neutral; it does not exist as a mere means to enable certain functions, necessary or otherwise, in distinction from a self-contained, social realm. Money, once it inserts itself into interpersonal relationships, remakes the social in its own image, expanding its logic both internally (at the individual level) and externally, to become all-encompassing. Such is the organization of capital we refer to as neoliberal, but again the difference in the latter is one of degree and not kind: it is a potential that lies in money itself, because of the type of object that it is. Hence, Ingham maintains that "monetary space is sovereign space."⁵⁵

Although this social space is organized variously, at its root it is based on credit-debt relationships—because this is ultimately what money is. Ingham writes:

> All money is constituted by credit-debt relations—that is, social relations. First . . . the holder of money is owed goods; money is a claim on the social product. Second . . . money is a credit for the user because it is a debt (liability) for the issuer. (Issuers promise to accept back their own money in payment of a debt.) Thus, the holder of money is both owed goods and has the means of discharging any debt contracted in money of account that exists to be discharged in that monetary space. Money cannot be created without the simultaneous creation of debt. For money to *be* money presupposes the existence of a debt measured in money of account elsewhere in the social system and, more importantly, in the debt created by the issuer's promises to accept back it's money in settlement. In other words, the money debt is *assignable*—or transferable, or negotiable.⁵⁶

As Ingham points out, understanding money in terms of credit and debt shifts attention away from commodities to social relationships, and it adds another layer to our understanding of what is actually happening in exchange. The conceptualization of barter is largely one-dimensional, in that it assumes a simple exchange of goods. This is why, in the commodity theory of money, exchange is really just a more efficient form of barter: money provides the medium for exchange of goods, which means that one is really trading for the medium, for money. When money is understood along the lines of credit-debt and the relationships between creditor and

54. Vogl, *The Specter of Capital*, 26.
55. Ingham, *Nature of Money*, 71.
56. Ingham, *Nature of Money*, 72.

debtor, however, transactions take place along two, interrelated levels. As Ingham states, "Money is exchanged *for* goods; it is also the abstract value *by* which goods are priced and exchanged. Goods and money 'change hands,' but the money is also cancelling the *debt* incurred for the goods priced in the money of account in abstract value."[57]

Another way to put the matter is to say that money is really a promise, which means that it is based on trust. The trust involved, here, is not interpersonal trust, since that would take us back to more of a barter relationship, which is, as I said above, structurally distinct from a monetary relationship. Trust is, rather, impersonal, ultimately grounded not in the individuals involved in transactions but in a third party that backs what money promises, that is, its legitimacy as a means for paying accrued debts. Ingham thus notes, "Money is assignable trust. In the face of real-world radical uncertainty, self-fulfilling long-term trust is rooted in a social and political legitimacy whereby potentially personally untrustworthy strangers are able to participate in complex multilateral relationships."[58]

We can also take a broader, more theological view on the promissory nature of money. Money is certainly, as Ingham stresses, constituted in part through the promise that it is a legitimate and acceptable means for paying off the debt accrued in and through exchange, exchange being understood here in terms of credit-debt relations rather than in terms of commodities. So understood, promise quite literally makes exchange possible and, to the extent that society is constituted through exchange, society itself. But, at another level, it also promises a place within exchange for the actors involved. That is to say, money as promise is also based in and on competition, which means, as Goodchild emphasizes, that money is also threat. Goodchild writes:

> Money, as an absolute sign of wealth, combines the promise of wealth with the threat of poverty, for the wealth promised by money is only temporary. Only capital promises enduring wealth. For one who holds money and buys, the freedom to satisfy demands is a promise of wealth; once the purchase has taken place, however, the condition is replaced by one of the absence of money. The threat of poverty follows the promise of wealth. For one who sells to acquire money, money holds out the promise of freedom to satisfy demands. Yet failure to sell

---

57. Ingham, *Nature of Money*, 73; original emphasis.
58. Ingham, *Nature of Money*, 74.

holds out the threat of poverty. The threat of poverty precedes the promise of wealth.[59]

That threat, of course, is based at least in part on the myth of scarcity that lies behind and supports competition as the driving force of the economy in capitalist societies, but it is also based on simple and real needs, that is, survival itself. To the extent that money is tied to survival, in a very real way, then money is also based on coercion: we are forced to use money as a means to meet our needs, wants, and desires. Heidegger may have considered *Dasein* as thrown into the world, but the world into which we are thrown is not abstract but one in which money mediates our life, our being-in-the-world. To quote Goodchild again, "One can have security in such a society only if one has a dependable source of income. One can participate in such a society only to the extent that one has access to money or credit. While money promises the freedom of the market, it also threatens the constraint of exclusion."[60] One is, then, as Goodchild argues, constrained to use money, obligated to participate in activities associated with its acquisition. One can, theoretically at least, opt out, but that involves exclusion from relationships of interdependence, society, and—indeed—life itself. Opting out, in other words, is akin to death, or at least being-toward it.[61]

The power of money is not embodied in its promise alone, then; it is also embodied in the threat present within a market society, the threat that a market society poses to existence as such. Such is the contradiction at the heart of a money economy, a contradiction that is intensified under capitalism, especially its neoliberal variety: money promises security, increased standards of living, access to needs and desires, and overall well-being, while threatening all of these at the same time. The promise on which money is based, then, takes the form of a threat, and this has everything to do with the type of object money is, with its primary position in exchange relationships and its ties to sovereignty. Quoting Goodchild again:

> The initial impetus giving value to money is nothing less than its promise and threat. If, prior to the marketization of society, the promise carries more weight than the threat, then subsequent to

---

59. Goodchild, *Theology of Money*, 106–7.
60. Goodchild, *Theology of Money*, 107.
61. It is not surprising, then, that those who have willingly given up money, for whatever reason, also find themselves living to some extent outside of society, both ideologically and materially. There is a small, alternative literature that treats this theme. See, for instance, Sundeen, *Man Who Quit Money*. It is telling, however, that many who "quit money" do so not out of necessity, but out of choice: they have the means, in other words, to opt out.

the marketization of society both promise and threat are intensified: more relations can be constituted than ever before through the market; fewer relations can be reconstituted at all outside the market. Through the agency of money, the market effects a progressive colonization of society. Through the colonization of society, the market intensifies the demand for money.[62]

Money, and the market more generally, then, cannot be reduced to its variegated functions in exchange. Rather, it relies for its power on various external resources, that is, the force of promise as threat and threat as promise.

It is in light of all this that we can say that the impersonality that the market offers comes at a price. Money offers freedom through anonymity, but that freedom turns against itself, repackaging and generalizing the conditions it is ostensibly supposed to avoid and transposing them onto another plane. Such is, at least, Maurizio Lazzarato's argument concerning debt, in *The Making of the Indebted Man*. Money, as I have said, is essentially debt, which means that it is based on trust, however abstractly or minimally we may characterize the latter. In a complex, globalized economy, money according to Ingham thus "consists in vast networks of debtor-creditor relationships between issuers and users, and the seemingly obvious point that monetary systems involve the continuous contracting and discharging to debts must not be overlooked."[63] Numerous elements must be in place, of course, in order for that system to work, including effective means for transferring debts and credit, along with a stable, viable, and socially recognized currency. But crucial within that system is also the payment of debts. As Ingham says, "Debtors must be, first, willing and, second, able to pay."[64] That willingness and that ability is crucial to the production of money through debt, meaning that confidence on behalf of creditors with respect to debtors is key to the whole system. Such confidence is marked, in the current system, through complex measures of creditworthiness. Hence the importance of a credit rating or score, for countries, institutions, and individuals.

Measures of creditworthiness are largely impersonal, meaning that they rely on a series of ostensibly objective, economic measures, rather than interpersonal interaction, to determine willingness and ability to pay. Nevertheless, as Ingham points out, this anonymous network, which measures confidence and putatively assigns trust to purely external factors, depends on a "morality of indebtedness." As Ingham puts it, "the economic ties that are constituted by the vast network of credits and debts fundamentally

---

62. Goodchild, *Theology of Money*, 108.
63. Ingham, *Nature of Money*, 77.
64. Ingham, *Nature of Money*, 77.

comprise a 'moral' network that depends on the keeping of promises."[65] Otherwise put, that network entails that debtors understand their debts in terms of responsibility, responsibility for the debt itself and to the creditor(s) who extended and/or own it. Without a moral notion of individual and corporate responsibility, the system could not function in the way that it does, which is why notions of debt relief and forgiveness and, on the other side of the equation, debt resistance, remain problematic, even if they might, in some circumstances, make good economic sense.

It is this notion of responsibility for debt that, according to Lazzarato, capitalism generalizes, especially in its neoliberal instantiation. Like Ingham, Lazzarato's work is based on the observation that the creation of debt is not a hindrance to the economy but its very condition, especially under its neoliberal organization. The creation of and speculation on individual, collective, corporate, and sovereign debt is a major source of financial revenue and wealth creation, one that ultimately drives the global economy. Simply put, without the creation of debt through the extension of credit and its financial instrumentalization, the economy as we know it would grind to a halt and, perhaps, collapse.[66]

The real significance of Lazzarato's work, however, lies in his claim that the economic relationship between credit and debt also functions as a paradigm for social relationships, which means that there is a subjective quality to debt and its creation and maintenance. The relationship between credit-debt and creditor-debtor does not function merely at an economic level but shapes subjectivity itself: under neoliberalism we all understand ourselves, in one way or another, in terms of debt. Lazzarato writes, "It is debt and the creditor-debtor relationship that make up the subjective paradigm of modern-day capitalism, in which 'labor' is coupled with 'work on the self,' in which economic activity and the ethico-political activity of producing the subject go hand in hand. Debt breeds, subdues, manufactures, adapts, and shapes subjectivity."[67] It shapes us, in other words, as indebted subjects—we are our debt.

The indebted subject is not a by-product but, rather, essential to neoliberalism. On the one hand, neoliberalism requires materially indebted subjects, that is, subjects who must, for numerous reasons, take on and use numerous forms of debt, which in turn can be put into circulation in financial markets for the creation of wealth. On the other hand, neoliberalism

---

65. Ingham, *Nature of Money*, 77.

66. Though that debt must also be to some extent viable, as we know from the financial crisis of 2007–08. See, for instance, Marazzi, *Violence of Financial Capitalism*.

67. Lazzarato, *Making of the Indebted Man*, 38–39.

moralizes debt and the creditor-debtor relationship, so that the indebted subject understands his or her debt in terms of obligation, guilt, and responsibility.[68] Debt, we could say, functions biopolitically in neoliberalism, encompassing all aspects of life to shape the very being of the subject.[69]

Money, then, relies structurally on the extension of credit through debt, but its economic organization and functioning depends upon the dispersal of a certain morality, which allows it to leverage individuals on its behalf. Moreover, since the relationship between creditor and debtor is always and by definition asymmetrical, differentiating wealth, which I mentioned above, is a basic feature of the system. Debt depends on differentiating wealth, which in Miranda's terms means that debt lends itself to an unjust form of social organization.

None of this would be possible, however, if money were not also tied to sovereignty. Money is certainly legitimated trust, which means that money is created through debt and relies on a moral substrate of obligation, guilt, and responsibility. However, since money is not valuable in and of itself, that is, in its materiality, and cannot be reduced to interpersonal relationships or its function in exchange, then there must be some legitimating entity. The obvious candidate is, at least at present, the state, but the particular form that entity takes can vary, in both theory and practice. What matters, rather, is the extent to which the entity in question can exercise the power of coercion. I have already noted this coercive power above using different terms, when discussing the necessity of having and using money to enter into various spheres of exchange. That one cannot not use money represents the latter's particular force. Ingham, however, suggests that the real coercive power of money lies in taxation, the institution of which captures individuals and organizations within the power of the state. "[T]he monopolistic imposition of a money of account, and a refusal to accept any other than the approved credit tokens of the issuer," Ingham argues, "go hand in hand with the monopolization of physical force."[70]

The question of money, then, is also a question of sovereignty, and the value of money lies in the power of the entity that backs it in the form of debt, a power that, in a sort of feedback loop, relies on money. Indeed, as Maurizio Lazzarato has argued, if we really want to understand political economy and the role that money plays within it, we must begin with the question of sovereignty and the political constitution of money, which

---

68. Lazzarato cites Nietzsche's second essay from the *Genealogy of Morality* in support of this view. See Lazzarato, *Making of the Indebted Man*, 37–88.

69. Graeber makes similar claims in *Debt*.

70. Ingham, *Nature of Money*, 76.

includes the relation of credit and debt, not exchange. The former is, strictly speaking, prior to the latter, which means that exchange is grounded in the power of the state and its ability to tax its subjects. Noting that the model of political economy put forth by Marx in volume 1 of *Capital* begins, as I said above, with the commodity theory of money, Lazzarato writes, "Barter does not come first, then exchange and money as a means of equivalence, of circulation and payment, to finally end up at taxes exacted by the state apparatus of capture. Instead, we must start with the political constitution of a stock of money; and now it is taxes and not exchange that create the equivalence of goods and services through which money is able to function."[71] For Lazzarato, it is taxation that ensures the economy and the relationships within it, including that between creditor and debtor, and not the other way around, which means that taxation measures "the power and control exercised over the population."[72]

Lazzarato's argument is specifically addressed to advanced capitalist societies, but it is applicable more generally. As Goodchild notes, the establishment of the Bank of England at the end of the seventeenth century coincided with the systematic creation of money through credit, which became a model for banking generally down to the present. Nevertheless, that money had value and stability because it was, in effect, "underwritten by the power of the state to raise taxes."[73] Goodchild notes as well that, although the establishment of the Bank of England is a watershed for money and the development of capitalism, in that it "inaugurated the period when credit effectively functioned as money . . . the creation of money as credit does not so much change as reveal the essence of money."[74] Money is, and always has been, credit, or alternatively debt, but it has also always been tied to sovereignty, and hence coercion and violence.

JESUS, DEBT, STATE

I have focused on a broader understanding of money that understands it in terms of debt and sovereignty in addition to exchange because I think it provides another way to understand what Jesus says about mammon. Indeed, I would suggest that limiting our understanding of money to exchange leads to misunderstanding, giving an incomplete picture of what Jesus says about mammon. This, in turn, allows readers to blunt the force of

71. Lazzarato, *Governing by Debt*, 35.
72. Lazzarato, *Governing by Debt*, 36.
73. Goodchild, *Theology of Money*, 7.
74. Goodchild, *Theology of Money*, 7.

his pronouncements against money, wealth, and related matters. The sovereignty of money over exchange, the theological demarcation of money as the value of all values, can certainly be understood by appealing to the mechanisms operative in exchange. But the power of money can only be understood fully by taking into account the economic and moral relationship between credit and debt and sovereignty.

It is essential to emphasize, in this respect, that Jesus portrays his activity as one that is largely against debt. Jesus' campaign against debt, against the way it functions in terms of differentiating wealth and sovereignty, is not merely an aspect of his mission but is, rather, fundamental to it, a natural outgrowth of the disjunction between God and mammon.

Indeed, if we take that disjunction as central for understanding what Jesus taught and did, we can also understand why he is, generally speaking, against debt: debt forces one to serve mammon, rather than God. Debt is, in other words, a primary means to enact servitude and, in this sense, it functions as a mechanism for social and economic inequality, that is, for differentiating wealth.[75] Although debt and its servitude are, of course, articulated and leveraged variously throughout history and place, debt itself remains an essential feature of social maintenance and control. So much is true whether we are talking about the ancient or contemporary world, or worlds in between.[76]

Note that the first thing that Jesus does of any significance, at least according to Luke's Gospel, is challenge the notion of debt and proclaim its general release, a release, he claims, that is fulfilled in his person:

> When he came to Nazareth, where he had been brought up, he went to the synagogue on the sabbath day, as was his custom. He stood up to read, and the scroll of the prophet Isaiah was given to him. He unrolled the scroll and found the place where it was written: "The Spirit of the Lord is upon me, because he has anointed me to bring good news to the poor. He has sent me to proclaim release to the captives and recovery of sight to the blind, to let the oppressed go free, to proclaim the year of the Lord's favor." And he rolled up the scroll, gave it back to the

---

75. As Oakman, *Jesus, Debt*, 18 notes: "Debt was one of the major mechanisms whereby the rich kept getting richer, and the poor, poorer."

76. This is an important point to emphasize. Although much of the literature on debt treats it from the perspective of neoliberalism, we should not confine the economic and subjective power of debt to its contemporary form. Such is the broad contribution that Graeber's *Debt* makes, but Karatani (*Structure of World History*), also makes a similar point, noting the way in which debt functions historically through different modes of exchange. For more detailed studies of the role of debt in antiquity, see Hudson and Van De Mieroop, *Debt and Economic Renewal*.

attendant, and sat down. The eyes of all in the synagogue were fixed on him. Then he began to say to them, "Today this scripture has been fulfilled in your hearing." (Luke 4:16–21)

Jesus here connects "the year of the Lord's favor" in Isa 61 with the biblical tradition of Jubilee. Leviticus 25 legislates that every seventh year is to be "a sabbath for the LORD":

> Six years you shall sow your field, and six years you shall prune your vineyard, and gather in their yield; but in the seventh year there shall be a sabbath of complete rest for the land, a sabbath for the LORD; you shall not sow your field or prune your vineyard. You shall not reap the aftergrowth of your harvest or gather the grapes of your unpruned vine; if shall be a year of complete rest for the land. You may eat what the land yields during its sabbath—you, your male and female slaves, your hired and your bound laborers who live with you; for your livestock also, and for the wild animals in your land all its yield shall be for food. (Lev 25:2–7)

In addition, Leviticus also legislates the observance of a jubilee, which is to occur after a series of seven sevens, or in the fiftieth year. The jubilee year follows in many respects the pattern of the sabbath year and dictates, like the latter, a rest for the land. But it also includes a redistribution of property and social goods and, more generally, a release from debt: "you shall return, every one of you, to your property and every one of you to your family" (25:10).

To what extent such legislation was actually observed remains, in the end, unclear. The legislation certainly represents the ideal, if not always a literal and material reality.[77] Nevertheless, the notion of a jubilee, of a general release from debt, is not unique to the biblical traditions. Periodic restorations of economic parity and order through the release of debt, as Michael Hudson has shown, was a well-established institution among Bronze Age civilizations, which likely informed the biblical traditions themselves. Such economic restorations, it should be noted, were not necessarily undertaken for purely benevolent or altruistic reasons. Debt relief, although certainly beneficial for debtors, also allowed rulers to restore and preserve social order, consolidate their rule, and curry favor and loyalty among populations. Hudson notes that the biblical traditions of debt cancellation, which, he also insists, should not be taken as mere literary ideals, transformed the notion from a simple economic and political institution, albeit one with

---

77. For more on the economy of ancient Israel, see Boer, *Sacred Economy*.

metaphysical roots, to a covenantal obligation. That is, for the biblical traditions, instead of "debt cancellations being merely a military tactic to win or hold the loyalty of domestic populations, the biblical authors appealed to a national covenant with the Lord of Justice and Righteousness."[78]

It is not clear whether Jesus was proclaiming the observance of an actual Jubilee, but Hudson rightly notes that, in his use of Isaiah in Luke 4, Jesus "hardly could have chosen a passage more concerned with the debt burden."[79] Indeed, a significant aspect of Jesus' mission is to treat debt servitude as a real issue, one to which the notion of redemption is, in large measure, addressed. Consider, in this light, Jesus' Parable of the Unforgiving Servant, which Hudson also mentions as crucial for understanding Jesus' mission in light of the tradition of debt cancellation:

> For this reason the kingdom of heaven may be compared to a king who wished to settle accounts with his slaves. When he began the reckoning, one who owed him ten thousand talents was brought to him; and, as he could not pay, his lord ordered him to be sold, together with his wife and children and all his possessions, and payment to be made. So the slave fell on his knees before him, saying, "Have patience with me, and I will pay you everything." And out of pity for him, the lord of that slave released him and forgave him the debt. But that same slave, as he went out, came upon one of his fellow slaves who owed him a hundred denarii; and seizing him by the throat, he said, "Pay what you owe." Then his fellow slave fell down and pleaded with him, "Have patience with me, and I will pay you." But he refused; then he went and threw him into prison until he would pay the debt. When his fellow slaves saw what had happened, they were greatly distressed, and they went and reported to their lord all that had taken place. Then his lord summoned him and said to him, "You wicked slave! I forgave you all your debt because you pleaded with me. Should you not have had mercy on your fellow slave, as I had mercy on you?" And in anger his lord handed him over to be tortured until he would pay his entire debt. So my heavenly father will also do to every one of you, if you do not forgive your brother or sister from your heart. (Matt 18:23–35)

The parable is just as much about God and the kingdom of heaven as it is how we treat each other, and both focus on debt and its remission. The parable is also, though, weighted toward a critique of those who hold debt: the failure to release the debt of others incurs God's wrath. Ironically, God's

---

78. Hudson, "Lost Tradition," 37.
79. Hudson, "Lost Tradition," 41.

wrath takes the form a certain indebtedness: failure to forgive the debt of others results in one becoming indebted to God.[80]

If we read Jesus' call for the release of debt in light of his other claims, moreover, it seems that he is not just calling for a periodic jubilee but, rather, generalizing and universalizing the notion of jubilee itself. Jesus, that is, is not calling merely for a reset of social relationships but, more broadly, for a restructuring of social relationships and life as such according to the form of jubilee. Such an understanding fits with Jesus' attitudes toward work and family, which I will discuss in the next chapter, but also forms the basis of the prayer that he teaches his disciples, the so-called Lord's Prayer:

> Our Father in heaven,
>   Hallowed be your name.
>   Your kingdom come.
>   Your will be done,
>   on earth as it is in heaven.
>   Give us this day our daily bread.
>   And forgive us our debts,
>   as we have also forgiven our debtors.
>   And do not bring us to the time of trial,
>   But rescue us from the evil one. (Matt 6:9–13).

Setting the prayer within its sociohistorical context, Douglas Oakman concludes that it originally concerned "the reality of oppression, indebtedness, hunger, and social insecurity."[81] Specifically, the petition to "give us this day our daily bread" assumes a lack of bread, meaning that the prayer is concerned, at least in part, with the reality of hunger among the poor in an economically and socially stratified society. The petition for bread, in this sense, coincides with other aspects of Jesus' mission, namely various feeding and healing narratives, to the extent that the latter may be the result of malnutrition.[82] In this sense, the prayer for bread, or food more generally, should be understood as part and parcel of trusting in God and God's kingdom for one's needs, but not in an overly pious, passive way. The prayer is not, in other words, "opium for the masses," to borrow Marx's famous phrase, but expresses faith in a material reality that is possible because it is already present. Moreover, central to the reality expressed in the prayer is

---

80. This notion of indebtedness to God would become central to the theorization of atonement in the Christian theological tradition, in particular Anselm's so-called satisfaction theory, as outline in *Cur Deus Homo*. See Anselm of Cantebury, *Major Works*.

81. Oakman, *Jesus, Debt*, 90. The reading I provide draws on Oakman, even if, in certain places, I supplement his sociohistorical critical reading with my own concerns.

82. Oakman, *Jesus, Debt*, 63.

the forgiveness of debt. The centrality of debt in the prayer likewise responds to its sociohistorical context, in which chronic indebtedness plagued those at the lower strata of society.[83] In response and more generally, however, the prayer envisions a world without debt, one in which debts have been forgiven. The mention of debt in the prayer correlates with its other aspects: having one's needs met ("Give us this day our daily bread") undercuts one of the conditions that drives indebtedness: scarcity, leveraged by the rich against the poor.

Jesus' criticism of debt and his call for its release does not, however, take place solely within the orbit of individual responsibility. That is, it does not just concern how individuals treat each other, which absent a broader critique would bring us back into the realm of morality, of charity. Jesus' call for the release of debt is marked as well in terms of a distancing from the state, which is, as we have said, essential to the creation of money as debt. The latter requires any critique of debt to criticize as well the institutions that make it possible and, in turn, support its maintenance as a means of wealth extraction and social control.

Such is how we can understand Jesus' statements concerning the payment of taxes. We read in Mark, for instance, of a time when Jesus' opponents attempted to "trap him in what he said" (12:13):

> And they came and said to him, "Teacher, we know that you are sincere, and show deference to no one; for you do not regard people with partiality, but teach the way of God in accordance with truth. Is it lawful to pay taxes to the emperor, or not? Should we pay them, or should we not?" But knowing their hypocrisy, he said to them, "Why are you putting me to the test? Bring me a denarius and let me see it." And they brought one. Then he said to them, "Whose head is on this, and whose title?" They answered, "The emperor's." Jesus said to them, "Give to the emperor the things that are the emperor's and to God the things that are God's." And they were utterly amazed at him. (12:13-17; cf. Matt 22:15-22; Luke 20:20-26).

---

83. Oakman, *Jesus, Debt*, 18: "Many of Jesus' fellow Israelites labored under a crushing load of indebtedness (including taxes, tributes, tithes and religious dues, land rents, as well as 'borrowed money'). The problem of debt exacerbated the quality of relations between the owning class of agrarian first century Palestine and those who were forced for one reason or another into tenancy or wage labor. Debt was one of the major mechanisms whereby the rich kept getting richer and the poor, poorer. Through debt, ownership of the patrimonial land of the Judean and Galilean peasantry could be, and was, wrested from them. The 'rights' of the creditor were only a manifestation of an insensitive egoism that demanded security and securities to the detriment of the well-being of all."

At issue, here, is likely the Roman poll tax, which was one of the principal direct taxes on subjects, but not citizens, in the empire's provinces. The tax, then, functioned as a means of extracting resources from subject populations, and was roundly despised. The challenge to Jesus, in this passage, comes off as a fairly straightforward example of what I have previously referred to as a forced choice. Whatever answer he might give from within the accepted framework of the question risks inciting one party or another: if he answers "yes," that it is lawful to pay taxes, Jesus risks inciting the crowd against him and his work; if he answers "no," that it is not lawful, then he risks inciting the anger of the Roman authorities, whose system of taxation functioned simultaneously as a means of revenue and control.

Jesus, however, avoids the trap through the use of irony. His answer ("Give to the emperor the things that are the emperor's, and to God the things that are God's") simultaneously evades both presented options, so that, as Miranda has pointed out, he "would neither recognize authority nor be accused of denying the obligation to pay the tax."[84] Jesus' ironic non-answer has often been interpreted as granting legitimacy to government and its functions, specifically the power to tax its subjects. It has been taken, Miranda argues, in terms of a "pro-government theology," or, if not directly "pro" government, at least one that, apparently in line with Saint Paul, accepts government's legitimacy. "Be subject to the governing authorities," Paul reminds us in his Letter to the Romans, "for there is no authority except from God, and those authorities that exist have been instituted by God" (Rom 13:1). In the case of Jesus' own claim, such an interpretation rests on a division of spheres of influence, specifically between the so-called religious sphere and the so-called secular sphere, and there is no problem in acting in terms of such clearly demarcated functions. Jesus is understood as saying, that is, that some things belong to God, some things to the emperor; so long as this difference is respected, so long as one gives according to what is due to whom, then there is really no conflict.

Such an interpretation, however, largely ignores Jesus' ironic evasiveness and, to refer back to chapter 1, obviates the substance of the distinction between God and mammon. That is, a reading that assumes that Jesus renders the paying of taxes unproblematic by default attributes to him an answer of "yes" to the question of its lawfulness. Moreover, such a reading fails to take seriously that Jesus' apparent evasiveness is really a repetition of the primary disjunction between God and mammon, which is central to Jesus' teachings. Jesus is not, then, recommending a division of his followers' actions, as if it were possible to serve God and the emperor simultaneously.

---

84. Miranda, *Communism in the Bible*, 63.

He is, rather, reiterating the disjunction between God and mammon in slightly different terms, terms that, in addition, expose the façade of money as a neutral object. Crucial in this episode is the fact that the coin that Jesus requests bears the image of the emperor, of Caesar. That image, as Miranda has rightly pointed out, is the incarnation of civil authority, that is, the power of empire.

On a side note, a similar claim is made by John in the Revelation, albeit using much more vivid imagery. There, we read of the infamous "mark of the beast," whose name, when taken numerically, adds up to the number 666. Contemporary scholars have noted that the reference here is likely to Nero Caesar, whose name in Hebrew is equivalent to 666.[85] Considered by early Christians as the very incarnation of evil for his persecution, later emperors, such as Domitian, the emperor of John's time, were in turn identified with him. Nevertheless, when considered in light of the coin that bears the emperor's imprint, the infamous mark is, really, nothing other than money, mammon incarnate. Thus speaking of the beast that he sees in his apocalyptic vision, John relays that "it causes all, both small and great, both rich and poor, both free and slave, to be marked on the right hand or the forehead, so that no one can buy or sell who does not have the mark, that is, the name of the beast or the number of his name" (Rev 13:16–17). John puts those who have received the mark in contrast to the followers of Christ, who instead have "his name and his Father's name written on their foreheads" (Rev 14:1).

Nevertheless, as Miranda points out, Jesus' distinction between what is God's and what is the emperor's does not give government a pass but rather functions as a ploy to "deny all governmental authority, but in such terms that no one can accuse him before the governor."[86] Moreover, the very fact that that denial hinges on the question of taxes, that is, on what to do with money, shows the close connection between the two: money and governmental authority go hand in hand. Put in terms of the above discussion, money has value not merely through exchange but also in terms of the third party that grants it legitimacy, which here is the authority of empire or the state. If we cross Jesus' disjunction between God and mammon/emperor with John's vision of the beast, it is clear that the very use of money shifts one's allegiance away from the former and toward the latter. As Miranda points out, the Aramaic verb 'abad, which means "serve" ("You cannot serve

---

85. Identifying the number with Nero also accounts for alternative manuscript traditions that have the number as 616, so long as one considers alternative spellings of his name. See Metzger, *Breaking the Code*, 77.

86. Miranda, *Communism in the Bible*, 65.

God and mammon"), also means "adore," with connotations of divine service and acts of worship.[87]

Another detail in the episode is interesting to note as well. Before making his point with a denarius, Jesus has to ask for the denarius. Of course, that may just be part of the ploy, done for rhetorical effect similar to the way in which a common street magician may ask his or her subject for a coin with which to perform his or her trick. It may also indicate a lack of money or, at least, an unwillingness to carry it on his person. We should not make too much of such a minor detail, at least in isolation, especially when it is arguably not pertinent to the overall thrust of his claims. Nevertheless, it would be consistent with the way in which Jesus and his entourage apparently handled money. The Gospel of John tells us that they carried a "common purse" (John 12:6; 13:29), and when Jesus sends his followers out to do his work, he bids them to "[c]arry no purse, no bag, no sandals" and instead rely on the generosity of others (Luke 10:1–12). I will return to the latter point in chapter 4, but nevertheless it does not seem incidental that, according to the narrative accounts that we have, the one who eventually betrays Jesus, Judas, is also the one in charge of the common purse. John refers to him as a "thief," who would "steal what was put into [the purse]" (John 12:6), and Judas, we know, ultimately ends up selling Jesus out for thirty pieces of silver (Matt 26:15), for mammon.

These are usually taken as negative marks against Judas's character, as indications, that is, of base moral weakness. That is, of course, largely how the tradition, including certain aspects of the biblical tradition, have read such details. But shifting the perspective away from Judas and toward mammon offers a different way to take matters. That is, Judas is not a thief first, who then has access to money but is, rather, made a thief through his access to money, through holding the "common purse." It is, in other words, mammon itself that determines who Judas is and what he does, including his ultimate betrayal of Jesus. Perhaps that is why Jesus seemingly does not handle money on a regular basis, and it is telling, in this respect, that Judas's repentance, according to Matthew, involved attempting to give back the thirty pieces of silver that he received, as if he recognized that his guilt were wrapped up in his money (Matt 27:3–10).

Judas, according to Matthew, then commits suicide, although in Acts we are told that he bought a field with his proceeds, "and falling headlong he burst open in the middle and all his bowels gushed out" (Acts 1:18). Whatever the case may be, it is important to point out that, although roundly vilified by the theological and ecclesiastical tradition, Judas finds himself in

---

87. Miranda, *Communism in the Bible*, 64.

the same structural position as the rich man and the rich young ruler. This is the case even if his immediate offense is more extreme, especially when the theological identification of Jesus as the Son of God is taken into account. Like the rich man in the Parable of the Rich Man and Lazarus, Judas remains blind to the effects of money, to the way that money influences his actions; and like the rich young ruler who comes to Jesus seeking eternal life, Judas's attachment to money limits the extent to which he can really become Jesus' follower. That attachment, moreover, contributes to his siding, at least in his actions, with the religious authorities seeking Jesus' demise and, ultimately, the Roman Empire itself.

Judas, of course, knows better, knows the power of money, and in this much he is, again, like the rich man whose wealth blinds him to the plight of Lazarus. In John's Gospel we read of the time when Jesus and his disciples arrived in Bethany at the house of Lazarus, on their way to the Passover celebration in Jerusalem. During the dinner that Lazarus and his house host for him and his disciples, Mary "took a pound of costly perfume made of pure nard, anointed Jesus' feet, and wiped them with her hair. The house was filled with the fragrance of perfume" (John 12:3–4). Judas questions Mary's expenditure, saying, "Why was this perfume not sold for three hundred denarii and the money given to the poor" (John 12:5). John's commentary on Judas's question stresses that it is not really genuine, that he was interested in the money for himself ("He said this not because he cared for the poor, but because he was a thief; he kept the common purse and used to steal what was put into it" [John 12:6]). Jesus responds, in John's highly developed theology, by appealing to his death and burial, and seemingly prioritizing his immediate situation over the poor: "Leave her alone. She bought it so that she might keep it for the day of my burial. You always have the poor with you, but you do not always have me" (John 12:7–8). I will return to these and parallel passages in Matthew, Mark, and Luke in the final chapter, since when combined with other passages, they show that Jesus' criticism of money and wealth does not entail an otherworldly asceticism. Nevertheless, the very fact that Judas could appeal to the poor, despite his intentions, shows that he knows well his responsibilities with respect to money, even if he apparently acts disingenuously with respect to them.

Returning to the question of taxes, this is also the case with the religious authorities. They know very well their responsibilities with respect to money, which is why they can attempt to lay a trap for Jesus in the first place. Moreover, they likely would, in principle, accept Jesus' response: "Give to the emperor the things that are the emperor's and to God the things that are God's." Indeed, that distinction, whether stated implicitly or explicitly, seems to inform the piety of the religious authorities, as we see in the Parable of the Pharisee and the Tax Collector:

> Two men went up to the temple to pray, one a Pharisee and the other a tax collector. The Pharisee, standing by himself, was praying thus, "God, I thank you that I am not like other people: thieves, rogues, adulterers, or even like this tax collector. I fast twice a week; I give a tenth of all my income." But the tax collector, standing far off, would not even look up to heaven, but was beating his breast and saying, "God, be merciful to me, a sinner!" I tell you, this man went down to his home justified rather than the other; for all who exalt themselves will be humbled, but all who humble themselves will be exalted. (Luke 18:9–14)

The parable is often read mostly in light with the last statement ("for all who exalt themselves will be humbled, but all who humble themselves will be exalted"), as an example of the contrast between hubris and humility. Despite being a tax collector, an occupation which, because it has to do with taxes, entails a certain amount of exploitation on behalf of the state and for personal gain. Nevertheless, he finds favor in Jesus' eyes and, of course, God's, because he meekly acknowledges his own sin. This is in contrast to the Pharisee, whose personal piety with regard to the law results in self-exaltation over others. Unlike the tax collector, he cannot see the log in his own eye, which blinds him to the ways in which his stated moral and religious vigilance leads him in the opposite direction, away from what God desires. To borrow Pauline language, his literalness with regard to keeping certain commandments keeps him from the spirit of the law, a spirit that the tax collector understands well despite what we could call his "dirty hands." The log in the Pharisee's own eye, in other words, obstructs his view of what God really wants: not observance of the law for its own sake but, as the prophet Micah famously put it, "to do justice, and to love kindness, and to walk humbly with your God" (Mic 6:8). Such is, as Jesus states, the whole point of the law and the prophets, that is, the love of God and neighbor (Matt 22:37–40; Luke 10:27).

That reading is not wrong, as it exhibits the basic sense of the text, one that, moreover, exhibits Jesus' privileging of social outcasts and the oppressed. But we also should not ignore the apparent connection with Jesus' statements concerning paying taxes when the role of mammon is emphasized. It is no accident, in this regard, that the Parable of the Pharisee and the Tax Collector involves, to a large extent, the issue of money. The Pharisee emphasizes that he is careful to tithe a tenth of his income, and he contrasts himself with thieves and rogues, all of which, of course, puts him in apparent opposition to the tax collector, whose relationship to money is self-serving and exploitative. If we bracket for a moment the Pharisee's obvious self-satisfied pride, he can appear, oddly enough, as someone who has done exactly what Jesus elsewhere says: at the level of his actions, he renders to God the things that are God's.

Given the thrust of the parable, that cannot be what Jesus means, but we should also resist the temptation of reducing matters to internal disposition alone, assuming that rendering to God the things that are God's involves only an internal disposition expressed in humility, kindness, generosity, and the like. Those are all certainly admirable qualities, but what is at stake also concerns mammon itself. More specifically, rendering to God the things that are God's cannot take the form of rendering to the emperor the things that are the emperor's, which means that the former cannot take the form of mammon, the principle of the latter.

Here we can recall the infamous temple incident, which is likely the final straw that leads to Jesus' arrest and eventual execution:

> Then Jesus entered the temple and drove out all who were selling and buying in the temple, and he overturned the tables of the money changers and the seas of those who sold doves. He said to them, "It is written, 'My house shall be called a house of prayer;' but you are making it a den of robbers." The blind and the lame came to him in the temple and he cured them. But when the chief priests and the scribes saw the amazing things that he did, and heard the children crying out in the temple, "Hosanna to the Son of David," they became angry and said to him, "Do you hear what these are saying?" Jesus said to them, "Yes; have you never read, 'Out of the mouths of infants and nursing babies you have prepared praise for yourself'?" He left them, went out of the city to Bethany, and spent the night there. (Matt 21:12–17; cf. Mark 11:15–19; Luke 19:45–48; John 2:13–22)

The historical details of this episode remain somewhat vague, but the overall sense of the narrative fits with the distinction between God and mammon. The outer court of the temple, known as the Court of the Gentiles, functioned as something like an outdoor bazaar. During the Passover, when this episode occurs, it would have been extremely crowded, with perhaps as many as 400,000 Jews on pilgrimage for the holiday. Among the various items sold were animals for sacrifice (the "doves" mentioned above, though other animals as well); currency was also exchanged for Tyrian shekels, which were used to pay the half-shekel temple tax required of Jews aged twenty and older, and vice versa.

Although an accepted and expected part of religious observance and, specifically in the case of the tax, basic upkeep of the temple, Jesus criticizes the scene, labeling it as robbery over against prayer, that is, as real devotion. Indeed, Jesus' healing of the blind and lame, who likely lacked the means necessary to participate in the temple and its rituals, shores up this contrast: Jesus' actions show the form that devotion should take. That form, moreover, is completely disjunct from mammon, which appears as the real principle guiding the temple and its sanctioned or even tolerated practices. Here it is not a question of abuse, of shifting or reforming the institution. The violence of Jesus' response—which, it is important to point out, is the only such incident we have reported in the gospels—suggests a more radical approach. Read in line with the trajectory I have been tracing, the problem is not in corruption and abuse but, more specifically, in mammon itself, because it leads inevitably in that direction. That is just what it means to distinguish between God and mammon, and thus Jesus' "cleansing" of God's house entails cleansing it of mammon.

CHAPTER 3

Against Work and Family

In the last chapter, I outlined an understanding of money that, by taking into account its role in exchange and its relationship to debt and sovereignty, emphasizes its coercive nature. The coercive nature of money obviously manifests itself in differentiating wealth and debt, but it is the type of thing that money is that makes these possible. Money promises access to life and all that goes along with it, but it does so in the form of threat: if money provides access to life, then to choose not to use money, to the extent that is possible, portends death. Money presents itself to us in the form of a forced choice, which means that one's relationship to money qua mammon is, for most people most of the time, not a choice at all.

Understanding money in these terms brings into stark relief the disjunction that Jesus insists on between God and mammon, which also means that it rules out responding to the problem of money through moral appeals primarily or only. Insofar as the latter ultimately rest upon an appeal to individualized and internalized desire and the limitation of consumption, such appeals do little to dislodge money itself from its sovereign position over life. Even if one does achieve some amount of detachment from money in his or her day-to-day dealings, even if one appears to prioritize God over mammon, the very use of money implies capture in and, hence, fealty to, the system of exchange, debt, and sovereignty. Having it both ways, serving two masters, as Jesus says, is impossible: it is God or mammon, and he appears to leave little room in between. Nevertheless, in order to serve God instead of—and, it seems, against—mammon, a thoroughgoing, subjective destitution is required. Given the way that money functions in actuality, however, that destitution also implies a material destitution, but one that, as I will suggest, does not take the form of asceticism.

Explaining what the latter involves negatively and positively in its idea, if not in terms of a program, is the goal of this and the next chapter. We have already seen in chapter 1 that it certainly involves, at least at some level, a literal and not just metaphorical denial of money and wealth. Such is the sense of the Parable of the Rich Man and Lazarus, which also critiques differentiating wealth, and the story of the rich young ruler. In the latter story, the rich young ruler finds it impossible to dispense with his wealth, but this isn't the case, it seems, for Jesus' inner circle, even if they did not similarly, it seems, possess such wealth. In response to the harshness of Jesus' requirements, they do not hesitate to remind Jesus, "we have left our homes and followed you" (Luke 18:29). Jesus assures them, "Truly I tell you, there is no one who has left house or wife or brothers or parents or children, for the sake of the kingdom of God, who will not get back very much more in this age, and in the age to come eternal life" (Luke 18:29–30).

Gaining "eternal life," then, involves giving up one's wealth, but this also means leaving family and, along with it, work (cf. Mark 1:16–20). The connection that Jesus draws between these three—money, work, and family—is not incidental, but is rooted in the sphere of money itself. Otherwise put, a critique of mammon is insufficient if it does not also involve a critique of work and family.

NOT JUST WORK, BUT ANTI-WORK

Before discussing the relationship that Jesus has to work or, more appropriately, anti-work, it is worth stating up front that the notion of work or labor is notoriously difficult to define, at least if we are looking for something like the being of work as a specific mode of human activity.[1] Like many other aspects of life, we often know what work is through a sort of "common sense" perspective: we know work when we see it, do it, and—if it is of the

---

1. I use the terms "work" and "labor" interchangeably, even if others, such as Hannah Arendt and the Marxist tradition more generally make distinctions between the two. In doing so, I follow Kathi Weeks here, who emphasizes that collapsing the distinction between the two allows for a more radical, anti- and post-work critique of economic and social organization and practice. Weeks notes that refusing to distinguish between "work" and "labor" takes the form of a wager: "by blocking access to a vision of unalienated and unexploited work in the guise of living labor, one that could live up to the work ethic's ideals and labor's necessity and virtues, and be worthy of the extravagant praise the ethic bestows, I hope to concentrate and amplify the critique of work as well as to inspire what I hope will be a more radical imagination of postwar futures." See Weeks, *Problem with Work*, 15.

difficult or taxing type—feel it. Still, what counts as work versus something like leisure or play is, to a certain extent, in the eye of the beholder, at least if we take the perspective that work corresponds to an identifiable essence. The difficulty in pinning down what work is, is one of the things that contributes to the blurring of the distinction between work and other aspects of life that we see manifest especially in many contemporary labor practices.

It is obvious that what we call "work" has some relationship to human being and activity. Hannah Arendt famously distinguished between labor, work, and action,[2] and more recently Bruno Gulli has sought to provide an ontology of labor that sees labor as the vital force of life, but a force that is indifferent or neutral to its capture within specific economic, political, and social structures.[3] Labor, for Gulli, is in this sense just another name for human activity, but this human activity can be put to use in various ways, some of them beneficent, some of them deleterious. Work, then, is always determined by economic, political, and social conditions, but these conditions do not—and can never—exhaust its ontological plenitude. Such discussions are important for understanding the being of human activity, but they also invite ambiguity in seeking to carve out the space of work proper.

Without necessarily dismissing such ontological considerations, in what follows I focus on the relationship between work and money. It may seem obvious to emphasize the relationship between the two. Money, as I argued in the previous chapter, is the means through which we gain access to the market, and our access to money is, for most of us most of the time, mediated through work: we work to get money to secure our needs, wants, and desires; we work, in other words, to gain access to life. Although there are exceptions, the profound simplicity of this basic fact often gets lost in the thicket of ideology, which ascribes to work an extra-economic meaning. Sure, work provides us with income, but work is also, we are told variously, a meaningful activity, one in which we realize our truest selves and human potential more generally and, is so doing, contribute to the good of society as a whole.

Since I am interested in the relationship between work and money, I define work quite simply in terms of a wage relationship. Although the wage system of labor as we know it is wrapped up in the development and expansion of capitalism, I understand it more broadly as a relation of subordination, in which one is forced to sell one's activity and/or its products—whether these be physical, mental, or affective—for the purpose of gaining access to means of subsistence. Such a broad view allows us to appreciate

2. Arendt, *Human Condition*.
3. Gulli, *Ontology of Labor*.

work's invariability and continuity despite historical and sociocultural differences, both in the past and, at least, into the near future.[4] Work, in this sense, invariably corresponds to money, especially nowadays, and because money is distributed differentially, work implies hierarchical interpersonal and social relationships. Work is the way in which we gain access to money, to life, but because of the type of thing that money is, it is also one of the ways in which we are disciplined to accept it as the medium through which life is gained, including the various socioeconomic inequalities that get marked in terms of differentiating wealth. That remains the case, even if we "enjoy" our work, or find "meaning" in it, as is common to say.

To define work in such a manner is in certain respects limiting, in that it does not take into account "work" done outside wage relationships. Left out specifically are household duties and childbearing and -rearing, activities that have, of course, traditionally fallen to women. Indeed, in many ways, the system of wage labor has historically depended upon a mass of unpaid, gendered activity. Under a capitalist economic organization, for instance, the production of surplus value does not depend solely on the wage relationship, on the labor power sold to capitalists. It also depends on the family, understood as the basic unit of reproduction, broadly conceived. Work or labor, then, depends on unpaid housework (e.g., bearing and raising children, cooking, cleaning, etc.). Sylvia Federici thus argues that such unpaid labor allows us to see housework as "the most pervasive manipulation, the most subtle and mystified violence that capitalism has ever perpetrated against any section of the working class."[5] Moreover, unlike the promises made surrounding work, it does not even pretend to offer the appearance of freedom, equality, and dignity:

> The wage gives the impression of a fair deal: you work and you get paid, hence you and your boss are equal; while in reality the wage, rather than paying for the work you do, hides all the unpaid work that goes into profit. But the wage at least recognizes that you are a worker, and you can bargain and struggle around and against the terms and the quantity of that wage, the terms and the quantity of that work. To have a wage means to be part of a social contract, and there is no doubt concerning its meaning: you work, not because you like it, or because it comes naturally to you, but because it is the only condition under which you are allowed to live. But exploited as you might be, *you are not that*

---

4. Indeed, the structure of work itself appears to be shifting away from stable employment to a more precarious, gig-based economy, usually euphemistically dubbed "the sharing economy." See Sundararajan, *Sharing Economy*.

5. Federici, *Wages against Housework*, 1.

work. Today you are a postman, tomorrow a cabdriver. All that matters is how much of that you have to do and how much of that money you can get.[6]

This is, of course, not the case with housework and the role that women play with respect to it. Housework is, clearly, work in a very basic sense, and often extremely difficult and taxing work at that, much more so than most jobs, especially the "bullshit" ones to which David Graeber has drawn attention.[7] Nevertheless, it is socially constructed as not being work, as being, rather, a natural component of women's activity as such. Federici thus notes that "not only has housework been imposed on women, but it has been transformed into a natural attribute of our female physique and personality, an internal need, an aspiration, supposedly coming from the depth of our female character."[8] It is the putative "naturalness" of housework that allows it to be defined as not work and, thus, justified as unwaged. In turn the unwaged condition of housework reinforces the assumption that it is not work.

One could, of course, argue that the gendered component in play here has lessened, as more men take on household duties and as families themselves become more diverse.[9] That may be the case, to an extent, but even when men do take on such duties, it is not considered "natural" but rather a choice or, in some instance, a sacrifice. The opposite is usually the case for women: they "choose" to go outside the home to work, which involves making a host of "sacrifices." Moreover, even if we take into account multiple other familial and cohabitation situations, including same-sex relationships, housework itself still remains unwaged. If we follow Federici's logic, this means that it is still conceived along gendered lines.

My use of the term "work" to refer primarily to wage-labor, broadly construed, is not meant to exclude such considerations, and to the extent that wage-labor remains operative, fighting to include housework and other activities that have traditionally fallen along gendered lines remains important. Nevertheless, the problem in elevating such activity to the level of work, at least theoretically, is that it tends to assume the wage relationship as the ultimate horizon of possibility. The goal instead is to challenge that

6. Federici, *Wages against Housework*, 2.

7. Graeber, "On the Phenomenon of Bullshit Jobs." For Graeber, bullshit jobs refer primarily to administrative and service sector jobs, broadly construed. Such jobs, according to Graeber, serve no real economic need, and have more to do with moral and political disciplining. Graeber writes, "It's as if someone out there were making up pointless jobs just for the sake of keeping us all working."

8. Federici, *Wages against Housework*, 2.

9. For a discussion of this shift, see Smith, *Daddy Shift*.

very relationship: in other words, rather than elevating activity undertaken outside the wage relationship to the status of work, the purpose in what follows is to devalue work to develop an anti-work position.[10]

Developing an anti-work position in dialogue with the teachings and activity of Jesus may at first glance appear as a non-starter. Modern and contemporary theologies have, generally speaking, sought instead to develop theologies of work, as a means of understanding the salutary role that work can, does, and should play in human flourishing.[11] Various components of the biblical materials and narratives and numerous theological themes can be mobilized for this broad purpose, but the most important for the argument developed here is the line of thought that grounds the dignity of work in Jesus himself.

Such a line is displayed prominently in Pope John Paul II's *Laborem exercens*, the basic arguments of which go back at least to Leo XIII's *Rerum Novarum*.[12] In concluding his encyclical on the importance and dignity of work, John Paul II seeks to develop a "spirituality of work . . . which will help all people to come closer, through work, to God, the Creator and Redeemer, to participate in his salvific plan for man and the world and to deepen their friendship with Christ in their lives by accepting, through faith, a living participation in his threefold mission as Priest, Prophet, and King, as the Second Vatican Council so adequately expresses."[13] Work is thus endowed with a soteriological significance, understood as a vital component of God's plan for human beings, from the beginning to the end. From the book of Genesis—the first "gospel of work," according to the Pontiff—we understand that work is one means through which human beings share in the creative activity of God, in fidelity to the *imago dei* and in obedience to God's command to subdue and rule over the earth (cf. Gen 1:28). Genesis teaches us "what the dignity of work consists of: it teaches that man ought to imitate God, his creator, in working, because man alone has the unique characteristic of likeness to God."[14]

This truth, however, is revealed most prominently in Jesus Christ who, because he enters fully the human condition, comes to humankind as,

---

10. Kathi Weeks' discussion in *Problem with Work*, 113–50 is important here as well. Surveying and critiquing second-wave feminist literature surrounding the issue of wages for household work, Weeks argues instead for less work and a basic income.

11. The literature on this theme is fairly extensive at this point, and ranges across political spectrums. See for instance Volf, *Work in the Spirit*; Cosdon, *Theology of Work*; Witherington, *Work*; Jensen, *Responsive Labor*.

12. John Paul II, *Laborem exercens*; Leo XIII, *Rerum Novarum*.

13. John Paul II, *Laborem exerens*, 50.

14. John Paul II, *Laborem exerens*, 51.

among other things, a worker. His gospel can be understood, in this sense, as a "gospel of work," because as John Paul II states, "*He who proclaimed it was himself a man of work*, a craftsman like Joseph of Nazareth."[15] Although John Paul II rightly emphasizes that Jesus gave no specific or special commands in regard to work, a point to which I will return below, nevertheless,

> the eloquence of the life of Christ is unequivocal: he belongs to the "working world," he has appreciation and respect for human work. It can indeed be said that *he looks with love upon human work* and the different forms that it takes, seeing in each one of these forms a particular facet of man's likeness with God, the Creator and Father. Is it not he who says: "My Father is the vinedresser," and in various ways puts *into his teaching* the fundamental truth about work which is already expressed in the whole tradition of the Old Testament, beginning with Genesis?[16]

The claim is buttressed through appeal to various work-related metaphors and references from the Hebrew Bible/Old Testament and the teaching of Paul who, contrary to Jesus, did give specific commands related to work. "Whatever your task, work heartily, as serving the Lord and not men, knowing that from the Lord you will receive the inheritance as your reward" (Col 3:23–24; quoted in 55). Thus, even if work often involves "sweat and toil," we find glimmers of redemption in it, and look forward to its final redemption in Christ's death and resurrection, in the "new good" promised therein.[17]

It is worth dwelling more deliberately on the problem of work at this point. Although the social teaching on work that we see expressed in *Laborem exercens* and other encyclicals, especially *Rerum novarum*, aims to distinguish itself from Marxist critique by emphasizing the importance of private property,[18] in emphasizing the importance of dignified work the two traditions share much in common.

15. John Paul II, *Laborem exerens*, 53.
16. John Paul II, *Laborem exerens*, 53–54.
17. John Paul II, *Laborem exerens*, 58.
18. Leo XII in *Rerum Novarum* states, for instance: "It is surely undeniable that, when a man engages in remunerative labor, the impelling reason and motive of his work is to obtain property, and thereafter to hold it as his very own. If one man hires out to another his strength or skill, he does so for the purpose of receiving in return what is necessary for the satisfaction of his needs; he therefore expressly intends to acquire a right full and real, not only to the remuneration, but also to the disposal of such remuneration, just as he pleases. Thus, if he lives sparingly, saves money, and, for greater security, invests his savings in land, the land, in such case, is only his wages under another form; and, consequently, a working man's little estate thus purchased should be as completely at his full disposal as are the wages he receives for his labor. But it is precisely in such power of disposal that ownership obtains, whether the property consist

The traditional Marxist critique of work does not begin from the assumptions of theological dogma, of course, but in the notion of alienation. For Marx, the essential component of labor, or work, is found in the relationship between the worker and production. This relationship is one marked by alienation, but the estrangement involved is twofold. On the one hand, Marx argues that the worker is estranged from the product of his labor, from the object that he or she produces. The object of his or her labor is, in this sense, labor objectified, but as an alien object, an externalized thing that the worker has no purchase on, set as it is over against him or her. It does not matter what the object actually is, that is, what the worker produces. Alienation is worked into the capitalist mode of production itself, irrespective of what workers produce. Marx writes: "Whatever the product of his labor is, he is not. Therefore, the greater this product, the less is he himself. The *alienation* of the worker in his product means not only that his labor becomes an object, an *external* existence, but that it exists *outside him*, independently, as something alien to him, and that it becomes a power on its own confronting him. It means that the life he has conferred on the object confronts him as something hostile and alien."[19] Marx refers to this as "estrangement of the *thing*."[20]

On the other hand, Marx insists that the alienation of the worker from the products of his or her labor is merely a "summary" of a deeper alienation found in productive activity itself. Marx writes: "If then the product of labor is alienation, production itself must be active alienation, the alienation of activity, the activity of alienation. In the estrangement of the object of labor is merely summarized the estrangement, the alienation, in the activity of labor itself."[21] Marx will thus say that labor in the capitalist mode of production is external to the worker, by which he means that it does not belong to his "intrinsic nature."[22] Again, the process here is doubled. On the one hand, the worker is divided from his intrinsic nature, from a type of work that would allow him to affirm himself in who he actually is. Rather than

---

of land or chattels. Socialists, therefore, by endeavoring to transfer the possessions of individuals to the community at large, strike at the interests of every wage-earner, since they would deprive him of the liberty of disposing of his wages, and thereby of all hope and possibility of increasing his resources and of bettering his condition in life. What is of far greater moment, however, is the fact that the remedy they propose is manifestly against justice. For, every man has by nature the right to possess property as his own" (§5–6).

19. Marx, *Economic and Philosophic Manuscripts*, 29.
20. Marx, *Economic and Philosophic Manuscripts*, 31.
21. Marx, *Economic and Philosophic Manuscripts*, 30.
22. Marx, *Economic and Philosophic Manuscripts*, 30.

being something through which he can affirm himself, work in the capitalist mode of production is a form of denial: it dialectically reverses what should constitute work. Marx writes, "[I]n his work, therefore, he does not affirm himself but denies himself, does not feel content but unhappy, does not develop freely his physical and mental energy but mortifies his body and ruins his mind. The worker only feels himself outside his work, and in his work feels outside himself."[23] For this reason, Marx insists, labor is "not voluntary, but coerced; it is *forced labor*."[24] On the other hand, if labor does not belong to the "intrinsic nature" of the individual through the process of work, it is also external to the self through the simple fact that someone else owns the labor. Simply put, one works for someone else and, because such work is coerced, a forced labor, Marx can say that "in it he belongs, not to himself, but to another."[25] There is, Marx insists, a close connection here with religion: "Just as in religion the spontaneous activity of the human imagination, of the human brain and the human heart, operates on the individual independently of him—that is, operates as an alien, divine or diabolical activity—so is the worker's activity not his spontaneous activity. It belongs to another; it is the loss of his self."[26] Marx refers to this loss as "self-estrangement."[27]

Moreover, the process of labor also has a more universal alienating effect, in that it ultimately collectively estranges human beings from what Marx calls their species-being. The species-being of humankind refers to humankind's labor on the objective world. Of course, all animal and vegetal existence works on the world for its subsistence, in the sense that it must extract from "nature" the means for its survival. It is in this sense that nature functions as a part of organic life, as the body of organic life. Marx, as a materialist, makes it clear that we are no different in this respect, when he writes: "Nature is man's *inorganic body*—nature, that is, insofar as it is not itself human body. Man *lives* on nature—means that nature is his *body*, with which he must remain in continuous interchange if he is not to die. That man's physical and spiritual life is linked to nature means simply that nature is linked to itself, for man is a part of nature."[28] Yet the relationship between humans and nature here is not immediate in the sense of other animals. Nature is certainly a means to satisfy basic needs, which enables the human to

23. Marx, *Economic and Philosophic Manuscripts*, 30.
24. Marx, *Economic and Philosophic Manuscripts*, 30.
25. Marx, *Economic and Philosophic Manuscripts*, 30.
26. Marx, *Economic and Philosophic Manuscripts*, 30.
27. Marx, *Economic and Philosophic Manuscripts*, 31.
28. Marx, *Economic and Philosophic Manuscripts*, 31.

survive in the world, but human beings also relate to nature and themselves in terms of excess: that is, human beings are not tied to mere subsistence. Marx refers to this as the "life-activity" of human beings, which is found in "free, conscious activity."[29] It is this that is reversed in the estrangement discussed above, meaning that in the capitalist mode of production, we are estranged from our species-being but also, because of this, from other human beings, insomuch as we relate to them primarily as workers.

The goal, in light of this multileveled and intertwined notion of alienation, is to push past it through organized worker and class struggles, so as to achieve unalienated labor, or at least a modicum of it. The problem with this goal, however, is that in articulating a vision of unalienated labor, it gives too much away to the capitalist system of labor in that it presupposes work as the horizon of individual and social realization. The dream of unalienated labor is really a vision of work's redemption, which is where it dovetails with the social teaching found in *Rerum Novarum* and *Laborem exercens*. Thus, as Nicholas Thoburn notes in his discussion of the anti-work politics of Italian *operaismo*, "work is always already a capitalist relation."[30] The problem, in other words, is not alienated labor vis-à-vis unalienated labor, but labor itself, since it is this that capitalism captures. Simply put, work is the problem.

Moreover, the discourse on alienated labor often fails to take account of the fact that work under various capitalist modes of production has itself taken on unalienated characteristics, not just rhetorically but also in practice. If alienated labor remains a potent source of subjectivity and, hence, socioeconomic change, then the owners of labor have just as much stake in reconciling the individual with their work, perhaps even more so. Thus, in many ways, the dream of human beings being reconciled to their selves, their work, and the products of their labor—this dream of an organic connection between human being and activity—has passed to the capitalist wage system, if not always in practice then at least in terms of a horizon of possibility.

The identification of capitalism itself with a vision of unalienated labor is by no means straightforward or seamless. Frédéric Lordon, for instance, has emphasized that in late capitalism, it is no longer enough to simply be good at one's job, to be a productive and, ultimately, profitable worker. One must identify with the desires of one's employer and find personal meaning

---

29. Marx, *Economic and Philosophic Manuscripts*, 31.

30. Thoburn, *Deleuze, Marx and Politics*, 111. See also Weeks's discussion of *operaismo* in *Problem with Work*, 79–112.

in serving and executing them.³¹ But the ideological mechanism at work works best when it is self-motivated. Franco Berardi has argued along these lines in reference to high tech workers who, because their labor is so specialized and non-interchangable, "consider labor as the most essential part of their lives, the most specific and personal."³² For Berardi, whereas the industrial workers with whom Marx was concerned "invested mechanical energies in their wage earning services according to a depersonalized model of repetition, high tech workers invest their specific competences, their creative, innovative, and communicative energies in the labor process; that is, the best part of their intellectual capacities."³³

Identification and investment, however, are not confined to the tech industry or intellectual labor more broadly, to what is often referred to as the "creative class."³⁴ Even lower-wage workers in the service sector are often expected to buy into the values of their employers, to align their interests and desires with the company. One is no longer simply a worker or an employee, but a "team member," a designation that signifies, among other things, that one's identity and activities are an essential, meaningful part of a greater whole. The quality and value of one's work, in this respect, are measured by the extent to which one is "part of the team." Otherwise put, one's worth as an employee and the value of one's work is not just a matter of production but, in addition, one's personal investment in production, in the company's identity.

A good illustration of this demand for personal investment can be found in the cult classic *Office Space*, a satire of contemporary work written and directed by Mike Judge. Joanna, played by Jennifer Anniston, works as a server at Chotchkie's, a clear parody of the casual-dining chain restaurant TGI Friday's. Chotchkie's requires their servers to wear "flair"—buttons, pins, and other accessories—as a way to personalize both their service and the customer experience. At one point in the film, Joanna's manager Stan, played by Mike Judge, questions how many pieces of flair she is wearing:

> **Stan, Chotchkie's Manager:** We need to talk about your flair.
>
> **Joanna:** Really? I . . . I have fifteen pieces on. I, also . . .
>
> **Stan, Chotchkie's Manager:** Well, okay. Fifteen is the minimum, okay?
>
> **Joanna:** Okay.

31. Lordon, *Willing Slaves of Capital*.
32. Berardi, *Soul at Work*, 68.
33. Berardi, *Soul at Work*, 70.
34. See Florida, *Rise of the Creative Class*.

Stan, Chotchkie's Manager: Now, you know it's up to you whether or not you want to just do the bare minimum. Or . . . well, like Brian, for example, has thirty-seven pieces of flair, okay. And a terrific smile.

Joanna: Okay. So you . . . you want me to wear more?

Stan, Chotchkie's Manager: Look. Joanna.

Joanna: Yeah.

Stan, Chotchkie's Manager: People can get a cheeseburger anywhere, okay? They come to Chotchkie's for the atmosphere and the attitude. Okay? That's what the flair's about. It's about fun.

Joanna: Yeah. Okay. So more then, yeah?

Stan, Chotchkie's Manager: Look, we want you to express yourself, okay? Now if you feel that the bare minimum is enough, then okay. But some people choose to wear more and we encourage that, okay? You do want to express yourself, don't you?

Joanna: Yeah, yeah.

Stan, Chotchkie's Manager: Okay. Great. Great. That's all I ask.

What makes Joanna a good server is not simply a skill set but, rather, her investment in the brand, understood here along the lines of expressing herself. Such expression has to exceed the required minimum, because a good employee would seek to do more than management requires of her. How much is required in excess is, naturally, left intentionally vague, and functions, to borrow from Žižek, as a sort of superego supplement to the explicit letter of the law: the supplement determines how the law should be taken. Joanna should, in other words, be existentially invested in her work enough to "know" the point at which her labor manifests genuine expressiveness, above and beyond the bare minimum officially required. That she does not know—or even, apparently, care—shows that she is not really invested in the company and its goals and, hence, is not a good employee.

The emotional and psychic investment required of employees also increasingly manifests itself materially and temporally, as the distinction between work and non-work gradually blurs, to the point where the line demarcating the two shifts or even gets erased altogether. Technological development, as well as the rise of the so-called gig economy, certainly facilitates the collapse of that distinction: it enables a constant virtual connection to work-related activities, demands, and pressures, whether one officially "works from home" or not. But the encroachment of work into areas previously deemed non-work is not just reflected outside the workplace but in it as well, as it becomes increasingly domesticized as a means of extracting more productive energy in the form of time. It is well known that Google, for instance, offers its employees numerous perks, including meals, onsite healthcare services, free haircuts, massages, laundry and dry-cleaning services, and more. Such generous amenities, Google insists, are about making its employee's lives "better and easier,"[35] but they also ensure that there is no reason not to be at work: work has co-opted other aspects of life but also, in so doing, has made these aspects more enjoyable, along, of course, with work itself. The Google work environment thus enables "Googlers to live longer, healthier and more productive lives."[36]

Such perks, along with better-than-average salaries, mean that Google is consistently rated in the business press and general media as one of the best places to work. But such labor practices stand in sharp contrast with the horrendous, inhuman conditions that two-thirds of the world's workers face at work, work upon which companies like Google depend in a very real, material sense to produce a profit. Such conditions are generally well known, so there is no need to document them here. Nevertheless, at a formal level, capital requires that both sets of workers commit their lives to their work, in their own way. Differentiating wealth on a global scale, along with a host of other political, social, and economic factors, dictates the shape that commitment takes and its content, and values life differently depending on whose life is at stake. Not all lives matter, at least in the same way.[37] Whereas the Google employee is promised a longer, healthier life, the labor of the poor often promises only trauma, sickness, and death. Despite the contrast, in both cases it is still life that is at stake.

For workers at the bottom of the economic pyramid, the commitment of one's life to work is, to a large extent, forced: it is often one of the only means left available to gain the money necessary for access to subsistence goods and services. At the upper echelons, however—and globally speaking, that includes the so-called middle class—one often trades one's life for "private" comfort. Andre Gorz has argued that individuals accept many of the contradictory values and demands that work requires, including the sheer amount of time that work takes up, largely because of compensation and, hence, consumption. Gorz writes:

---

35. https://www.google.com/about/careers/lifeatgoogle/benefits/.

36. https://www.google.com/about/careers/lifeatgoogle/proof-in-the-perks.html.

37. This is, of course, the point behind the slogan #blacklivesmatter and the social movement of the same name. For information on the movement, see http://blacklivesmatter.com.

> Within large organizations, professional success requires a will to succeed according to the purely technical efficiency criteria of the functions one occupies, irrespective of content. It demands a spirit of competition and opportunism, combined with subservience toward superiors. This will be recompensed—and *compensated*—in the private sphere by a comfortable, opulent, hedonistic lifestyle. In other words, professional success becomes the *means* of achieving private comfort and pleasures that have no qualities demanded by professional life.[38]

With decades-long wage stagnation combined with rising prices for goods, services, and rents, debt has come to supplement compensation to enable consumption of needs, wants, and desires, and drive economic development. Nevertheless, consumption still functions as the force driving us to work. Another way to put the matter is to say that work is the sacrifice we make for consumption.[39]

Theologies of work do, of course, often touch on the basic issues discussed above, but mostly for the purpose of making work more humane.[40] That is fair as far as it goes, but it only goes so far. The appeal to more humane working conditions, or to use Marxist terminology, unalienated labor, largely assumes the necessity of the wage-relationship and, hence, work itself. Work itself is, for the most part, never called into question, mainly for ideological reasons: the individual, social, and theological significance of work is assumed rather than made subject to criticism. On this view, the problems that result from particular organizations of labor systems are inessential by-products, intentional or unintentional distortions of something that is fundamentally good. Many of the issues I have discussed above, however, are not by-products but features of work itself, at least in its current articulation. Indeed, so long as work is the primary means through which

---

38. Gorz, "The Divorce Between Working and Living," in *Critique of Economic Reason*, 36.

39. Though as Matthew Tiessen has suggested, as debt has come to play a more prominent role in relation to consumption, debt-repayment rather than consumption, understood in terms of desire, may play a greater role as a motivating factor. He notes that "debt-repayment has—for many—become *the* primary—and perpetual—source of motivation. Debt's appetite, in other words, orients peoples' energies and keeps people working as indentured servants of capital. Debt-free desires are necessarily postponed or abandoned as debt-servicing takes pride of place in an ever shorter list of priorities." See Tiessen, "Infinite Debt," 124.

40. Such is ultimately the position of *Laborem exercens*. But see also Jensen, *Responsible Labor*, 115, where the issue is with fostering "good work," that is, work that can flourish in "contexts that value workers as persons, honor gifts and rest, and encourage having through giving."

we gain access to money—which means to life itself—work is, as Bob Black has argued in his famous essay "The Abolition of Work," a means of control, one of the main disciplinary techniques used to make individuals pliable to social, political, and economic demands. Work is, Black insists, "forced labor, that is, compulsory production."[41] The task, then, is not to humanize labor but to challenge work itself, to develop the lines of an anti-work position.

JESUS AGAINST WORK

Rerum novarum, I said above, finds the truth of work manifest in Jesus, who comes to us as a worker and points to the redemption of work in his death and resurrection. The theological argument that buttresses work, here, is even more interesting in what it omits.

When situating Jesus within the biblical traditions concerning work, *Rerum novarum* appeals to the Old Testament or Hebrew Bible and to Paul but not, really, to Jesus himself and his actual activity and life. The encyclical does mention, to be sure, that many of Jesus' parables on the kingdom of God reference work, but that is about it. The lack of attention given to Jesus' activity and life, at least as presented in the gospels, cannot be accidental. Although Jesus is referred to as a *tekton* (Mark 6:3; cf. Matt 13:55), which is usually translated as "carpenter," but refers more generally to a skilled trade, and uses various work-related images in his teaching, we never actually witness this "man of work" working himself. Such an omission may not mean much in and of itself, but it is curious, given the weight that later readers attach to his identity as a *tekton*.

Indeed, Michael J. Sandford has argued that Jesus' supposed identification as a *tekton* has the opposite effect. That is, it functions not to identify Jesus as a worker but negatively, in the sense that it disassociates Jesus from the work that he should be doing. When the question is raised in Mark 6:3, "Is this not the carpenter, the son of Mary and brother of James and Joses and Judas and Simon, and are not his sisters here with us?," and in Matt 13:55, "Is this not the carpenter's son?," it functions less as a positive identification and more as an accusation that Jesus is shirking his familial and social responsibilities with respect to work. Sandford writes that these questions "are significant not because they describe the work that Jesus does, but because they highlight the work that he does not do, or is no longer doing. Thus, far from being a carpenter of any kind, the gospels do not depict Jesus as engaging in work at all. In this respect, previous discussions have

---

41. Black, "Abolition of Work."

distracted from the fundamental point that Jesus, in the gospels, is quite simply not a *tekton*."[42]

The gospels are, no doubt, limited in intent and scope, and Jesus certainly did a host of things not explicitly mentioned in the scant records that we have, and he most certainly worked at some point in his life. There is no mention of Jesus using the bathroom in the gospels, for instance, and he certainly did that![43] That is a somewhat crude way to say that a simple argument based on omission is not really all that compelling, when taken on its own terms. Nevertheless, when that omission is combined with other facets of Jesus' life, his words and deeds, it does become significant, in that we can find resources for developing an anti-work position in the latter.

We should be careful, however, in how we deal with the material, notably because the fact that Jesus does not work may have to do with specific, uncontrollable circumstances, circumstances that should not be fetishized. Robert Myles, for instance, has argued that the circumstances of Jesus' life have been romanticized by biblical scholars and the theological tradition, notably his itinerancy or, put otherwise, his homelessness. What many readers of the gospels have failed to account for is the ways in which Jesus' homelessness may have been not an individual choice, but the result of socioeconomic forces, forces that for Jesus and his followers entailed hardship and the loss of agency.[44]

Such ideology critique is certainly important, and it can do much to correct the often bucolic images that readers have a tendency to import into the biblical texts. But it can also reinforce the very lack of agency that it criticizes, to the extent that it fails to take account of the myriad ways in which the constraints of a particular system can be harnessed for constructive purposes and, ultimately, used against it. Ideological mechanisms do not function unilaterally, over against subjects but, rather, are themselves subject to a back-and-forth, to the ways in which subjects find agency within systems of control.[45] Finding agency within constraint cannot be reduced to making "the best of the situation," which is an ideological recommendation if there

---

42. Sandford, "Luxury Communist Jesus," 251.
43. Although there are early theological traditions that deny this.
44. See Myles, *Homelessness of Jesus*.
45. Michel de Certeau's discussion of use, tactics, and strategies is important here. De Certeau draws attention to the way in which people twist the officially sanctioned sense of language, culture, and economic reality for their own purposes and desires. Power, in other words, is not total, but negotiated in and often undermined by the discrete actions of individuals with respect to it. See de Certeau, *Practice of Everyday Life*, 29–42.

ever were one. Rather, it is about using a forced situation to see through its cause, as a means of thinking an alternative.

That said, I am less interested in why Jesus may have not worked than the statements and actions that flow out of his seeming lack of work. Whatever Jesus' circumstances may have been and whether they were forced or freely chosen, it is clear that he enjoins his followers to participate in them, by adopting a stance that is opposed to work.

We read, for instance, that when Jesus was passing "along the Sea of Galilee, he saw Simon and his brother Andrew casting a net into the lake—for they were fishermen. And Jesus said to them, 'Follow me and I will make you fish for people.' And immediately they left their nets and followed him. As he went a little farther, he saw James son of Zebedee and his brother John, who were in their boat mending the nets. Immediately he called them; and they left their father Zebedee in the boat with the hired men, and followed him" (Mark 1:16–20). We should not treat this episode metaphorically, similarly to how the theological tradition often treats the relationship between money and desire, as discussed in chapter 1. Reducing Simon and Andrew's abandonment to some putative internal sense (i.e., that it indicates some general "sacrifice" that all must make to follow Jesus) tends to downplay its material significance. For Simon and Andrew to leave "their father Zebedee" involves not just leaving family but also any modicum of socioeconomic security, and from both angles. That is, although it certainly signifies a loss of security for Simon and Andrew, that loss also applies to Zebedee, who, although he has "hired men" certainly relies on the labor of his sons as a way to earn a living. That loss, moreover, would seem to extend to other members of the family as well, such as wives and children, if we assume that they were married, which is entirely reasonable. What is interesting, here, is that this voluntary abandonment of security—voluntary, that is, for Simon and Andrew—takes the form of an abandonment of work. If they are to follow Jesus, in other words, Simon and Andrew must leave all behind, including their work, the means of their and their family's livelihood.

We see a similar pattern in Jesus' calling of Levi, a tax collector. Levi is, we are told, at work "sitting at the tax booth." Just as Jesus had done with Simon, Andrew, and James, Jesus tells Levi, "Follow me." We then read that Levi "got up, left everything, and followed him" (Luke 5:27–28; cf. Mark 2:14; Matt 9:9). As Sandford puts it, Levi leaves his work "literally in the middle of a shift, at Jesus' command."[46] What's even more interesting about this episode, at least in terms of its narration, is that after, Levi throws "a

---

46. Sandford, "Luxury Communist Jesus," 252.

great banquet for him in his house; and there was a large crowd of tax collectors and others sitting at the table with them" (Luke 5:29). The banquet serves as a pretext for contrasting the company that Jesus keeps among social outcasts with the closed piety of the religious leaders. The Pharisees and the scribes complain that Jesus eats and drinks with "tax collectors and sinners" (Luke 5:31). Jesus responds that is precisely the point: it is the "sick" who are in need of a physician, and not the other way around. Nevertheless, what interests me here is that Levi's abandonment of his work also does not result in apparent poverty or asceticism, either with him or Jesus and his disciples. There is no forced austerity but rather the opposite: plenitude and excess, in the form of a banquet.

I will return to this idea of excess in chapter 4, but Jesus' command to "follow him" in both of these examples takes a rudimentary anti-work form, a form that, moreover, is irretrievably crossed with the distinction between God and mammon that I have analyzed in previous chapters. That is, for Jesus work is not on the side of dignity, a basic aspect of human existence understood in concert with the work of God but, rather, on the side of mammon. So much is clear if we return to the story of the rich young ruler. Recall that the rich young ruler's wealth prevents him from following Jesus. Although the wealth in question, here, certainly refers to money and material possessions ("sell all that you own and distribute the money to the poor" [Luke 18:22]), the story also assumes that one must as well cut oneself off from the means through which wealth is produced and amassed ("Truly I tell you, there is no one who has left house or wife or brothers or parents or children, for the sake of the kingdom of God, who will not get back very much more in this age, and in the age to come eternal life" [18:29–30]).

Of course, not all of Jesus' dealings with work and the wage-relationship appear so starkly, in light of the disjunction between God and mammon. At times, Jesus seems at first glance to express an opposite sentiment, one that extols the value of work and service to one's employer or master. The Parable of the Workers in the Vineyard is a case in point.

> For the kingdom of heaven is like a landowner who went out early in the morning to hire laborers for his vineyard. After agreeing with the laborers for the usual daily wage, he sent them into his vineyard. When he went out about nine o'clock, he saw others standing idle in the marketplace; and he said to them, "You also go into the vineyard, and I will pay you whatever is right." So they went. When he went out again about noon and about three o'clock, he did the same. And about five o'clock he went out and found others standing around; and he said to them, "Why are you standing here idle all day?" They said

> to him, "Because no one has hired us." He said to them, "You also go into the vineyard." When evening came, the owner of the vineyard said to his manager, "Call the laborers and give them their pay, beginning with the last and then going to the first." When those hired about five o'clock came, each of them received the usual daily wage. Now when the first came, they thought they would receive more; but each of them also received the usual daily wage. And when they received it, they grumbled against the landowner, saying, "These last worked only one hour, and you have made them equal to us who have borne the burden of the day and the scorching heat." But he replied to one of them, "Friend, I am doing you no wrong; did you not agree with me for the usual daily wage? Take what belongs to you and go; I choose to give to this last the same as I give to you. Am I not allowed to do what I choose with what belongs to me? Or are you envious because I am generous?" So the last will be first, and the first will be last. (Matt 20:16)

Here, work functions metaphorically and analogically to indicate how the kingdom of heaven or God takes place through a reversal of values. The landowner, usually identified with God, pays each of the laborers the same wage, irrespective of the length of time they have worked, that is, served God. Everyone gets paid the same—so long that one works, that is. So understood, the parable equates service of God with work or labor and, in so doing, gives value to the latter, precisely in the sense that we have seen in a document like *Rerum novarum*.

Although the parable itself is not about work per se, the metaphor is telling: serving God is akin to work, and it is easy to turn things around, to the point where work itself becomes service to God. Such is the sense, generally speaking, of Max Weber's famous thesis on the development of early capitalism out of Protestant Christianity: the latter endows the values of hard work, frugality, and thrift with individual and spiritual significance, values that in turn drive economic development and growth.[47] The parable can also be used in service of social and political reform, in support of, for instance, a just and living wage. On such a reading, the "last" correspond with the poor, the oppressed, and the outcast and, on this account, the parable functions as an exhortation to treat them justly. The parable, in this sense, calls for an "economics of need" that is human-centered, above and beyond the cold calculation of a wage-based system.[48]

---

47. Weber, *The Protestant Ethic*.
48. This is Mark Davis's argument in "Politics of Just Wages."

There are, however, other ways to read the parable. William R. Herzog II has suggested that rather than reading the parable in terms of the generosity of the landowner, we read it in terms of the laborers themselves. The very fact that the marketplace in the parable teems with laborers would seem to indicate a high degree of unemployment, a situation of which the landowner is taking advantage. The landowner is, as Herzog notes, exploiting an unemployed work force to meet his labor needs "by offering them work without a wage agreement."[49] Indeed, although the value of the wage itself, a denarius, is difficult to determine, it is likely not that generous and, instead, probably amounted to little more than a subsistence wage, which the workers had to accept due to a lack of other viable options. Herzog writes of the situation:

> In a market where the labor pool is larger than the number of jobs available, he offers a subsistence or lower-than-subsistence wage to the first-hired workers before abandoning all pretense of negotiation. The workers are so desperate that they go to the vineyard at his command, hoping to receive some portion of a denarius to maintain their precarious existence.[50]

The earlier-hired laborers' consternation at receiving the same pay as the later-hired laborers is, from this perspective, entirely understandable, even justified: they have been insulted and exploited. If we follow this line of thinking, the landowner's response to their grumbling does not come off as generous but ironically cold, as his so-called charity is little more than a ruse to assert his economic position and power over the workers: "Friend, I am doing you no wrong; did you not agree with me for the usual daily wage? Take what belongs to you and go; I choose to give to this last the same as I give to you. Am I not allowed to do what I choose with what belongs to me? Or are you envious because I am generous?" (Matt 20:16).

Such a reading to a large extent depends upon a form-critical approach to the texts, which attempts to isolate an "original" form of the parable before its redaction and theological deployment at the textual level. Herzog, for instance, ultimately has to bracket the theological framing of the parable as unoriginal, to make his reading work ("So the last will be first, and the first will be last"). But even if we accept the final, received form of the text for the purpose of analysis, it is possible to give a different emphasis to the parable once we bracket attachment to the ideology of work. Although the parable certainly raises the "last" to the position of the "first," equalizing what is due, it also equalizes the notion of what is due itself as connected to

49. Herzog, *Parables as Subversive Speech*, 86.
50. Herzog, *Parables as Subversive Speech*, 90.

work. In giving to the "last" the same amount as the "first," the parable, that is, unbinds wages from work: the parable illustrates that labor and wages are not immediately convertible to each other. In challenging the link between money and the amount of labor expended, both in terms of physical effort and time, the parable thus challenges the relationship between work and life. What one is due, the parable says, is in excess over one's work, which also means that in telling this story, Jesus severs life from work and money, from the idea that we must work to gain money in order to have access to our needs, wants, and desires.

Jesus continues to express this notion through the lens of work and the employer-employee relationship in this parable. But the basic idea—that work and life are disjunct, correlative to the opposition between mammon and God—is more explicitly expressed elsewhere, although in somewhat enigmatic terms. In Matthew's gospel, immediately after instantiating the distinction between God and mammon, Jesus goes on to say:

> Therefore I tell you, do not worry about your life, what you will eat or what you will drink, or about your body, what you will wear. Is not life more than food, and the body more than clothing? Look at the birds of the air; they neither sow nor reap nor gather into barns, and yet your heavenly Father feeds them. Are you not of more value than they? And can any of you by worrying add a single hour to your span of life? And why do you worry about clothing? Consider the lilies of the field, how they grow; they neither toil nor spin, yet I tell you, even Solomon in all his glory was not clothed like one of these. But if God so clothes the grass of the field, which is alive today and tomorrow is thrown into the oven, will he not much more clothe you—you of little faith? Therefore do not worry, saying, "What will we eat?" or "What will we drink?" or "What will we wear?" For it is the Gentiles who strive for all these things; and indeed your heavenly Father knows that you need all these things. But strive first for the kingdom of God and his righteousness, and all these things will be given to you as well. (Matt 6:25–33)

Similar to the way in which we often treat the disjunction between God and mammon, as discussed in chapter 2, it is all too easy to read this statement as indicative of an internal disposition. Jesus' statement, that is, primarily concerns, for lack of a better word, a vertical rather than horizontal shift, a shift in how we carry ourselves with regard to material necessities. The emphasis, in other words, is on worry, on the anxiety that drives us to seek security in our various attempts to control our lives. This dispositional emphasis no doubt has much to do with the severity and apparent impracticality of Jesus' suggestions, which we have seen before.

Money, I have said, provides access to our needs, wants, and desires, and the primary means through which we gain access to money is through work, meaning that labor is linked to life. Jesus' statement here, however, seeks to show that that entanglement primarily rests on anxiety, but that anxiety is material as well as internal. The issue, that is, is not just with one's disposition but with work itself, since work is one of the forms that anxiety takes. We work because we worry about life, about the very real needs, wants, and desires that existence entails. Separating anxiety from work treats the former as secondary or epiphenomenal: we work not only because it is a necessity (how else would we gain access to money, and hence life?) but also because it is valuable in and of itself. It is in and through work that we realize ourselves or, more theologically put, that we find our place as co-creators with God in God's creation. Any anxiety we feel about matters is what we bring to the table, and not, from this perspective, an aspect of the work/money system itself, of mammon.

The assumption behind this line of reasoning is that the market is a neutral sphere. I argued in the last chapter, however, that one's participation in the market—in exchange, but also in the wage relationship—is coerced or forced: one must opt in or else be subject to death. Indeed, in actuality, there is no "opting in" in the first place, since one's participation in the economy is ideologically and materially determined as necessary, as "just part of life." Hence when problems arise within this system and its various constellations, the solution—individually, collectively, and institutionally—is usually conceived in terms of parameters dictated in advance, parameters already symbolically sanctioned. A financial crisis calls for financial solutions, whether we are dealing with investors on Wall Street or individuals on so-called Main Street.[51]

Jesus commands his followers, however, not to worry, not to harbor anxiety over how one's needs, wants, and desires will be met. He contrasts the anxiety that goes along with serving mammon with seemingly bucolic images drawn from the natural world, the birds of the air and the lilies and grasses of the field. These, he insists, rely on the providence of God for their material needs, which means that they live in the world without anxiety. One could, of course, say that this is because a different relationship to being is at work, here. The birds of the air and the lilies and grasses of the field do

---

51. For Konings, *Emotional Logic of Capitalism*, 58, this is because money is not "an external authority but a sign invested with subjective meaning, characterized by an extraordinary capacity to activate the chains of connections that link it to our most personal, differentiated concerns."

not "care" for their being in the same way as human beings do; they do not, that is, raise the question of being and, because of this, cannot even participate in the structure of anxiety. The sundry creatures of the "natural" world exist in the world as water in water, as Bataille might say, with no separation between themselves and their environment.[52] Or, as Heidegger would put it, they do not exist toward their own death.[53]

Perhaps, but similar to the way in which "ultimate concern" for Jesus is not an abstract category but has to do primarily with money, anxiety should not be understood in generalized, ontological terms. It is, rather, material, attached to work and, ultimately, money. Hence Jesus does not articulate reliance on God as an antidote to anxiety in terms of a simple shift in attitude but, rather, as the cessation of work: the birds "neither sow nor reap nor gather," the lilies neither "toil nor spin."

We should not dismiss the radical point that Jesus is making. One contemporary commentator, for instance, stresses that "the challenge to trust in God's providence does not exclude working and having property. [Jesus'] words are directed to people involved with sowing, reaping, storing in barns, toiling, and spinning, but who are called to see that their life is not based on these things. Such people are not called upon to become birds or lilies, but to consider God's providence for all creation, including birds, lilies, and human beings."[54] Not only does this claim ignore that elsewhere Jesus does urge his followers to become "like" his stated examples (cf. Matt 18:3), which suggests that the literal sense of his so-called metaphors should not be so quickly dismissed. It also misses the entire point: work inevitably entails basing one's life on "these things" (sowing, reaping, toiling, spinning, storing), meaning that if one is to trust in God's provisions one must become like the birds and the lilies. To recall Goodchild's words, it is a question of time, attention, and devotion, but these need to be understood materially: it is a question of what we actually spend our time doing, of what we actually devote our attention to. For most of us, now and then, that is work. Insofar as "natural" beings do not participate in the world in this way, they are not just aspects of God's creation but examples to be emulated.

The contrast here with Paul's admonition to work is sharp. In one of his letters to the Thessalonians, Paul closes with a command:

> Now we command, you, beloved, in the name of our Lord Jesus, to keep away from believers who are living in idleness and not according to the tradition that they received from us. For

---

52. Bataille, *Theory of Religion*, 17–26.
53. Heidegger, *Being and Time*, 219–46.
54. Boring, *Matthew*, 210.

> you yourselves know how you ought to imitate us; we were not idle when we were with you, and we did not eat anyone's bread without paying for it; but with toil and labor we worked day and night, so that we might not burden any of you. This was not because we do not have the right, but in order to give you an example to imitate. For even when we were with you, we gave you this command: Anyone unwilling to work should not eat. For we hear that some of you are living in idleness, mere busybodies, not doing any work. Now such persons we command and exhort in the Lord Jesus Christ to do their work quietly and to earn their own living. (2 Thess 3:6–12)

Paul's words, here, can certainly be abused, and like many things biblical, they often have as justification for eschewing aid to those in need.[55] But even if we rightly grant that Paul's claims here do not easily translate into policy prescriptions but, rather, express a sentiment made under specific pressures (some had apparently stopped working in anticipation of Jesus' promised return), they still contrast with Jesus' own attitudes toward work.

Whereas Paul works so as not to be a burden on others, Jesus relies heavily on the resources of others, seemingly without working, which means that he is, from a Pauline perspective, a "burden" or, if you will, a "freeloader." We read, for instance, in Luke's gospel of the time when Martha offered him hospitality by welcoming him into her home. We read that Martha

> had a sister named Mary, who sat at the Lord's feet and listened to what he was saying. But Martha was distracted by her many tasks; so she came to him and asked, "Lord, do you not care that my sister has left me to do all the work by myself? Tell her then to help me." But the Lord answered her, "Martha, Martha, you are worried and distracted about many things; there is need of only one thing. Mary has chosen the better part, which will not be taken from her." (Luke 10:38–42)

We can, of course, read this episode piously. The "better part" that Mary has chosen, on this account, coincides with the presence of Jesus himself. Jesus praises Mary, in other words, because of her attention to him and his teachings, rather than the many "tasks" that constitute household work, on which Martha devotes her attention. Nevertheless, it is important to emphasize

---

55. For instance, in 2013 Rep. Stephen Fincher (R-TN) used Paul to justify making cuts to funding for the Supplemental Nutrition Assistance Program (SNAP). Echoing Paul, Fincher said, "The one who is unwilling to work should not eat." See Raferty, "Ax Hovers Over Food Stamp Program."

two things. First, the episode is a clear illustration of Jesus' normal pattern of relying on the generosity of others for his needs. Second, his reliance on others, here, becomes a pattern for others to follow. Mary's lack of attention toward her work, whether expressed in terms of failure or refusal, should not be read simply in terms of pious devotion but, rather, in line with other aspects of Jesus' teaching and actions. Like Simon and Andrew, she apparently "leaves" her work to "follow" Jesus, and in this sense her actions correspond with the general pattern that Jesus recommends for his disciples. Moreover, the contrast between Mary and Martha, the latter of whom keeps at her work, correlates with the more generic command: "Therefore I tell you, do not worry about your life, what you will eat or what you will drink, or about your body, what you will wear" (Matt 6:25).

The contrast between Martha's worry or distraction and Mary's faith, which here takes the form of ignoring her tasks, of not working, also lines up with the prayer which, in Luke's gospel, immediately follows. Jesus famously teaches his disciples to pray:

> Father, hallowed be your name.
>> Your kingdom come.
>> Give us each day our daily bread.
>> And forgive us our sins,
>>> for we ourselves forgive everyone indebted to us.
>> And do not bring us to the time of
>>> trial. (Luke 11:2–4)

To pray to God for one's sustenance, for one's bread, is to assume that it is God who provides, not oneself through one's labor. One could argue, as is often done, that it is through work that God provides, but that assumption cannot be held consistently on the basis of Jesus' teachings and also ignores the structural limitations that work poses. Work is not a neutral activity, one in which we have the option of recognizing and acknowledging God or not. It is not a matter, in other words, of how we relate to work, of how we feel about it and conceive of what we are doing through it, personally, socially, and theologically. In its connection to mammon, work works against God and God's kingdom, by redirecting and shaping time, attention, and devotion, to borrow Goodchild's phrase again. In the story of Mary and Martha, Mary embodies the material shift indicated in Jesus' comments and thus the substance of his prayer.

Another way to think about Jesus' attitudes toward work is to focus on sabbath, that is, on rest, cessation from work. Walter Brueggeman has recently drawn attention to the subversive element of sabbath in the biblical texts but more generally as well. For Brueggemann, sabbath should not be understood in overly moralistic terms but rather in terms of resistance and alternative. Brueggemann notes that our contemporary societies require almost constant activity. We are, he says, a "society of 24/7 multitasking in order to achieve, accomplish, perform, and possess. But the demands of market ideology pertain as much to consumption as they do to production. Thus the system of commodity requires that we want more, have more, own more, use more, eat and drink more."[56] Insofar as sabbath names the cessation of normal activity, its celebration can serve as "an act of both resistance and alternative. It is resistance because it is a visible insistence that our lives are not defined by the production and consumption of commodity goods.... It is an alternative to the demanding, chattering, pervasive presence of advertising and its great liturgical claim of professional sports that devour all our 'rest time.'"[57]

Brueggemann is right to shore up the disruptive potential of sabbath. It is, he writes, "an occasion for reimagining all of social life away from coercion and competition to compassionate solidarity."[58] Nevertheless, in the end Brueggemann remains too indebted to a vision of work's redemption through sabbath. I think we can push Brueggemann further, though, by reading what Jesus says about sabbath in light of an anti-work stance. We read, for instance:

> One sabbath he was going through the grainfields; and as they made their way his disciples began to pluck heads of grain. The Pharisees said to him, "Look, why are they doing what is not lawful on the sabbath?" And he said to them, "Have you never read what David did when he and his companions were hungry and in need of food? He entered the house of God, when Abiathar was high priest, and ate the bread of the Presence, which it is not lawful for any but the priests to eat, and he gave some to his companions." Then he said to them, "The sabbath was made for humankind, and not humankind for the sabbath; so the Son of Man is lord even of the sabbath." (Mark 2:23–28)

The episode is, on the one hand, meant to highlight and criticize the strict observance of the sabbath among Jesus' opponents. In castigating Jesus for working on the sabbath, which is a violation of the law (cf. Exod 20:8–11; 34:21; Deut 5:12–15), Jesus' opponents show their inflexibility but also, more seriously, their misunderstanding of the law. The sabbath, Jesus insists, was not created merely to be followed, as if observing the sabbath is

---

56. Brueggemann, *Sabbath as Resistance*, xii. Crary, *24/7*, is relevant here as well.
57. Brueggemann, *Sabbath as Resistance*, xiii–xiv.
58. Brueggemann, *Sabbath as Resistance*, 45.

akin to checking the correct boxes. To conceive of the sabbath in such terms is to mistake it for a rule. Said differently, it turns sabbath, a day of rest, into work, if not entirely in content then at least in form: the line demarcating work and sabbath thus blurs. This is why Jesus says that humankind was made for the sabbath, and not the other way around: it is rest rather than toil, gift rather than law.

In plucking heads of grain on the sabbath, Jesus, too, blurs the distinction between work and sabbath, but from the other direction. Whereas Jesus' opponents envision sabbath in the image of work, Jesus envisions work in terms of sabbath, which also puts Jesus at odds with contemporary attempts to collapse non-work into work. The apparent ease with which Jesus and his disciples move through the field, plucking heads of grain, is reminiscent of the activity of the lilies of the field and the birds of the air and expresses the basic sentiment of the prayer that Jesus teaches his disciples: "give us each day our daily bread." The point, in other words, is not that Jesus "works" on the sabbath but that work itself is dissolved in sabbath. Whereas, as I said above, current labor practices tend to erase the line demarcating work and life in favor of work, Jesus advocates for the same, but on the side of life.

On this basis, we can give a different reading of that "first gospel of work," the opening chapters of Genesis. Recall that in *Laborem exercens*, work is sanctified to the extent that it mirrors and participates in God's own creative activity, which in Gen 1 extends over six days and finds its end or rest on the seventh, that is the sabbath. Hence we are reminded in Exodus that the sabbath is to be observed as a day without work, because "in six days the LORD made heaven and earth, the sea, and all that is in them, but rested the seventh day; therefore the LORD blessed the sabbath day and consecrated it" (Exod 20:11). The connection between work and sabbath makes rest into a metaphysical principle, but it also has the unfortunate effect of doing the same with work: we work and rest alternatively because that is the pattern laid down in the beginning by God, whose own activity follows that pattern.

But we could also easily read differently, emphasizing sabbath not in terms of an alternating pattern but in terms of real cessation, as the completion of God's creative activity. Paul LaFargue makes this point, noting that the creation narrative is not so much about work as it is rest, or anti-production: in Gen 1 God gives "his worshipers the supreme example of ideal laziness; after six days of work, he rests for all eternity."[59] Indeed, although in the second account of creation in Gen 2 the man is placed in the garden of Eden "to till it and keep it," the type of activity involved here seemingly falls

---

59. Lafargue, *Right to Be Lazy*, 8.

out of pattern. It is only after the human beings have violated the command not to eat from the tree of the knowledge of good and evil that work starts to carry negative connotations.

> To the woman he said,
>
>> "I will greatly increase your pangs in childbearing;
>>> in pain you shall bring forth children,
>> yet your desire shall be for your husband,
>>> and he shall rule over you."
>
> And to the man he said,
>
>> "Because you have listened to the voice of your wife,
>>> and have eaten of the tree
>> about which I commanded you,
>>> 'You shall not eat of it,'
>> cursed is the ground because of you;
>>> in toil you shall eat of it all the days of your life;
>> thorns and thistles it shall bring forth for you;
>>> and you shall eat the plants of the field.
>> By the sweat of your face
>>> you shall eat bread
>> until you return to the ground,
>>> for out of it you were taken;
>> you are dust,
>>> and to dust you shall return."

One could, of course, contrast the two "works" here in terms of redeemed and unredeemed or alienated and unalienated labor, along the lines of a theology of work. But it is important to emphasize that the alternating pattern of work and rest only makes sense in light of the negative view of work established after the human beings ate from the forbidden tree. It is only then that work becomes something from which one needs rest, which means that any "tilling" and "keeping" prior looks more like what the lilies of the field and the birds of the air do or, rather, do not do: "they neither toil not spin."

Work, in this sense, is more "punishment" than anything else, which is why in the Genesis narrative it coincides with expulsion from the garden. Calvin captured this sense well, in typical overdrawn fashion:

> Before the fall, the state of the world was a most fair and delightful mirror of the divine favor and paternal indulgence towards man. Now, in all the elements we perceive that we are cursed. And although (as David says) the earth is still full of the mercy of God (Ps 33:5), yet, at the same time, appear manifest signs of

his dreadful alienation from us, by which if we are unmoved, we betray our blindness and insensibility.[60]

For Calvin, however, this does not lead to a denial of work but to its acceptance, as a means of submitting to God and God's grace:

> It is, however, to be observed, that they who meekly submit to their sufferings, present to God an acceptable obedience, if, indeed, there be joined with this bearing of the cross, that knowledge of sin which may teach them to be humble. Truly it is faith alone which can offer such a sacrifice to God; but the faithful the more they labor in procuring a livelihood, with the greater advantage are they stimulated to repentance, and accustom themselves to the mortification of the flesh; yet God often remits a portion of this curse to his own children, lest they should sink beneath the burden.[61]

It is this sentiment, of course, that is expressed in the so-called Protestant work ethic, mentioned above: given work's value, hard work and success become a sign of God's favor.

This is the exact opposite of what we find in Jesus and his teachings. God's favor for Jesus is not found in work, in toiling for security, but in the opposite: in abandoning any and all means that direct our attention away from God and God's kingdom. This does not just have to do with making labor more just, moreover. Jesus certainly considers an act done against the poor, the oppressed, and the downtrodden as an act done against him and, thus, deserving of punishment or reward as appropriate. The Parable of the Laborers in the Vineyard, moreover, can function, at least in part, as an implicit critique of the employer-employee relationship, neutralizing it in favor of the employee. Nevertheless, Jesus' critique of work is much more thoroughgoing, in that he challenges the basis on which such practices are based: the need to gain security in the world through labor. Because of this, work is on par with money, mammon, as set in opposition to God. This does not mean, of course, the end of human activity, which would obviously be absurd, at least as a general principle. Jesus is not a pious ascetic, and does not advocate a passive reliance on God for one's needs. We will discuss this in more detail in the next chapter, but his point is to reconfigure human activity in terms of the birds of the air and the lilies of the field, in terms, that is, of a material relationship to the earth that does not involve anxiety

---

60. Calvin, *Calvin's Commentaries*, chapter 3.
61. Calvin, *Calvin's Commentaries*, chapter 3.

and that is anti-productivist. To refer it back to Genesis, Jesus' vision is one of Eden.

AGAINST FAMILY

The critique of work discussed above is thus a component of the critique of mammon, and this is because the two go hand in hand: money mediates life, but it is through work that we gain access to money. Jesus' critique of work, which takes the form of a rudimentary anti-work position in his actions, recommendations, and parables, extends to family as well. The link between work and family, on the one hand, should be obvious: in Jesus' immediate context and, for the most part until very recently, the family functions as the primary locus of production. Work may, of course, take place outside the locus of the family proper, but it always turns back to the household, meaning that work, to a large extent, remains within the latter's sphere. Indeed, the term "economy" originally signifies as much: it is management of the household.

I mentioned above Federici's critique of the gendered nature of work, which also implies that the family is also a means of exploitation. Nevertheless, in addition, such management, whether we understand it in terms of the original sense of "economy" or in more contemporary terms, where the family functions as a means of supporting and reproducing consumption and the means of production, almost inevitably tends in a more conservative direction. That is, family inevitably tends to turn inward on itself and, when it does turn outward, does so with its own concerns in mind.

This is partly Michael Hardt and Antonio Negri's point in *Commonwealth*, in which they seek to develop a notion of the common that would allow the multitude to sever their relationship to capital. Hardt and Negri take social institutions as essential for thinking the common, in that the former must draw on the latter for their creation and continued existence and maintenance. But it is necessary to separate the positive from the negative in such institutions, as a means of distinguishing the common at work in them from its corruption.

Hardt and Negri note that the family is one such institution, in addition to the corporation and the nation. On the one hand, the family, as Hardt and Negri emphasize, is a site of the common—indeed, it is, for many, the primary institution through which one experiences the common. The family is "the principal if not exclusive site of collective social experience, cooperative labor arrangements, caring, and intimacy," Hardt and Negri write.[62] Yet,

---

62. Hardt and Negri, *Commonwealth*, 160.

at the same time, it corrupts the common on which it is based, mobilizing it into "a series of hierarchies, restrictions, exclusions, and distortions." Specifically, it does so across four, interrelated terrains. First, Hardt and Negri note that the family is, on the whole, "a machine of gender normativity that constantly grinds down and crushes the common."[63] Gains have, of course, been made on this front, at least in certain quarters, but it still remains the case that overall the family functions to reinforce patriarchy, a gendered division of labor, and a heteronormativity based on gendered hierarchies and norms. It is important to point out that this remains the case even as we have seen the notion of "marriage" expand to include same-sex couples.

Although opening the institution of marriage to previously excluded individuals certainly represents an improvement in the struggle for equal rights, so long as marriage entails certain individual and social benefits, it prevents recognizing in any substantial way other forms of relationality.[64] This is Hardt and Negri's second point on the negative aspects of the family when it comes to fostering the common, that it constrains the very diverse ways in which human beings relate to each other to one, specific pattern. They write, "All alternative kinship structures, whether based on sexual relationships or not, are either prohibited or corralled back under the rule of the family. The exclusive nature of the family model, which carries with it inevitably all of its internal hierarchies, gender norms, and heteronormativity, is evidence of not only a pathetic lack of social imagination to grasp other forms of intimacy and solidarity but also a lack of freedom to create and experiment with alternative social relationships and nonfamily kinship structures."[65]

Such a constrained vision of relationality, which envisions other forms of the latter in terms of the family, also acts centrifugally. Thus, third, although one of the purposes of the family is to provide a launching pad for individuals to extend themselves outward, toward the larger community and world, it often does so in the form of narcissism and individualism. Navigating the broader social sphere, that is, takes the form of doing what is best for one's family. Although, as Hardt and Negri point out, acting in such a manner is often framed in terms of altruism, it actually represents the "blindest egoism."[66] For instance, "Political discourse that justifies interest in the future throughout the logic of family continuity . . . reduces the common to a kind of projected individualism via one's progeny and betrays an

---

63. Hardt and Negri, *Commonwealth*, 160.
64. Lehr discusses this as well in *Queer Family Values*.
65. Hardt and Negri, *Commonwealth*, 161.
66. Hardt and Negri, *Commonwealth*, 161.

extraordinary incapacity to conceive the future in broader social terms."[67] Hence the seeming ubiquity of rhetoric about "our children" and "future generations" surrounding many policy recommendations and prescriptions. Emphasis on the family, in other words, fosters what Lee Edelman has called a politics of "reproductive futurism."[68] Such egoism correlates to Hardt and Negri's fourth and final point, which is that the family serves as the "core institution for the accumulation and transfer of private property."[69] Otherwise put, the family is one of the main drivers of the sort of differentiating wealth that I have critiqued throughout.

It should go without saying that Christianity has often reinforced these negative components of the family, even if its view of the latter is by no means monolithic.[70] Although official dogma in many quarters emphasizes that the sacrament of baptism serves to incorporate the individual into the body of Christ over and above purely natural ties, such ultimately rests on a sacralized understanding of the family. The *Catechism of the Catholic Church*, for instance, locates marriage between a man and a woman in the order of creation itself, and emphasizes the importance of the family that results from such union for individual, collective, and ecclesiastical well-being. Quoting *Gaudium et spes*, the *Catechism* emphasizes that the "well-being of the individual person and of both human and Christian society is closely bound up with the healthy state of conjugal and family life."[71] Hence, the *Catechism* refers to the family home as "the domestic church," that is, "a community of grace and prayer, a school of human virtues and of Christian charity."[72] Even among individual congregations and other denominations that criticize the attendant patriarchy, heteronormativity, and myopia that this vision of the family has often sanctified, the tendency is still to reinforce the basic structure, however open that structure may be viewed. The focus, in other words, remains on the family, as a basic unit that should be nurtured, both individually and socially. The extension of marriage beyond the confines of "one man, one woman," although a gain, is in this sense quite traditional: the inclusion involved also simultaneously extends the reach of the notion of "family," without calling the latter into question.

---

67. Hardt and Negri, *Commonwealth*, 161.
68. Edelman, *No Future*.
69. Hardt and Negri, *Commonwealth*, 161.
70. For different views of the family in Greco-Roman culture and in the history of Christianity, as these influence contemporary views, see Radford Reuther, *Christianity*.
71. *Catechism of the Catholic Church*, Part II, 2.3, §1603.
72. *Catechism of the Catholic Church*, Part II, 2.3, § 1666.

That is, however, precisely what Jesus does, in the form of urging his followers to abandon their families, and the individual, social, and economic security that goes along with them. As I have mentioned previously, when Simon and Andrew decide to follow Jesus, they also, apparently, leave behind their families (" . . . and they left their father Zebedee in the boat with the hired men" [Mark 1:20; cf. Matt 4:22; Luke 5:11]). Likewise, in the story of the rich young ruler, upon telling his disciples that it is virtually impossible for a rich person to gain eternal life, the disciples are quick to remind Jesus that they have left their livelihood, including their homes, to follow him. Jesus then assures his followers, "Truly I tell you, there is no one who has left house or wife or brothers or parents or children, for the sake of the kingdom of God, who will not get back very much more in this age, and in the age to come" (Luke 19:29–30).

Such a claim is consistent with his much stronger claim about "hating" family. Thus in Luke 14, for instance, we read of Jesus addressing the "large crowds traveling with him" as follows:

> Whoever comes to me and does not hate father and mother, wife and children, brothers and sisters, yes, and even life itself, cannot be my disciple. Whoever does not carry his cross and follow me cannot be my disciple. For which of you, intending to build a tower, does not first sit down and estimate the cost, to see whether he has enough to complete it. Otherwise, when he has laid a foundation and is not able to finish, all who see it will begin to ridicule him, saying, "This fellow began to build and was not able to finish." Or what king, going out to wage war against another king, will not sit down first and consider whether he is able with ten thousand to oppose the one who comes against him with twenty thousand? If he cannot, then, while the other is still far away, he sends a delegation and asks for the terms of peace. So, therefore, none of you can become my disciple if you do not give up all your possessions. (Luke 14:25–34)

One can, of course, interpret what Jesus says here as a question of priority, similar to the way in which the relationship between God and mammon is often interpreted. Jesus, that is, does not actually bid his followers to "hate" familial ties and their own lives but is, rather, using hyperbole to shock them out of their complacency. So understood, when Jesus uses the term "hate" (*misei*, from *miseo*) as indicative of what it means to follow him, he really means something like "priority," the importance of loving family "less" than Jesus. This is at least how Matthew would appear to interpret such matters, rendering them seemingly more palatable: "Whoever loves father or mother more than me is not worthy of me; and whoever loves son or daughter more than me is not worthy of me; and whoever does not take up the cross and follow me is not worthy of me. Those who find their life will lose it, and those who lose their life for my sake will find it" (Matt 10:27–39).

To interpret it in that way, however, internalizes the sense of what Jesus commands, which like the relationship between God and mammon, disavows the force of the disjunction. It likewise ignores how Jesus' own disciples have taken such claims, at least according to the Gospels. They apparently took them literally, as referring also to material realities rather than mere internal dispositions, and it is their actual leaving of family, work, and possessions that marks them as disciples. Moreover, Matthew's own telling can only appear easier to the extent that we ignore how he has Jesus preface the "more than me":

> Do not think that I have come to bring peace to the earth; I have not come to bring peace, but a sword. For I have come to set a man against his father, and a daughter against her mother, and a daughter-in-law against her mother-in-law; and one's foes will be members of one's own household. (Matt 10:34–36)

It is only after these stark words of separation that Jesus introduces the notion of priority, or "more than me." What it means to love Jesus more than father and mother, son or daughter, is, then, found in the sword, in the separation that following Jesus introduces into familial ties and responsibilities. Otherwise put, when it comes to family, those who follow Jesus should "let the dead bury their own dead" (Matt 8:22).

We find this "sword" in Jesus' own identity as well, in the way in which his own self-understanding vis-à-vis himself and his disciples depends upon an interruption of familial ties, a denial of their significance. We read, for instance, that

> [w]hile he was still speaking to the crowds, his mother and his brothers were standing outside, wanting to speak to him. Someone told him, "Look, your mother and your brothers are standing outside, wanting to speak to you." But to the one who had told him this, Jesus replied, "Who is my mother, and who are my brothers?" And pointing to his disciples, he said, "Here are my mother and my brothers! For whoever does the will of my Father in heaven is my brother and sister and mother."

I argued in the last chapter that money, too, interrupts family, that is, natural or organic ties, in favor of self-determination and exchange-based relationships. Nevertheless the "what" Jesus advocates is decidedly different.

Whereas capital demands the severing of familial relations for the sake of consumption, production, and accumulation, Jesus demands the same for something different, namely, love: "I give you a new commandment, that you love one another. Just as I have loved you, you also should love one another" (John 13:34).

One way to interpret this "new" commandment is as an internal feeling expressed vertically (toward God) and horizontally (toward others), outwardly expressed in appropriate doses of sympathy and empathy and, when necessary, charity. "You shall love the Lord your God with all your heart, and with all your soul, and with all your strength, and with all your mind; and your neighbor as yourself," Jesus famously says (Luke 10:27). When individualized in this manner, however, the command may come off as an unobtainable ideal, which is, perhaps, another way to say that it is pious nonsense. That was Freud's opinion of the claim. For Freud, no amount of "reason" could recommend the injunction. Despite the various unconscious motivations involved, love, for Freud, is "a valuable thing that I have no right to throw away without reflection. It imposes obligations on me which I must be prepared to make sacrifices to fulfill. If I love someone, he must be worthy of it in some way or another. . . . I shall even be doing wrong if I do, for my love is valued as a privilege by all those belonging to me; it is an injustice to them if I put a stranger on a level with them."[73] Indeed, far from being an object of love, the other, my neighbor, has more of "a claim to my hostility, even to my hatred," precisely to the extent that he or she does not act toward me according to the command to love.[74] Hence, for Freud, "universal love" makes no practical, moral, or psychoanalytic sense.

In a way, Freud is right: Jesus' command to love does not make sense, so long as it is read according to a pre-established ethical framework that, in the end, privileges familial bonds. This is, at least, Lacan's take on Freud's disgust with the command. Lacan notes that Freud's hesitancy with regard to the command to love one's neighbor is, to an extent, "quite right," since it raises the issue of "what is worth loving."[75] Freud recognizes that love is "something precious," something that cannot be doled out so easily, especially on command. Lacan will thus say that Freud "reveals how one must love a friend's son because, if the friend were to lose his son, his suffering would be intolerable. The whole Aristotelian conception of the good is alive in this man who is a true man; he tells us the most sensible and reasonable

---

73. Freud, *Civilization and Its Discontents*, 38.
74. Freud, *Civilization and Its Discontents*, 39.
75. Lacan, *Ethics of Psychoanalysis*, 186.

things about what it is worth sharing the good that is our love with."[76] For Lacan, however, love of neighbor cannot be reduced to altruism and, in this sense, doesn't have the good as its horizon, as Freud appears to assume. What Freud misses, on Lacan's reading of him and the command, is the way that the latter opens "on to *jouissance*."[77] In this sense, Freud's horror at the commandment is precisely its point, because the commandment points to the problem of *jouissance*. Lacan writes that

> every time that Freud stops short in horror of the consequences of the commandment to love one's neighbor, we see evoked the presence of that fundamental evil which dwells within this neighbor. But if that is the case, then it also dwells within me. And what is more of a neighbor to me than this heart within which is that of my jouissance and which I don't dare go near? For as soon as I go near it, as *Civilization and Its Discontents* makes clear, there rises up the unfathomable aggressivity from which I flee, that I turn against me, and which in the very place of the vanished Law adds its weight to that which prevents me from crossing a certain frontier at the limit of the Thing.[78]

Another way to put the matter is to say that the other, when encountered under the injunction to neighbor love, poses a threat to my being, because that injunction forces me to confront the *jouissance* that structures my subjectivity and the threat the other poses to it. This is why, for Lacan, love of neighbor cannot be reduced to an image of the good, to mere altruism. On the contrary, a certain amount of altruism enables us to remain inside ourselves, so to speak, precisely because it conceives of the other in our own image. Lacan notes, "It is a fact of experience that what I want is the good of others in the image of my own. That doesn't cost so much. What I want is the good of others provided that it remain in the image of my own."[79] Love of neighbor, in contrast, forces us "to confront the fact that my neighbor's jouissance, his harmful, malignant jouissance, is that which poses a problem for my love."[80]

Such ambivalence with regard to love can be purposed into a more radical conception of it. Alain Badiou has emphasized as much, conceiving of love in terms of a truth procedure. For Badiou, the experience of love

---

76. Lacan, *Ethics of Psychoanalysis*, 186.
77. Lacan, *Ethics of Psychoanalysis*, 186.
78. Lacan, *Ethics of Psychoanalysis*, 186.
79. Lacan, *Ethics of Psychoanalysis*, 187.
80. Lacan, *Ethics of Psychoanalysis*, 187.

is an experience of truth, specifically, "of what it is to be two, not one."[81] Although within Badiou's conception of truth procedures, "the two" here refers primarily to the amorous relationship, his discussion of the notion in Saint Paul would seem to warrant generalizing the notion of what happens in "the two" toward new forms of social organization.[82] Love, in this sense, draws the individual out of his or her subjective isolation, which can include the so-called natural ties that bind the individual to family, reshaping his or her subjectivity according to the truth of difference. Such reshaping, in turn, forces a new perspective on the world from the position of the two, or the truth of love more generally. Better put, love re-creates the world in its own image, and does so through fidelity to the event contained within it. Badiou's conception of love is, in this sense, radical and interruptive or, as he puts it "combative."[83] The external, social structures with which we often associate love, should not, then, be substituted for love. Something like the family, Badiou insists, functions as a means of socializing its impact, similar to the way in which the state represses political enthusiasm and truth for the calculated logic of management.[84]

Badiou criticizes Christianity itself for ultimately having too passive an understanding of love, trading immanence for transcendence. Love, in other words, is not a truth in its own right but only a means to direct attention elsewhere, to the Other. Badiou writes:

> In the final analysis, religions don't speak of love. Because they are only interested in it as a source of intensity, in the subjective state it alone can create, in order to direct that intensity towards faith and the Church and encourage this subjective state to accept the sovereignty of God. The main outcome is Christianity substitutes devout, passive, deferential love for the combative love that I am praising here, that earthly creation of the differentiated birth of a new world and a happiness won point by point. Love on bended knee is no love at all as far as I am concerned, even if love sometimes arouses passion in us that makes us yield to the loved one.[85]

Christianity has certainly often been guilty as charged, but it remains open whether the latter image of love is coextensive with Jesus' own. Indeed,

---

81. Badiou, *In Praise of Love*, 39.
82. Badiou, *Saint Paul*, 86–92.
83. Badiou, *In Praise of Love*, 66.
84. Badiou, *In Praise of Love*, 54.
85. Badiou, *In Praise of Love*, 67.

Jesus' notion of love, I would suggest, is closer to Badiou's own conception than he realizes.

Michel Henry's discussion of love in the gospels in terms of the difference between reciprocity and non-reciprocity is helpful, in this respect. As Henry points out, human relationality is normally governed through a basic understanding of reciprocity, which tends to privilege so-called natural bonds and a sort of tit for tat mentality. Reciprocity, that is, trades in like versus like, upholding "the living and spontaneous relations which unite members of the same family" as a model which, outside the familial sphere, determines forms of relationality according to a strict principle of just deserts. Relationality, in other words, is really about exchange. Jesus, in contrast, intervenes in this logic of reciprocity, interrupting it from within and, thus, "turning the human condition upside down."[86] As I indicated above, Jesus makes leaving family a precondition for following him, meaning that following him entails a loosening of the "natural" ties that otherwise found human relationality. To quote the passage again, "Do you think that I have come to bring peace to the earth? No, I tell you, but rather division! From now on five in one household will be divided, three against two and two against three" (Luke 12:51–52).[87]

But this disruption extends to the principle of just deserts as well, rendering "what is due" moot, indicative of a logic that cuts against the intent of God and God's kingdom. Rather than rendering like for like, Jesus urges his followers to relate to others without regard to what is normally due. Jesus, that is, urges his followers to act in excess over the logic that normally governs human relationships. Hence we are told:

> You have heard that it was said, "You shall love your neighbor and hate your enemy." But I say to you, Love your enemies and pray for those who persecute you, so that you may be children of your Father in heaven; for he makes his sun rise on the evil and on the good, and sends rain on the righteous and on the unrighteous. For if you love those who love you, what reward do you have? Do not even the tax-collectors do the same? And if you greet only your brothers and sisters, what more are you doing than others? Do not even the Gentiles do the same? Be perfect, therefore, as your heavenly Father is perfect. (Matt 5:43–48)

To use different terminology, borrowed from Badiou, we could say that Jesus' words and deeds recommend a reconfiguring of human relationality in terms of its generic potential, a potential that renders all forms of

---

86. Henry, *Words of Christ*, 33.

87. Henry quotes this passage as well is support for his claim, in *Words of Christ*, 32.

identification, including familial ties, ultimately insignificant in light of the truth of love.

We see this, for instance, in Jesus' own person, from his birth to his death. Despite Matthew's and Luke's attempt to ground Jesus genealogically, the notion of the "virgin birth" upon which they rely symbolically deconstructs the notion of lineage itself. Although placed within the history of Israel, a history that Luke traces back to Adam, Jesus is also without father. Put more exactly, he has God as his father, which puts Jesus on par with Adam, whom Luke tells us was also "son of God" (Luke 3:38).[88] In the context of remarks on the issue of gay marriage, Michel Serres has emphasized that the proper model for understanding Jesus and what he suggests for family more generally is, in this sense, adoption. It is worth quoting Serres at length on this point:

> But let us examine the Holy Family. In the Holy Family, the father is not the father: Joseph is not Jesus' father. The son is not the son: Jesus is the son of God, not the son of Joseph. Joseph, he has never made love to his wife. Concerning the mother, she is the mother indeed, but she is a virgin. The Holy Family, that's what Levi-Strauss called the elementary structure of kinship. A structure that breaks completely with ancient genealogy, based until then on filiation: one is Jewish through the mother. There are three types of filiation: natural filiation, recognition of paternity and adoption. In the Holy Family, what is blocked is both natural filiation and recognition; only adoption remains. Thus, since the Gospel according to Luke, the Church proposes as model for the family an elementary structure based on adoption: it is no longer a question of making children, but of choosing oneself, to the point where we are parents, you will be parents, father and mother, only if you say to your child "I have chosen you," "I adopt you because I love you," " it is you I wanted." And reciprocally, the child also chooses his parents because he loves them.[89]

Jesus, then, generalizes the notion of adoption as a means of disrupting accepted patterns of filiation. What this ultimately entails, however, is that one's relationship to God, understood in terms of doing God's will, substitutes for familial ties:

---

88. It is this identification of Jesus with Adam that allows Irenaeus to read their relationship in terms of recapitulation. See Irenaeus, *Against Heresies*.

89. Joris, "Michel Serres on Gay Marriage."

> While he was still speaking to the crowds, his mother and his brothers were standing outside, wanting to speak to him. Someone told him, "Look, your mother and your brothers are standing outside, wanting to speak to you." But to the one who had told him this, Jesus replied, "Who is my mother, and who are my brothers?" And pointing to his disciples, he said, "Here are my mother and my brothers! For whoever does the will of my Father in heaven is my brother and sister and mother." (Matt 12:46–50)

As Henry puts it, Jesus substitutes a divine genealogy for a human genealogy, which turns non-reciprocity into a new reciprocity that is based in "life in common."[90]

Nevertheless, it is important to stress that the achievement of this "life in common" proceeds asymmetrically. As Henry points out, Jesus can certainly say that God "makes the sun rise on the evil and on the good, and sends rain on the righteous and on the unrighteous" (Matt 5:45). But the equalizing that this implies is always weighted in practice toward the economic and social outcast. Jesus' overturning of values, in this sense, is a real overturning, one that takes the initial form of privileging economic and social outcasts over against all others. To use the language of liberation theology, it manifests itself as a "preferential option for the poor" or, to put it in Miranda's terms, a critique of "differentiating wealth." Such a preference, or real overturning, still remains inside the generic, since the generic is not the same thing as sameness. In Badiou's terminology, a generic procedure takes place from the position of an excluded part of a situation, whose trajectory when traced functions to change the logic of the situation itself. A generic procedure, in this sense, is asymmetrical, because it proceeds on the basis of the excluded as a means to achieve the universal.[91]

In the last chapter, I noted that money functions similarly, in that it, too, promises to disrupt the so-called natural ties that bind human relationality and exchange. Because money inserts itself as an abstract third party in the midst of exchange, it promises a certain amount of freedom. That freedom remains elusive in real terms, because money still has exchange as its horizon which, as I argued in the last chapter, entails inequalities. But whereas exchange under mammon still relies on a notion of reciprocity, Jesus' emphasis on the non-reciprocal challenges the notion of exchange itself:

---

90. Henry, *Words of Christ*, 36–37.

91. For a discussion of the technical aspects of Badiou's notion of the generic, see Badiou, *Being and Event*, 327–87.

> If you love those who love you, what credit is that to you? For even sinners love those who love them. If you do good to those who do good to you, what credit is that to you? For even sinners do the same. If you lend to those from whom you hope to receive, what credit is that to you? Even sinners lend to sinners, to receive as much again. But love your enemies, do good, and lend, expecting nothing in return. Your reward will be great, and you will be children of the Most High; for he is kind to the ungrateful and the wicked. Be merciful, just as your Father is merciful. (Luke 6:32–36)

Jesus' recommendation, here, cannot be reduced to charity, since it challenges the very system that renders charity necessary. Acting in excess of the logic of exchange, in excess of natural ties and just deserts, is also, then, acting against mammon.

To sum up, the distinction between God and mammon is not just about money, but work and family as well, since all three contribute to an economic logic that cuts against what Jesus refers to as the kingdom of heaven or God. Jesus' critique of these institutions, which takes an anti-work and anti-family form, however, should not be read in terms of passivity or a denial of relationality but, rather, as instigations toward thinking these along new lines. When Jesus says, for instance, that we should be like the birds of the air and the lilies of the field, for instance, it is meant not only as a challenge to the way in which we organize our lives in terms of production and work but also as an incitement to think of our activity otherwise, in terms of the birds of the air and the lilies of the field. Likewise, when Jesus indicates that it is necessary to leave family behind to follow him, he implies that the form of the family is, ultimately, irrelevant to the kingdom of God or heaven. Indeed, the family, for Jesus, is on the side of mammon, hence the importance of rethinking relationality apart from familial parochialism and the latter's assumed economic necessity.

CHAPTER 4

Excess Against Asceticism

I have argued in the previous chapters that one line present in Jesus' teachings and activities is a total critique of money and its related institutions, specifically work and family. That critique is, I have suggested, condensed in the disjunction between God and mammon, a disjunction that takes different forms as it cuts across interrelated spheres. I have argued that we should not understand the disjunction hierarchically, that is, in terms of priority but in absolute terms: there is no in-between space, no prioritizing one over the other, since it is impossible to serve both simultaneously. That goes, apparently, for work and family as well. The position that I have drawn out from Jesus, then, is one that is anti-money, anti-work, and anti-family, at least on an initial pass.

At this point, it is tempting to read Jesus' position on these matters as resulting in an otherworldly asceticism, understood more or less strictly. Such was Nietzsche's critique of Christianity, at least as a whole: it devalues this world by turning attention away from it and toward the next. Nietzsche's critique of Christianity, to be sure, was directed more at its dominant Pauline articulation, which he understood as a codification of *ressentiment*. Still, he expresses ambivalence about Jesus himself. Nietzsche can, on the one hand, insist that Jesus is the only "true Christian," to the extent that his life and his teachings coincide. Nietzsche says, for instance, that "[t]his bearer of 'glad tidings' died the way he lived, the way he *taught—not* to 'redeem humanity,' but instead to demonstrate how people need to live. His bequest to humanity was a *practice*: his behavior toward the judges, toward the henchmen, the way he acted in the face of his accusers and every type of slander and derision,—his conduct on the *cross*."[1] Jesus, it seems, found a joy in life, despite all external pressures, and it is this that Nietzsche can respect, if not totally buy into. On the other hand, one of the foundations of Jesus' praxis is exactly what Nietzsche despises: the elevation of the poor, the sick, the weak, and the like. To quote Nietzsche again, "Everything pitiful, everything suffering from itself, everything tormented by base feelings, the whole *ghetto-world* of the soul suddenly *on top!*"[2] As I have suggested throughout, Jesus' reversal of values, of which this elevation is part and parcel, is not different from the disjunction between God and mammon but part of its very logic.

Nevertheless, the mainstream of the Western ecclesiastical and theological traditions has tended to take Jesus' intervention in ascetic terms, in both theory and practice. To be sure, wholesale asceticism, that is, a total renunciation of the things of the world in exchange for heavenly reward, has never really been on the table, at least across the board. Such a path is, of course, not absent, and it can manifest itself with varying degrees of intensity. At the most extreme end is someone like Anthony the Great, who considered material deprivation and isolation the highest form of emulation. Indeed, as Athanasius narrates his life, it is irretrievably shaped by the command to the rich young ruler to sell his possessions and give to the poor, which Anthony takes literally.[3] Even if the monastic path does not always or even necessarily take the form of such immoderation, it still has usually been reserved for a select, called few, who vow poverty, chastity, and obedience.

All of which is to say, the monastic orientation of life has never really been understood as universal in scope, in part because of its sheer impracticality if taken literally. To be blunt, it is not a very attractive option to most people and, moreover, in short time would have eventually entailed the dissolution of the Christianity itself as a religion and form of social organization via the church. It is hard to pass down a tradition through generations when the very means of generation (i.e., sexual intercourse) is denied tout court.[4] Moreover, even the most self-sustaining monastic communities usually, at some point, make use of the world in order to sustain themselves,

---

1. Nietzsche, *Anti-Christ*, §35.
2. Nietzsche, *Anti-Christ*, §59.
3. See Athanasius, *Life of Antony*, §2.
4. Such is the lot of a group like The United Society of Believer's in Christ's Second Appearing, known as the Shakers. Although numerous reasons could be cited for the groups dissolution, the practice of covenantal celibacy did not help. For a history of the group, see Stein, *Shaker Experience*.

selling their products in the marketplace.⁵ Monasticism, in other words, is only possible if the majority of any given population is not only not monastic but also does not want to be.

The relationship between the two is, we could say, parasitic, in the sense that Michel Serres gives to that term.⁶ For Serres, parasitism is not confined to specific organisms that we normally label as parasites but is, rather, an essential component of interaction, relationality, and the basic functioning of systems, making these possible in the first place. It does so, however, by functioning under the radar, so to speak, and becomes visible in the interruptions and disruptions that parasites also provoke in and to their hosts. Take human beings, for instance. Although we do not commonly label humans as parasites, Serres argues that collectively we are the "universal parasite."

> Man milks the cow, makes the steer work, makes a roof from the tree; they have all decided who the parasite is. It is man. Everything is born for him, animals and beings. . . . But history hides the fact that man is the universal parasite, that everything and everyone around him is a hospitable space. Plants and animals are always his hosts; man is always necessarily their guest. Always taking, never giving. He bends the logic of exchange and of giving in his favor when he is dealing with nature as a whole. When he is dealing with his kind, he continues to do so; he wants to be the parasite of man as well. And his kind want to be so too. Hence rivalry.⁷

Just as human beings in general feed off their environment, so too does monasticism feed off non-monastics and the world for material sustenance. We could also say, however, that non-monastics parasite "spiritual" benefit from the work and prayers of monastics, who essentially assume the burden of the vows in their place, the burden, that is, of apparently taking what Jesus said and did more literally. The exchange between the parties, here, is diagonal rather than horizontal, in that the material is exchanged for the spiritual and vice-versa.⁸

---

5. To give just one example, the monks at Mepkin Abbey, located outside of Charleston, South Carolina, cultivate mushrooms to sell to the general public. For information about what they refer to as their "work," see http://mepkinabbey.org/wordpress/our-work/

6. Serres, *Parasite*.

7. Serres, *Parasite*, 24.

8. Serres, *Parasite*, 34ff.

Monasticism may, in this sense, function as an ideal, even if it cannot be implemented practically on a large scale. Nevertheless, because it is an ideal, the values that monasticism recommends and cultivates still hold sway more broadly, albeit in weakened, more piecemeal fashion. The bulk of Christian morality thus has focused at least one way or another on desire, as discussed in chapter 1. The problem is not money, work, and family in their own right but the way that we relate to them, along with other aspects of life. For the majority, then, the practical import of Jesus' teachings is not to withdraw from the world but to constrain ourselves with respect to it. Paul notes in Romans, for instance, that we should transform our minds rather than conform to the world, as a means of discerning "the will of God—what is good and acceptable and perfect" (Rom 12:2). The point, in other words, is to rein in our desires through the cultivation of habits and dispositions, that is, virtues, which allow us to live and act in the world responsibly.[9]

When combined with a critique of capitalism, emphasis is usually put on the problem of consumption or, more accurately, overconsumption. Daniel M. Bell Jr., for instance, understands capitalism in terms of "desire gone wild." On the one hand, capitalism, for Bell, unleashes desire from its proper ends; in so doing, desire becomes something of an end in itself, something we seek to fulfill for its own sake. Bell uses Mardi Gras as symbolic of out-of-control capitalist desire, here: it shows, for him, desire without reserve.[10] Although the untethering of desire promises us liberation, the freedom to become "true selves," Bell argues that it is really a form of discipline: the market forms and shapes human desire "such that economy does not so much serve human ends as subdues and shapes human desire in service of capitalist ends."[11] Capitalist freedom, which takes the form of desire's liberation, is thus for Bell really a form of servitude. Bell's solution is, in part, to acknowledge desire's redemption, so as to reorient it toward its true

---

9. Among contemporary authors, the work of Stanley Hauerwas is significant here. Hauerwas advocates for a type of virtue ethics, as a means for cultivating certain habits and dispositions that identify one as Christian over against the world and as part of the church. See, for instance, Hauerwas, *Vision and Virtue*; Hauerwas, *Community of Character*; Hauerwas, *Character and the Christian Life*.

10. Although Bell is right to point to certain problematic features of Mardi Gras, at least in how it is executed, I find Bell's reading of it horribly simplistic and moralistic. A better take on it would emphasize its celebratory aspects, along with the way in which farce may function as political critique. Although dated, Harvey Cox's *The Feast of Fools* remains an important resource in this respect. For a more contemporary take on the importance of festivity written for a general audience, see Ehrenreich, *Dancing in the Streets*.

11. Bell, *Economy of Desire*, 79.

end. In terms of consumption, that means learning how to consume rightly, not only in what and how we consume but in terms of quantity, as well.[12]

Such critiques and proposed solutions have a point: unnecessary overconsumption contributes to a host of problems, not only for individuals but also for social and natural environments. Indeed, current ecological and climate crises are, in many ways, directly related to issues related to consumption, in terms of what we consume, how much, and the enormous amount of waste generated throughout the process. Hence the need to be mindful of our consumption patterns at the individual level, as a means of counteracting the effects of a destructive system.

In light of this emphasis on the relationship between desire and consumption, we can read certain of Jesus' statements as recommending constraint or, to use the language of virtue, prudence and temperance. The notion of unconstrained desire as it relates to wasteful consumption is central, for instance, to the Parable of the Prodigal Son.

> Then Jesus said, "There was a man who had two sons. The younger of them said to his father. 'Father, give me the share of the property that will belong to me.' So he divided his property between them. A few days later the younger son fathered all he had and traveled to a distant country, and there he squandered his property in dissolute living. When he had spent everything, a severe famine took place throughout that country, and he began to be in need. So he went and hired himself out to one of the citizens of that country, who sent him to his fields to feed the pigs. He would gladly have filled himself with the pods that the pigs were eating; and no one gave him anything. But when he came to himself he said, 'How many of my father's hired hands have bread enough and to spare, but here I am dying of hunger! I will get up and go to my father, and I will say to him, "Father, I have sinned against heaven and before you; I am not longer worthy to be called our son; treat me like one of your hired hands."' So he set off and went to his father. But while he was still far off, his father saw him and was filled with compassion; he ran and put his arms around him and kissed him. Then the son said to him, 'Father, I have sinned against heaven and before you; I am no longer worthy to be called your son.' But the father said to his slaves, 'Quickly, bring out a robe—the best one—and put it on him; put a ring on his finger and sandals on his feet. And get the fatted calf and kill eat, and let us eat and celebrate; for this son of

---

12. See also Cavanaugh, *Being Consumed*.

mine was dead and is alive again; he was lost and is found!' And they began to celebrate." (Luke 15:11–24)

If the father stands in for God, then the main point of the parable seems to be to illustrate God's generosity and forgiveness, the sheer delight that God takes in the recovery of the lost. That joy, it is important to note, is directly opposed to the response of the father's other son, who can only look at the way the father treats the prodigal with utter disgust:

> Listen! For all these years I have been working like a slave for you, and I have never disobeyed your command; yet you have never even given me a young goat so that I might celebrate with my friends. But when this son of yours comes back, who has devoured your property with prostitutes, you killed the fatted calf for him! (Luke 15:29–30)

The parable, in this sense, mirrors other parables of loss and return, such as the Parable of the Lost Sheep (Luke 15:1–7) and the Parable of the Lost Coin (Luke 15:8–10), which occur directly before, but also the Parable of the Laborers in the Vineyard (Matt 20:1–16). At least in the details, the parable can also function as a cautionary tale about the squandering of wealth, about being irresponsible with one's possessions. Indeed, it is the prodigal's excessive consumption that leads to his downfall, and the parable does not hesitate to label it as a sin.

We see a similar view in Clement of Alexandria's "Who Is the Rich Man Who Will be Saved?" which I discussed in chapter 1. Recall that, for Clement, wealth as such is not the problem but one's disposition toward it; what is important, that is, are "the passions of the soul." Thus with regard to our relationship to wealth, Clement states, "But if one is able in the midst of wealth to turn from its power, and to entertain moderate sentiments, and to exercise self-command, and to seek God alone, and to breathe God and walk with God, such a poor man submits to the commandments, being free, unsubdued, free of disease, unwounded by wealth."[13] On this account, the problem with the prodigal is precisely that he does not know how to act rightly with respect to wealth, along with the world more generally. The prodigal's story is a cautionary one, one that conveys to us what not to do, even as it expresses grace in the midst of individual folly.

There is obviously some merit to this line of thought. Insofar as capitalism relies on continual consumption in order to shape desire toward the accumulation of wealth, suggestions that we limit consumption may harbor some critical import. Žižek has recognized this at a general level, in terms

---

13. Clement of Alexandria, "Who Is the Rich Man?" xxvi.

of saying "I would prefer not to."[14] If capitalism as a system relies on constant activity, including consumption, then refusing to act, refusing to (over) consume may, at the very least, throw a wrench in the otherwise smooth functioning of the relationship between production, consumption, and economic growth. Nevertheless, this sort of soft asceticism, as I would call it, is severely lacking, to the extent that it addresses itself primarily to individuals. It may certainly contribute to the cultivation of individual virtue, which is not bad in and of itself. But it tends to function as the theological equivalent of tackling climate change by choosing to drive a Prius or observing "Meatless Mondays." Moreover, this emphasis on individual desire can be appropriated easily enough, as the market adjusts itself to consumer demand. Being a "conscious consumer," that is, paying attention to what and how we consume, becomes its own niche, with a corresponding set of products and affects designed to reinforce a more "ethical" pattern of desire and consumption.

To give an example, while writing this section I'm staring at a bag of "Skinny Quinoa Sticks," a snack food constituted primarily from a mix of quinoa, corn, and rice flours that I purchased at a well-known natural and organic supermarket. "With only 140 calories I'm super low in guilt but super high in taste!," the bag advertises to me. "Yay for being cleverer than potato chips." The snack is labeled as vegan and certified gluten-free, a claim which is obvious if one reads the list of ingredients on the back but appeals to the conscious shopper. The bag thus seeks to assure me that my consumption of what is essentially a junk food is not all that bad, or at least better than the alternative—it appears friendlier, for lack of a better word, and unlike the bag of chips, it is packed with "ancient grains." Yet in terms of nutritional value, it is not much different from the bag of chips in my pantry, which claims 150 calories per serving and, in comparison, has a higher daily value of key nutrients. The chips, I assume, are also far less processed, as it is much easier to fry a potato than make a uniform stick-like concoction from a mix of grains.

Moreover, the theological discourse about limiting consumption, although understandable and often intended for good, assumes that we actually have a choice with regard to what and how much we consume. Suggesting that a privileged, middle- or upper-middle class (North) American can reign in his or her desire is one thing. But to propose constraint as a universal norm for desire can come across as insensitive and paternalistic when applied to the mass of impoverished who inhabit the world, especially when their poverty is, more often than not, directly and indirectly related to

14. See Žižek, *Parallax View*, 272–386.

the consumption patterns and economic position of the former. Suggesting that we constrain desire, in this sense, may correlate with a specific set of advantages in the marketplace, but it also ignores the way that desire functions mimetically.[15]

Nevertheless, what interests me is that it is questionable to what extent Jesus himself actually adopts this approach in his own teaching and actions, at least solely. Philip Goodchild has, for instance, rightly drawn attention to one of the particularities of Jesus with regard to money and wealth. As mentioned in chapter 1, Jesus is not alone among religious founders and intellectuals in his denunciation of wealth. It is, frankly, par for the course. What sets him apart, however, is that that denunciation does not result in renunciation and asceticism, even if some later theological thinkers and practitioners took him as recommending such. Goodchild writes, "Jesus, by contrast, warned against wealth while feasting and drinking himself."[16] When combined with Jesus' economic critique, which I have discussed in the previous chapters, Goodchild suggests that "Jesus may therefore be regarded as among the most radical of religious political thinkers."[17]

Jesus himself appears to recognize the irony in his stance, which is also a cause of misunderstanding and opposition. Thus, when speaking to the crowds about John the Baptist, he says:

> For John came neither eating nor drinking, and they say, "He has a demon"; the Son of Man came eating and drinking, and they say, "Look, a glutton and a drunkard, a friend of tax collectors and sinners!" Yet wisdom is vindicated by her deeds. (Matt 11:8-19; cf. Luke 7:33-35)

The contrast suggests that opposition is opposition, no matter what: the powerful will always find reason to oppose movements against them. The content of the contrast is, however, equally important, in the difference that it marks with regard to Jesus' approach to the world. His approach is not an ascetic approach, as is John's, but neither does it obviously recommend the soft asceticism of moderation, especially when it is read in light of other passages. Indeed, although the accusations against him are likely overdrawn to an extent, as they are in any smear campaign, they still must be somewhat descriptive of the reality. If they were not, they would not be plausible in the first place and could not function as a tool of accusation.

15. On a related note, see Sung, *Desire, Market, and Religion*, 30–50, where he discusses consumption in terms of mimetic desire. Suggesting that others limit consumption, on this account, ignores mimesis.

16. Goodchild, *Theology of Money*, 2.

17. Goodchild, *Theology of Money*, 3.

Jesus' reputation, moreover, cannot simply be reduced to the company he keeps but, rather, has more to do how he understands his mission, actions, and—indeed—himself.

Consider, for a moment, the well-known story of the wedding at Cana (John 2:1–12), which in John's Gospel is Jesus' first recorded miracle. Jesus, his mother, and his disciples attend a wedding at Cana in Galilee, but the wine, a crucial component to weddings then and now, unfortunately runs out too early. Mary, his mother, recognizes the problem and brings it to Jesus' attention, and much to the chagrin of fundamentalist preachers, teetotalers, and more than a few soft ascetics, Jesus famously proceeds to turn water into wine, specifically the water normally used for Jewish rites of purification. After performing the miracle—which, given the structure of the narrative, comes off without much fanfare—Jesus instructs that some be given to the chief steward, who would have been in charge of organizing the affair. We then read:

> When the steward tasted the water that had become wine, and did not know where it came from (though the servants who had drawn the water knew), the steward called the bridegroom and said to him, "Everyone serves the good wine first, and then the inferior wine after the guests have become drunk. But you have kept the good wine until now." (John 2:9–11)

According to Raymond Brown, there is no specific attestation for this custom in other literature, but it is not hard to speculate about the circumstances. The good wine would have been served first, before the guests had gotten drunk, because they presumably would have picked up on issues of quality at that point. The inferior wine, that is, wine of a lower quality, would have been brought out only after the guests had gotten drunk, because at that point they would not even notice or likely care. There must be only so much wine to go around, and it makes sense to ration along these lines. As Brown puts it, it is "the type of shrewd practice that is common to human nature."[18] Jesus' "miracle," however, takes the form of a reversal of this logic: it makes it look as if the good wine were kept for last. Not only does this episode illustrate Jesus' opposition to asceticism, it also shows more positively that his practices are wrapped up in abundance and excess.

In John's Gospel, the turning of water into wine anticipates the miraculous feeding in John 6, the only miracle that occurs in all four gospels.

> A large crowd kept following him, because they saw the signs that he was doing for the sick. Jesus went up the mountain and

---

18. Brown, *Gospel According to John*, 101.

sat down with his disciples. Now the Passover, the festival of the Jews, was near. When he looked up and saw a large crowd coming toward him, Jesus said to Philip, "Where are we to buy bread for these people to eat?" He said this to test him, for he himself knew what he was going to do. Philip answered him, "Six months' wages would not buy enough bread for each of them to get a little." One of his disciples, Andrew, Simon Peter's brother, said to him, "There is a boy here who has five barley loaves and two fish But what are they among so many people?" Jesus said, "Make the people sit down." Now there was a great deal of grass in the place; so they sat down, about five thousand in all. Then Jesus took the loaves, and when he had given thanks, he distributed them to those who were seated; so also the fish, as much as they wanted. When they were satisfied, he told his disciples, "Gather up the fragments left over, so that nothing may be lost." So they gathered them up, and from the fragments of the five barley loaves, left by those who had eaten, they filled twelve baskets. When the people saw the sign that he had done. They began to say, "This is indeed the prophet who has come into the world." (John 6:2-14)

Like the wedding at Cana, the episode draws attention to Jesus' ability to manifest abundance or excess, over against apparent material deprivation. I will say more about this below, in relation to Bataille's notion of a general economy. Nevertheless, although a lack of food may appear as reality, Jesus shows that it is appearance only, turning it into overflow. Moreover, the excess that Jesus makes present is completely detached from any sort of exchange or labor, hence the disjunction between "buying" and "wages" and Jesus' multiplication of the bread and fish. Indeed, the latter action has nothing to do with any sort of economic rationality but is, rather, concealed underneath the apparent lack of resources. Once economic rationality no longer counts as the condition governing the situation ("Where are we to buy bread for these people to eat?," "Six months' wages would not buy enough bread for each of them to get a little"), Jesus is able to harness abundance, which is made manifest in its distribution, without regard to any external constraints. To stress again, such excess is not the result of the labor of production but, rather, from materiality as such. It is the same experience of the world as that of the lilies of the field and the birds of the air.

We should not read these and similar instances of excess or abundance as mere miracles, as exceptions whose main purpose is to affirm who Jesus ostensibly is. Jesus himself often rejects such a view of his deeds. He refers, for instance, to those who seek signs as "evil and adulterous" (Matt 12:39) and implies that doing so is a sign of weakness (John 4:48). Such instances or miracles, as they are referred to, should instead be understood as markers of what Jesus refers to as the kingdom of heaven or kingdom of God. These markers, moreover, should not be read in eschatological terms but, rather, as present possibilities, in the here and now. These so-called miracles, then, only look like exceptions, so long as we take the present order of things and the world as the sole horizon of possibility. The exceptions that Jesus makes present are, rather, standard according to the logic that Jesus invokes and provokes: the logic of the kingdom of heaven or God. Hence Jesus' claim in Luke, in response to the Pharisees' question concerning when the kingdom of God might come, "The kingdom of God is not coming with things that can be observed; nor will they say, 'Look, here it is!' or "There it is!' For, in fact, the kingdom of God is among you" (Luke 17:21–22).

One way to understand the notion of excess that I am drawing attention to here is to refer to Georges Bataille's distinction between specific or restrictive economy and general economy. Crucial to this distinction is Bataille's claim that living matter constitutes itself in and through excess, a surplus of energy that cannot be reduced to its particular instantiations. Bataille refers to this excess as a general economy, but he notes that we usually do not consider it on its own terms, that is, as surplus. Rather, we tend to focus only on particular instantiations, operations, or organizations of the general economy, mistaking these for the whole when, in actuality, they are only a part. We restrict, in other words, the excess of the general to the limited ends of the particular. Such restriction, Bataille argues, is especially evident in regard to economic activity and its theorization:

> The human mind reduces operations, in science as in life, to an entity based on typical *particular* systems (organisms or enterprises). Economic activity, considered as a whole, is conceived in terms of particular operations with limited ends. The mind generalizes by composing the aggregate of these operations. Economic science merely generalizes the isolated situation; it restricts its object to operations carried out with a view to a limited end, that of economic man. It does not take into consideration a play of energy that no particular end limits: the play of *living matter in general*, involved in the movement of light of which it is the result. On the surface of the globe, for *living matter in general*, energy is always in excess; the question is always posed in terms of extravagance.[19]

---

19. Bataille, *Accursed Share*, 23.

The notion of scarcity, which is at the base of mainstream economic theory and, we are told, drives competition and economic growth is, on this view, limited to a particular perspective. For Bataille, the living organism always receives more energy than is necessary for maintaining itself, and it is this that constitutes the material basis of life, not scarcity. The question for Bataille, then, is not how to make do with and distribute adequately and fairly limited resources or limit consumption. Rather, for Bataille, the question is how to squander the limitless wealth that constitutes living matter in the "glorious operation" of a "useless consumption." The latter operation, which one could characterize as an expenditure without reserve, achieves the perspective of general economy, in which our being and doing coincide with "the useless and infinite fulfillment of the universe."[20]

Consider for a moment Matt 22, in light of Bataille's distinction:

> The kingdom of heaven may be compared to a king who gave a wedding banquet for his son. He sent his slaves to call those who had been invited to the wedding banquet, but they would not come. Again he sent other slaves, saying, "Tell those who have been invited: Look, I have prepared my dinner, my oxen and my fat calves have been slaughtered, and everything is ready; come to the wedding banquet." But they made light of it and went away, one to his farm, another to his business, while the rest seized his slaves, maltreated them, and killed them. The king was enraged. He sent his troops, destroyed those murderers, and burned their city. Then he said to his slaves, "The wedding is ready, but those invited were not worthy. Go therefore into the main streets, and invite everyone you find to the wedding banquet." Those slaves went out into the streets and gathered all whom they found, both good and bad; so the wedding hall was filled with guests. But when the king came in to see the guests, he noticed a man there who was not wearing a wedding robe, and he said to him, "Friend, how did you get in here without a wedding robe?" And he was speechless. Then the king said to the attendants, "Bind him hand and foot, and throw him into the outer darkness, where there will be weeping and gnashing of teeth." For many are called, but few are chosen.

The kingdom of heaven, as Jesus proclaims it, does not manifest itself in asceticism, austerity, or constraint but, rather, as a banquet. If we pay attention to the language used, the kingdom of heaven is a kingdom of excess, one that makes itself known over and above mere needs and the logic of means and ends. It is a kingdom where overconsumption and squandering reigns,

20. Bataille, *Accursed Share*, 21.

where it is all "oxen and fat calves." The banquet extolled here is basically that found in the Parable of the Prodigal Son: the son's return is met with an excess that is on par with the wedding banquet. His return, that is, is marked with luxury, an extravagance well beyond what is required, well beyond living strictly within the limits of desire. Indeed, if anyone is criticized in the parable, it is the other son, the one who appears to urge constraint at the return of his brother, whom he despises because of the wealth the latter has squandered.

We should not reduce such instances of excess to eschatological realities, as if they are only exceptional, proleptic indications of how things will be when "God may be all in all," as Paul tells us in 1 Cor 15 (15:28). Understanding Jesus' miracles and parables along these lines not only ignores their presentness, their immanence to the world (water is turned into wine, here and now; people are fed bread and fish, here and now). Similar to attitudes toward money that I discussed in the first chapter, doing so can also function as a means of disavowal: so long as we can push off Jesus' claims on reality as impractical in the here and now, even impossible for mere humans, there is no need to act accordingly, except in limited, piecemeal fashion. Charity steps in to fill in the gap in this line of thought, as I discussed in chapter 1.

One might object, of course, that such criticism is misplaced, in that it ignores the role of the church as the embodiment of eschatological reality on earth. What looks impossible from the perspective of the world is, on this account, possible in and for the church, which constitutes itself as an alternative community over against the structure of the world. It is the church, in other words, that fulfills Jesus' instantiation of the kingdom of God or heaven, at least on this side of the eschaton. And it can be fulfilled in the church because the church is, ideally, composed of those who claim to follow Jesus.

Jesus does speak of his church, and connects it with the sphere of those who follow him. Thus, upon confessing Jesus as Messiah, Jesus says to Peter, "And I tell you, you are Peter, and on this rock I will build my church, and the gates of Hades will not prevail against it. I will give you the keys of the kingdom of heaven, and whatever you bind on earth will be bound in heaven, and whatever you loose on earth will be loosed in heaven" (Matt 16:18–19). Indeed, we see the prototype of this alternative community in Acts, as I mentioned at the end of the last chapter, where it appears to instantiate the actions and teachings of Jesus among its members:

> Now the whole group of those who believed were of one heart and soul, and no one claimed private ownership of any possessions, but everything they owned was held in common. With

> great power the apostles gave their testimony to the resurrection of the Lord Jesus, and great grace was upon them all. There was not a needy person among them, for as many as owned lands or houses sold them and brought the proceeds of what was sold. They laid it at the apostles' feet, and it was distributed to each as any had need. (Acts 4:32–35)

Any sort of change to the current system that organizes the world, which in this book I have examined through the intertwined problematic of money, work, and family, will likely require the creation of similar communities. But it would be a mistake to conflate the latter with the church as it exists now, in the past, or even in its ideality. Doing so reeks of nostalgia, and ignores how structures simultaneously function to extend and limit possibilities. Although the church may be a bearer of Jesus' ideas and practices, it is the latter that remain essential, not a particular structure. Otherwise put, we should not reify the church, virtually or actually, as their vehicle. As Badiou points out, although structures may help facilitate the transmission of truths, they almost inevitably attempt to control them as well by limiting their interruptive potency. In so doing, structures, once in place, tend to strain toward their own perpetuation rather than that of the event itself.[21]

ACCUMULATION, NOT CONSUMPTION

I have argued that Jesus is not an advocate for asceticism, no matter how soft it may be. Although major strands of the theological and ecclesiastical traditions have taken him in this manner, his discourse and actual practices are, in many ways, diametrically opposed to an ascetic stance. This also means, however, that critiques of capitalism that focus primarily on consumption or desire miss the mark, despite their intentions. Overconsumption, as I have said, remains a real problem, especially when as a practice it depends on money and wealth. Access to the latter to a large extent determines consumption patterns and, when differentiating wealth is taken into account, entails that others consume less. Overconsumption is thus always related to underconsumption, relatively speaking, and both rely on a narrative that emphasizes the scarcity of resources. Limiting consumption may attempt to redress the imbalance present here, while also corresponding to the cultivation of virtue, of desiring and consuming rightly. Another way to put the matter is to say that the emphasis is on living within one's means, materially, morally, and spiritually. Ultimately, limiting consumption is about respecting finitude, our own as human beings and the world's.

21. See Badiou, *Being and Event*

There is little doubt that capitalism, both ideologically and in practice, depends on constant consumption both to maintain itself and drive economic growth. Capitalism, then, certainly depends on the cultivation of individuals as consumers, meaning that calls to limit consumption, although usually expressed in moral terms, may have some critical import: such calls would be the equivalent of what Žižek would refer to as a Bartleby politics, where the response to the mandate to consume is "I prefer not to."[22] Nevertheless, I want to suggest that Jesus focuses his attention elsewhere, not on consumption but on possession and accumulation. Although the two are certainly related, that emphasis makes all the difference, and ties as well into the themes that I have been discussing throughout.

A focus on accumulation, moreover, addresses the problem of consumption by other means, without the addition of a moralizing discourse based on desire. If, as I suggest, excess should be equated with expenditure, then it is possession—storing up treasures on earth, as Jesus puts it (Matt 6:19)—that leads us headlong into problems related to the relationships between consumption and wealth.

In using "accumulation" as one of the terms to signify Jesus' emphasis, I obviously have in mind the way the term functions for Marxist strands of thought. Marx emphasizes that the whole movement of capital seems to turn in a "vicious circle": "the accumulation of capital presupposes surplus-value; surplus-value presupposes capitalistic production; capitalistic production presupposes the preexistence of considerable masses of capital and of labour power in the hands of producers of commodities."[23] Similar to the way in which Adam's "original sin" supposedly explains the later sinfulness of all humanity, such accumulation depends upon a prior, "primitive" accumulation that is the "starting point" of the whole process. Primitive accumulation, in this sense, is a non-capitalistic mode of appropriation, possession, and accumulation that, in turn, drives capitalist appropriation, possession, and accumulation. Despite claims to the contrary, the former, Marx stresses, is far from benign. "In actual history it is notorious that conquest, enslavement, robbery, murder, briefly force, play the great part," he emphasizes.[24]

Capitalism, in this sense, is doubly determined by accumulation. Accumulation, in its "primitive" form, captures value in various ways for the purpose of making it available for further, capitalist accumulation. Although for Marx accumulation names this specific relationship and connects accumulation to production, we can give it a more general sense, as a

---

22. Žižek, *Parallax View*.
23. Marx, *Capital*, chapter 26.
24. Marx, *Capital*, chapter 26.

fundamental aspect of the way that capitalism organizes and controls life. As Todd McGowan has argued, accumulation is not neutral with regard to individuals but, rather, takes the form of a "superego imperative":

> That is, within capitalism, accumulation has the status of a moral obligation, and the capitalist subject inevitably hears an internal voice urging her or him on for "more." . . . Despite whatever efforts we might make at obedience, we can never quiet this voice or sate the superego's appetite: no amount of accumulation is ever enough, either for the individual capitalist subject or for the capitalist society as a whole. The debt to the superego, in other words, is infinite. The more we accumulate, the more we see there is for us to accumulate. Once we surrender to the demand for accumulation, we only get sucked further and further in by it.[25]

Accumulation thus functions as a means of entrapping the subject within the strictures of capitalist economy, and we should ground it as primary to consumption. That is, it is through accumulation, especially money, that we gain access to consumption. In this way, accumulation functions in tandem with money in terms of promise and threat: it mediates life to us.

It is all the more significant, then, that Jesus' own practice comes out against accumulation, a practice that is in line with other important biblical trajectories. Consider, for instance, the foundational story of the Exodus, specifically the period of wilderness wanderings that occur in the narrative after Israel's escape from Egypt and prior to the entrance into the promised land. In the desert and without food, YHWH provides quail and manna, bread from heaven, which we are told they ate for "forty years, until they came to a habitable land; they ate manna, until they came to the border of the land of Canaan" (Exod 16:25). At one level the story is meant to emphasize YHWH's care for the Israelites and the miraculous nature of their establishment as a people and, eventually, an empire, but more interesting for my purposes is the interplay that it grounds between consumption and accumulation. The Israelites consume as much as they need and even, as the text implies, much more than need alone would require, but they are prevented from accumulating any excess. Thus when commanded to gather the manna that appears overnight as a "fine flaky substance, as fine frost on the ground" (16:14), we read that the "Israelites did so, some gathering more, some less. But when they measured it with an omer, those who gathered much had nothing over, and those who gathered little had no shortage; they gathered as much as each of them needed" (16:18). YHWH via Moses

---

25. McGowan, *Enjoying What We Don't Have*, 63.

further commands the Israelites to consume, without remainder: "Let no one leave any of it over until morning" (16:19). When they do not listen, when they attempt to accumulate the manna that YHWH has provided seemingly without effort, the manna becomes useless: "it bred worms and became foul" (16:20). The only exception, of course, is the day before the Sabbath, when the future Israelites are able to gather twice as much in preparation for the "day of solemn rest, a holy Sabbath to the LORD" (16:23). If, then, we see in this narrative an image of a countereconomy, one based on faith in YHWH and YHWH's provisions, that economy only works to the extent that consumption is not tied to accumulation. Indeed, accumulation is, it would seem, prohibited, since it violates trusting in YHWH for one's needs, one's life. As Jesus will put it much later, "So do not worry about tomorrow, for tomorrow will bring worries of its own. Today's trouble is enough for today" (Matt 6:34).

The logic that we see expressed in the Exodus narrative is virtually the same as that at work in Jesus' miraculous feedings, which I discussed above. That logic, moreover, is not isolated to specific instances but is, rather, an insoluble component of what Jesus says and does and what he requires of his followers. I have already discussed the matter in slightly different terms in reference to the rich young ruler, who comes to Jesus seeking eternal life. When Jesus commands him to give up his possessions and redistribute the proceeds to the poor, the rich young ruler is not being commanded to give up his wealth only, as if this in and of itself were sufficient. He is, moreover, being asked to give up the principle or activity through which he was able to become wealthy in the first place. Jesus' command to the rich young ruler, then, is not simply about ends but means as well, the way in which having wealth (i.e., accumulation) determines one's subjectivity economically.

As mentioned previously, the rich young ruler is juxtaposed to the disciples, who have divested themselves of their possessions, work, and familial ties to follow Jesus. Such is the condition for being Jesus' disciple: "So therefore, none of you can become my disciple if you do not give up all your possessions" (Luke 14:33). Indeed, Jesus equates individual divestiture with bearing one's cross (Luke 14:27). The connection between the two may seem extreme, but once it is recalled that money and its related institutions literally mediate life, it comes off as an apt description: a type of death awaits those who refuse to possess.

The divestiture involved, here, is not a one-off affair but, rather, constitutes a permanent state that governs day-to-day activities, including those directly related to Jesus' mission. When Jesus sends his disciples out to "cure the sick, raise the dead, cleanse the lepers, [and] cast out demons" as a means of proclaiming the nearness of the kingdom of heaven or God, he commands them to "take no gold, or silver, or copper in your belts, no bag for your journey, or two tunics, or sandals, or a staff; for laborers deserve their food" (Matt 10:8–9). Such seeming poverty is meant to make the disciples reliant on the generosity of others, about which more shortly. Hence we read, "As you enter the house, greet it. If the house is worthy, let your peace come upon it; but if it is not worthy, let your peace return to you. If anyone will not welcome you or listen to your words, shake off the dust from your feet as you leave that house or town" (Matt 10:12–14). But it also serves to take the actions of the disciples and Jesus' mission as a whole outside of the normal parameters of exchange, in which a good turn—a miracle, say—is fairly compensated. Jesus thus reminds his disciples, "You received without payment; give without payment" (Matt 10:8).

All of this is to reinforce Jesus' claim made elsewhere that we are to be like the birds of the air and the lilies of the field, who neither work for what they have nor accumulate what they have received.

> Look at the birds of the air; they neither sow nor reap nor gather into barns, and yet your heavenly Father feeds them. Are you not of more value than they? And can any of you by worrying add a single hour to your span of life? And why do you worry about clothing? Consider the lilies of the field, how they grow; they neither toil nor spin, yet I tell you, even Solomon in all his glory was not clothed like one of these. But if God so clothes the grass of the field, which is alive today and tomorrow is thrown into the oven, will he not much more clothe you—you of little faith? (Matt 6:26–30)

I mentioned in the previous chapter that we should take this passage in a more literal fashion, rather than reducing it to a metaphor for appreciating God's provisions and overall providence. It is certainly about the latter, but such appreciation, for Jesus, is manifest in one's actions, which here correspond to modeling one's life after the birds, lilies, and grasses. What we might call the "natural" world, here, does not function in this passage as mere poetic flourish but, rather, as an example to emulate.[26] Take it as the equivalent of not storing up "treasures on earth" (Matt 6:19).

---

26. I put "natural" in quotation marks, here, to call attention to the problem with setting up an autonomous realm called "nature" over against human culture. There is already a substantial literature that interrogates this relationship, and the ways in which it has been constructed to privilege human exploitation of the earth and its resources. Nevertheless, that Jesus compares human beings to non-human beings would suggest a closer relationship between the two, even in regard to social organization. For a discussion of this latter theme at a general level, see Hartigan, *Aesop's Anthropology*.

To suggest as much is not to encourage passivity, which is one form that asceticism can take. The non-human world itself is not passive but interactive, in that needs are met ecologically, as various forms of life, non-organic matter, and energy interact with each other in systems to produce viable wholes. Jesus himself tends to gain what he and his disciples need by relying on the generosity of others, as we see, for instance, when Jesus visits the house of Mary and Martha, which I discussed in the last chapter. It is certainly possible to conceive of such reliance in terms of charity, but charity assumes accumulation, which Jesus is otherwise against. Charity, that is, arises out of excess, but it is an accumulated excess that makes charity possible. One can be charitable because one has accumulated more than one needs; on the flip side, one is subject to charity because one has less than one needs. The relationship between the two is mediated through accumulation and its lack, and assumes an underlying scarcity governing resources and their consumption.

Another way to put the matter is to say that charity does not assume any real, material change among the actors involved, to the extent that it takes place within a system governed by the lopsided accumulation of resources, which is another way of marking differentiating wealth. One of the ways to understand the lopsidedness involved is to return to Michel Serres' notion of parasitism, which I mentioned above in relationship to monasticism. Jesus' reliance on the generosity of others, which also determines his interactions and relationships with them, could be understood along the lines of this notion of parasitism. If we accept that monastics feed on non-monastics for material sustenance, while non-monastics feed on monastics for spiritual sustenance, Jesus would seem to take up the position of the monastic. It would seem, moreover, that both parties receive some benefit. In the case of Mary in the story of Martha and Mary, Mary trades hospitality for "the better part" (Luke 10:42).

But the relationship involved, here, need not be read in terms of charity. Charity, I have argued, takes place within a horizon of exchange and, in this sense, fails to recognize the parasitism that underpins it. Otherwise put, charity is a chosen activity, in the sense that it arises from an ostensible separation between the parties involved. As I discussed in chapter 1, charity supposedly mediates the relationship between giver and receiver and, thus, functions as a vehicle for God's grace. But the very fact that charity steps in to relate the parties involved implies that they are, fundamentally, unrelated: mediation, that is, assumes the prior existence of something that needs to be mediated. When put into the apparatus of exchange, the assumption is that one party gives "freely" out of his or her excess to the other for his or her benefit. The problem is that it assumes a prior sense of possession, of what is one's own in contradistinction from what is not.

It is in this sense that charity assumes, rather than dismantles, differentiating wealth, and it often expresses itself paternalistically, doling out needs from within a predetermined horizon of expectations. Michel Serres draws on La Fontaine's fable of "The Countryman and the Serpent" to illustrate a similar point, specifically the parasitic nature of charity and acts of goodwill. A "charitable" countryman comes across a snake, frozen from the winter air. Without regard for recompense, he brings the snake inside his house to revive him by the fire. Once warmed, La Fontaine tells us that the snake "raised his head, thrust out his forked tongue / Coiled up, and at his benefactor sprung." The countryman yells back, "Ungrateful wretch! . . . Is this the way / My care and kindness you repay?" He then proceeds to dismember the snake into three with an axe. The moral of the story is clear: "It's good and lovely to be kind; / But charity should not be blind; / For as to wretchedness ingrate, / You cannot raise it from its wretched state."[27]

Serres's reading of the fable produces a different moral, in that it takes the view of the snake rather than the countryman. From the snake's perspective, the countryman's act of charity is unwanted, because of the indebtedness that goes along with it, an indebtedness that in the fable is marked in the countryman's expectation of gratitude. Serres writes:

> The serpent is not a lessee; he was not looking for a haven; he was answered without having called. He was given an uncalled-for opinion. Someone made himself the serpent's benefactor, savior, and father. You are sleeping quite peacefully, and when you wake up you find yourself in debt. You live with no other need, and suddenly, someone claims to have saved your country, protected your class, your interests, your family, and your table. And you have to pay him for that, vote for him, and other such grimaces. Thus the serpent awakens obliged to another.[28]

Equating charity with parasitism, in the sense that Serres does here, may seem ungenerous and, moreover, cynical. Indeed, when Jesus speaks of charity—and he does, frequently and in variegated fashion—he reminds his followers to give without expectation of material return. He tells the crowd, for instance:

> If you love those who love you, what credit is that to you? For even sinners love those who love them. If you do good to those

27. The parable can be found at: http://www.lafontaine.net/lesFables/fableEtr.php?id=824.
28. Serres, *Parasite*, 22.

> who do good to you, what credit is that to you? For even sinners do the same. If you lend to those from whom you hope to receive, what credit is that to you? Even sinners lend to sinners, to receive as much again. But love your enemies, do good, and lend, expecting nothing in return. Your reward will be great, and you will be children of the Most High; for he is kind to the ungrateful and the wicked. Be merciful, just as your Father is merciful. (Luke 6:32–36)

The problem, however, is that expectation is worked into the notion of charity itself, at least in the matter in which it has been traditionally understood within Christianity. Although Jesus tells his followers to give without expectation of return, expectation is still involved on a different plane. The charitable will receive a great reward, which elsewhere Jesus equates with eternal life, as in the story of the rich young ruler. Thus, although Jesus can instruct his followers not to expect anything in return, he in other places appears to uphold a certain logic of exchange in relation to charity: "give, and it will be given to you. A good measure, pressed down, shaken together, running over, will be put into your lap; for the measure you give will be the measure you get back" (Luke 6:38).

One could argue that the difference between the material (this life) and the spiritual (eternal life) is crucial for elevating charity above the realm of exchange. This is basically Anderson's point, which I discussed in chapter 1: even if charity entails reward, its motivation is faith rather than calculation. That may be the case, but Serres argues that the trade of the spiritual for the material represents a logic that is, in essence, a parasitic invention. One can certainly trade the material for the material, as would be the case if one expected a material return, but exchange is still involved even if the material is traded for the spiritual: whatever the motivation (faith or calculation) one still gains what one wants through the act. In the case of La Fontaine's countryman, his anger results when that logic is interrupted, when he does not get what he wants. The snake, that is, does not repay the countryman's material generosity with gratitude, with the expected non-material reward. The snake's failure to honor the logic of exchange present is what leads to his death at the hands of the aggrieved countryman.

But Jesus also at times pushes charity to its extreme, to the point that it can no longer be recognized as charity but, rather, in terms of a different organization of the world, one in which excess is not possessed and given but is, rather, available to all. Consider the following vignette, often referred to as "The Widow's Offering":

> [Jesus] looked up and saw rich people putting their gifts into the treasury; he also saw a poor widow put in two small copper coins. He said, "Truly I tell you, this poor widow has put in more than all of them; for all of them have contributed out of their abundance, but she out of her poverty has put in all she had to live on." (Luke 21:1–4; cf. Mark 21:41–44)

Although both parties in the story, the rich people and the poor widow, act generously, Jesus praises the widow because unlike the rich people, she is not in a position to act generously at all but does so anyway. She contributes out of her poverty, Jesus emphasizes, while the others give out of their abundance. In praising the poor widow's actions, however, Jesus in effect moves away from charity as a model for the (re)distribution of wealth.

Jesus' response upends normal expectations regarding charity's recipient. One would expect the poor widow to be on the receiving end of any contribution; instead, she is the one who gives, and she gives more, relatively speaking, because her giving comes from a position of poverty rather than abundance. We should not read this episode in terms of a backdoor elevation of poverty as an ideal. Doing so would seemingly clash with Jesus' statements elsewhere that assume a reversal of values ("Blessed are you who are poor, for yours is the kingdom of God" [Luke 6:20]). It is, rather, a further illustration of that reversal. Not only does Jesus' reaction to the woman's act delink giving from individual excess, a connection which, I have emphasized, is one of the basic assumptions that governs charity. It also dissolves the relationship between material sustenance and money. The woman, in effect, puts her fate in God's hands, just as the lilies of the field and the birds of the air. That may sound pious and unsophisticated, but it is the same sort of act that Jesus calls for on behalf of someone like the rich young ruler. He comes from a position of wealth, but he is also called to give all, without remainder. Not only would calling the widow's trust in God naïve ring of paternalism; it also assumes the inviolability of one particular organization of the world. At his best, what Jesus says and does explodes that assumption, as the kingdom of God breaks into the present because it is already present as immanent reality. Using Bataille's terminology, we could say that the rich people in the story act on the basis of a restricted economy, while the woman strains toward the general.

This is what Jesus means when he refers to the kingdom of heaven or God: it is not an outstanding reality but is, rather, present in the here and now, underneath, beside, and in the gaps of the current organization of the world. "The kingdom of God is among you," Jesus says (Luke 17:21), and it is manifest in what Jesus says and does, but not him exclusively. The disciples, too, manifest this immanent alternative, when they go out—without money, without possessions—to "cure every disease and every sickness" (Matt 10:1). And it is present in the act of the widow. Such is the sense, then, of the "miraculous" feedings and healings, the magnificent signs down to what appear as the most mundane acts: they indicate that another world is possible, to borrow the well-known activist slogan, but possible because already present and enacted. One image that Jesus uses to describe it is the mustard seed. Jesus famously tells his disciples that having faith the size of a mustard seed will allow them to do the seemingly impossible: "For truly I tell you, if you have faith the size of a mustard seed, you will say to this mountain, 'Move from here to there,' and it will move; and nothing will be impossible for you" (Matt 17:20). But the kingdom of God itself is like a mustard seed, in terms of its growth relative to its size: "The kingdom of heaven is like a mustard seed that someone took and sowed in his field; it is the smallest of all the seeds, but when it has grown it is the greatest of shrubs and becomes a tree, so that the birds of the air come and make nests in its branches" (Matt 13:31–2). It is also, he says, like yeast (Matt 13:33), or weeds among wheat (Matt 13:24–30).

The theological tradition has ultimately condensed the sense of these and similar claims into the person of Jesus, into his supposed unique relationship with the Father, a relationship that marks him as divine. Bracketing such theological claims allows us to read along different lines. This is even the case with a more weighted theological passage, such as we find in the so-called Last Supper. Thus, the final meal that he shares with his disciples before his crucifixion:

> While they were eating, Jesus took a loaf of bread, and after blessing it he broke it, gave it to the disciples, and said, "Take, eat; this is my body." Then he took a cup, and after giving thanks he gave it to them, saying, "Drink from it, all of you; for this is my blood of the covenant, which is poured out for many for the forgiveness of sins. I tell you, I will never again drink of this fruit of the vine until that day when I drink it new with you in my Father's kingdom." (Matt 26:26–29)

The Eucharist constitutes the other main sacrament next to baptism, and functions, in this sense, as a vehicle of grace.[29] In its reception, that is, Christians partake of the body and blood of Christ, uniting with him and his

---

29. The Roman Catholic Church, of course, recognizes more than two. In addition to baptism and holy communion, it recognizes confirmation, confession, marriage, holy orders, and the anointing of the sick.

church, although individual denominations of course understand the sense of such participation variously.

The "grace" present in Jesus' gift of his body and blood, then, correlates to Jesus' uniqueness, to his assumed divine status. In this sense, the grace present really flows in one direction, at least in its impetus. It is a gift that originates with Jesus that, in turn, is meant to be given repeatedly, as Paul implies in 1 Corinthians:

> For I received from the Lord what I also handed on to you, that the Lord Jesus on the night when he was betrayed took a loaf of bread, and when he had given thanks, he broke it and said, "This is my body that is for you. Do this in remembrance of me." In the same way he took the cup also, after supper, saying, "This cup is the new covenant in my blood. Do this, as often as you drink it, in remembrance of me." For as often as you eat this bread and drink the cup, you proclaim the Lord's death until he comes. (1 Cor 11:23-6).

I am not so much interested in this episode because of later sacramental value but, rather, because it may suggest a different way to understand and construct relationality.

Although one can understand Jesus' offering of his body and blood in terms of gift, the initial form that gift takes coincides with a certain parasitism: the disciples literally feed on the body and blood of Jesus. His body and blood are, moreover, indistinguishable from the bread and wine, and this conflation, I would suggest, universalizes the parasitism involved. That is, what it implies is that the relationships that humans have to one another are not epiphenomenal, mediated through exchange and even community, but fundamentally intertwined and reciprocal. Our bodies are "food" for others, and theirs "food" for us, in the sense that basic sustenance and, moreover, luxury, depends upon a mutualism that passes from parasitism to symbiosis.[30] We can understand other forms of interaction, such as those found in and through exchange and the market more generally, as attempts to capitalize on this parasitism by denying it as fundamental, by twisting the logic of parasitism away from mutualism toward individualism and possession. Such is the sense that we can give to Jesus' statement to his disciples in the Gospel of John: "I do not call you servants any longer, because the servant does not know what the master is doing; but I have called you friends,

---

30. Michel Serres discusses this shift in numerous places, but see for instance *Natural Contract*. There, the passage from parasitism to symbiosis is essential for building new forms of relationality, to others and the earth. Given impending environmental collapse, for Serres the passage is literally about life and death: "either death or symbiosis" (34).

because I have made known to you everything that I have heard from my Father" (John 15:15).

We see this basic logic exhibited, I think, in the famous passage in Matthew concerning "the least of these":

> When the Son of Man comes in his glory, and all the angels with him, then he will sit on the throne of his glory. All the nations will be gathered before him, and he will separate people one from another as a shepherd separates the sheep from the goats, and he will put the sheep at his right hand and the goats at the left. Then the king will say to those at his right hand, "Come, you that are blessed by my Father, inherit the kingdom prepared for you from the foundation of the world; for I was hungry and you gave me food, I was thirsty and you gave me something to drink, I was a stranger and you welcomed me, I was naked and you gave me clothing, I was sick and you took care of me, I was in prison and you visited me." Then the righteous will answer him, "Lord, when was it that we saw you hungry and gave you food, or thirsty and gave you something to drink? And when was it that we saw you a stranger and welcomed you, or naked and gave you clothing? And when was it that we saw you sick or in prison and visited you?" And the king will answer them, "Truly I tell you, just as you did it to one of the least of these who are members of my family, you did it to me." Then he will say to those at his left hand, "You that are accursed, depart from me into the eternal fire prepared for the devil and his angels; for I was hungry and you gave me no food, I was thirsty and you gave me nothing to drink, I was a stranger and you did not welcome me, naked and you did not give me clothing, sick and in prison and you did not visit me." Then they also will answer, "Lord, when was it that we saw you hungry or thirsty or a stranger or naked or sick or in prison, and did not take care of you?" Then he will answer them, "Truly I tell you, just as you did not do it to one of the least of these, you did not do it to me." And these will go away into eternal punishment, but the righteous into eternal life. (Matt 25:31–46)

Here we have what appears as a reversal of the Eucharistic logic found in the Last Supper. Whereas in the latter, Jesus gives his body and blood to his disciples, here the disciples give to Jesus: their actions toward others, specifically those in need, literally affect Jesus. Such a reversal, however, fashions the supposed unidirectionality of the Eucharist as multidirectional: actions among the disciples, others, and Jesus are flattened, as they are fundamentally entangled. What such statements imply is that the other, in

Jesus' vision, is not transcendent but radically immanent to me and me to the other. One could say, perhaps, that every other is each other.[31] To say that the other is immanent to me and me to the other is not to conflate the two, through a denial of individuality; it is, rather, another way of acknowledging the basic parasitism that constitutes human relationality, a parasitism that can strain toward symbiosis. Or, to put the matter in different terms, it is to conceive of our relations to each other in terms of generic universality.[32]

Accumulation, however, cuts off this possibility. The problem with accumulation is not so much found in the mere fact of possessing. Jesus and his disciples have, it seems, divested themselves of all but the most essential possessions, and they certainly do not appear to own any property, which would provide a basis for wealth creation. The problem, rather, is with the way in which accumulation presupposes and, in turn, feeds mammon. The accumulation of wealth is one of the drivers of differentiating wealth, which means that it is always lopsided or asymmetrical. The two here go hand in hand: not only does accumulation lead to differentiating wealth, the promise of differentiating wealth—the promises of materially distinguishing ourselves from other in and in terms of the market—drives accumulation. One accumulates, seeking more and more vis-à-vis others in competition, not just for status but so as to better position oneself in the market and, indeed, life as a whole. It is not just greed, then, that drives this process, although that may certainly be a factor, but the promise of security, and the extent to which the latter is real or imagined really does not matter in terms of how it functions subjectively. At the root of accumulation is thus the myth of scarcity, which assumes the necessity of competition through various means for limited resources. Although one may seek to accumulate wealth for a variety of reasons, one of the main reasons is the assumption that one must get what one can, because there is only so much to go around. One accumulates wealth in part as a protective measure against the perceived scarcity of resources, which also means that challenging the myth of scarcity also challenges the need for accumulation.

I have mentioned previously the way in which Jesus challenges this myth by upholding and acting in light of excess rather than scarcity, toward a vision of a general economy versus a restricted one. In this light, Jesus' challenge to money, wealth, and accumulation does not coincide with asceticism or, as I will discuss below, clean hands with respect to one's actions but with genuine luxury. That may appear as a hopelessly contradictory

31. I am playing with and revising Derrida's "tout autre est tout autre," which in the *The Gift of Death* marks the inaccessibility of the neighbor to me as signal of ethical imperative. See Derrida, *Gift of Death*, 82–115.

32. Badiou, *Being and Event*, 327–43.

stance, but returning to Bataille implies otherwise. For Bataille, the critique of wealth need not issue in pious self-denial but, rather, should coincide with an utter indifference in expenditure rather than refusal. Generalizing from his discussion of various potlatch ceremonies, Bataille notes:

> The true luxury and the real potlatch of our times falls to the poverty-stricken, that is, to the individual who lies down and scoffs. A genuine luxury requires the complete contempt for riches, the somber indifference of the individual who refuses work and makes his life on the one hand an infinitely ruined splendor, and on the other, a silent insult to the laborious life of the rich. Beyond a military exploitation, a religious mystification and a capitalist misappropriation, henceforth no one can rediscover the meaning of wealth, the explosiveness that it heralds, unless it is in the splendor of rags and the somber challenge of indifference. One might say, finally, that the lie destines life's exuberance to revolt.[33]

In order to understand Bataille's point, here, recall the distinction between the restricted economy and the general economy. The distinction should not be understood as two, separate economies, but as separate, mutually implicated views of economy as such: the restricted economy is restricted because it restricts the general economy but, once restricted, the general remains latent in the restricted as its repressed content. To borrow language from Badiou's meta-ontology, the general economy is included in the restricted economy but does not belong to it, as an excess that constantly haunts and threatens to ruin the latter.[34] This means, on the one hand, that the restricted economy can only maintain itself under the threat of its own immanent dissolution, a dissolution that would come about on the basis of that on which it is founded, that is, the general economy. To use Badiouian language again, the consistency of the restricted economy, its one-count, can never be complete or whole, otherwise it would not be restricted in the first place. On the other hand, any sort of rupture with the restricted economy does not occur from elsewhere, in a pure position outside of its organization; it rather occurs internally, through a forcing of the restricted towards the general.

Derrida's reading of Bataille is helpful here. For Derrida, Bataille attempts to think general economy and, in other contexts, related concepts (sovereignty, etc.), not outside the dialectical interplay that constitutes the restricted economy or meaning more generally precisely because that

33. Bataille, *Accursed Share*, 76.
34. Badiou, *Being and Event*, 81–103.

"outside" can always be made "inside" through sublation. Bataille, rather, draws on the concepts that populate the restricted economy, playing with them in such a way that they fold in on each other and twist toward their nonsense. Derrida notes, "General economy folds these horizons and figures so that they will be related not to a basis, but to the nonbasis of expenditure, not to the *telos* of meaning, but to the *indefinite* destruction of value."[35] When reading Bataille, then, one cannot take the concepts he deploys ("experience," "interior," "mystic," "word," "material," "sovereign") at face value; one must, rather, pay attention to how the "face value" becomes suspended through the use to which Bataille puts them. The goal is, as Bataille says, to find a "usage of a function detached (liberated) from the servitude from which it springs."[36] One must read them, in other words, in light of the general economy, even if the "original" sense of the concept has its root in its restricted function.

It is in this sense that wealth can coincide with its critique. At the level of the restricted economy, such a claim can only appear as nonsense—wealth and critique are two separate principles, which can only coincide internally, so long as one cultivates a particular disposition that allows one to have it both ways, such as in discourses surrounding desire. From the perspective of the general economy, however, that coincidence is external or real, but this is because wealth is transposed into a different register. The "true luxury" that Bataille points to can only be had through critique because the wealth that he has in mind is not the wealth of the restricted economy.

We should understand Jesus' critique of wealth in similar terms. The opposition between asceticism/non-asceticism takes place under the purview of a restricted view of economy, one that, moreover, assumes scarcity. From the perspective of the latter, Jesus' actions come across as at times miraculous, at times impractical, even nonsensical. But labeling his actions nonsensical along these lines only makes sense so long as we ignore that Jesus assumes and acts in light of another organization of the world, one in which luxury or excess functions as norm. I have given examples of this above, but another way that Jesus' view of the world qua kingdom of God manifests itself is in terms of what Bataille might call useless consumption, an expenditure without reserve.

We get a glimpse of such expenditure in a story I have already discussed in another context and for other reasons, namely, Mary's anointing of Jesus. Recall that after Jesus and his disciples had eaten at the home of Lazarus, Mary "took a pound of costly perfume made of pure nard, anointed Jesus'

---

35. Derrida, "From a Restricted to General Economy," 271.
36. Quoted in Derrida, "From a Restricted to General Economy," 274.

feet, and wiped them with her hair. The house was filled with the fragrance of perfume" (John 12:3–4). The synoptic gospels contain a similar, though more generic story (see Mark 1:3–9; Matt 26:1–13; Luke 7:36–49). Theologically speaking, the story in its various articulations connects the anointing of Jesus with his impending death and, in the case of John, names Judas as the agent of the latter in contradistinction to Mary, who treats Jesus with the love that Jesus has for his own disciples (cf. John 13:1–3). Nevertheless, the theological conceptuality at work in the narrative is articulated through a basic economic contrast, one that we find throughout Jesus' teachings. In Matthew's, Mark's, and John's versions of the story, the woman who anoints Jesus (in John's version, Mary) is criticized for the extravagance of her act from the perspective of a closed, more calculating logic, even if, at least for Matthew and Mark, out of good intentions. In each case, Jesus' companions label the woman's apparently useless use of expensive perfume or ointment a waste: the perfume or ointment could have been sold for the purposes of helping the poor. Jesus, of course, shoots back, criticizing those who would criticize the woman, because, as John has Jesus say, "You always have the poor with you, but you do not always have me" (John 12:8).

Jesus' reasoning, here, need not be read in an overly pious way, and nor should it be read only as some sort of social commentary on the irremediable fact of poverty, given his trenchant critique of differentiating wealth. The narrative does, of course, assume that in other contexts Jesus' disciples are duty-bound to give to the poor, hence the ideology of charity that underpins much mainstream Christian ethics and politics, which I have already discussed. But whereas charity seeks a minimal redistribution of what are assumed to be scarce resources and relies on the logic of calculation, Jesus challenges that logic itself. His claim ("You always have the poor with you, but you do not always have me") should not be read as an individual exception but a genuine alternative. The woman's actions toward Jesus, that is, assume a different economy, one that is not calculated because it does not assume scarcity and in which "faith" coincides with "useless consumption."

It is interesting in this respect to bring up Luke's version of the narrative, which is markedly different from the others. Whereas in the other versions the issue is with what use the perfume or ointment has or should be put to, the issue in Luke's version is with the status of the woman who anoints Jesus and, in turn, Jesus' response.

> One of the Pharisees asked Jesus to eat with him, and he went into the Pharisee's house and took his place at the table. And a woman in the city, who was a sinner, having learned that he was eating in the Pharisee's house, brought an alabaster jar of

> ointment. She stood behind him at his feet, weeping, and began to bathe his feet with her tears and to dry them with her hair. Then she continued kissing his feet and anointing them with the ointment. Now when the Pharisee who had invited him saw it, he said to himself, "If this man were a prophet, he would have known who and what kind of woman this is who is touching him—that she is a sinner." (Luke 7:36–39)

Jesus' acceptance of the woman and her gift, in contradistinction to the silently expressed pious concern of the religious leader for purity, is for Luke part and parcel of Jesus' status as a "friend of tax collectors and sinners" (Luke 7:34). Jesus' acceptance of the woman and her gift, in this sense, overturn socioreligious mores and expectations. More interesting for my purposes, though, is the analogy that Jesus uses to explain his actions. Sensing the religious official's dis-ease with Jesus' contact with the woman, Jesus asks him to consider the following: "A certain creditor had two debtors; one who owed five hundred denarii, and the other fifty. When they could not pay, he canceled the debts for both of them. Now which of them will love him more?" (Luke 7:41–2). The religious leader, whose name, we are told, is Simon, rightly answers that the former will, to which Jesus responds with his point:

> Do you see this woman? I entered your house; you gave me no water for my feet, but she has bathed my feet with her tears and dried them with her hair. You gave me no kiss, but from the time she came in she has not stopped kissing my feet. You did not anoint my head with oil, but she has anointed my feet with ointment. Therefore I tell you, her sins, which were many, have been forgiven; hence she has shown great love. But the one to whom little is forgiven, loves little. (Luke 7:44–47)

MAKING FRIENDS THROUGH DISHONEST WEALTH

I have discussed the way in which Jesus critiques accumulation rather than consumption, and how this leads to a different way of imagining and organizing the world. The latter is what Jesus often refers to as the kingdom of heaven or God, and it should be understood as a present possibility, the reality of which bursts through piecemeal in Jesus' words and deeds. That kingdom is based on excess, an excess that always subtends and haunts particular organizations of the world.[37] I suggested that one way to understand

---

37. We could also speak of this excess in terms of a hauntology, in the sense that it

the relationship between the two is to borrow Bataille's distinction between general economy and restricted economy: Jesus acts on the basis of the former, activating it in critique of and as a real alternative to the latter.

Nevertheless, Jesus' words and actions do not always express that reality so explicitly. He continues to adopt a notion of charity at times, for instance, even if the critical import of his thought attempts to move beyond it, toward a world in which it is unnecessary. Jesus can proclaim release to the captives, in the spirit of Jubilee (Luke 4:18), and equate the kingdom of God with the elevation of the poor and the like (Luke 6:20ff); but he can also, it seems, emphasize the continuation of poverty and the structures that create it after his demise (see Matt 16:11). Part of the ambiguity, if not downright contradiction, can no doubt be chalked up to the agendas of the authors of the different gospels, as biblical critics would emphasize.[38] One could argue, in other words, that at least some of the ambiguity or contradiction is of my own creating, as I have intentionally, repeatedly, and freely run together different sources. Sticking to one portrait of Jesus would solve the problem, at least to an extent.

It is a fair point, but conceptually it assumes consistency or agreement as a marker of authenticity.[39] The more interesting critical problem is how to understand that inconsistency conceptually, assuming the philosophical viability of the materials themselves. Although differences in what Jesus says in and among the Gospels can no doubt be understood in light of differences in intention and the source materials used, they can also be read in terms of the tension in Jesus' message itself, which is scattered across the gospels. For, although Jesus proclaims the kingdom of heaven or God, he still has to live and act in the world as organized. This is, in part, inevitable, down to the language that he uses, but it is also chosen: I have emphasized that Jesus' message is not one of asceticism, meaning that he refuses permanent withdrawal from the world as an option for accomplishing his mission, to the extent that is even possible. Jesus' proclamation, I have stressed, can be understood as an anti-money, anti-work, and anti-family ethos, but on this side of things. Another way to put the matter is to say that he gives his followers the choice between God or mammon, which is the central

---

functions as a specter that haunts the presence of the present, destabilizing and interrupting it from within. See Derrida, *Spectres of Marx*.

38. As my former colleague Christopher Skinner likes to say of the gospels, they are "theologically stylized narratives with historical roots. Each has its own autonomous story to tell about Jesus."

39. Although he has different concerns in mind, Dolgopolski's *What Is Talmud?* is relevant here. Dolgopolski argues that disagreement is not a means to an end but the thing itself, in the sense that it constitutes human existence and relationality.

antagonism governing his actions, but it is a real choice, a choice between ways to live and act in this world, and not another.

Although I have emphasized the negative component of Jesus' stance, we should not reduce the options Jesus presents to a simple negation, as if it were always possible—or even desirable—to say no to mammon in one fell swoop. Jesus does, of course, recommend as much in places and to certain individuals, but the risk is that it tends toward an ascetic position, one that emphasizes a "clean hands" approach to the affairs of the world. Even if Jesus at times commends the former, he does not commend the latter. Indeed, his refusal to adopt a purist stance is what often leads to criticism, however self-serving that criticism might be. But nor can we understand Jesus' position in terms of priority, a position I have critiqued throughout. If the former option tends to result in asceticism, the latter devalues the force of the disjunction between God and mammon, as a means of making it more palatable and practical. Such is the logic of the discourse on desire in the theological tradition, I think, which emphasizes a reorientation of the self toward God without, however, necessarily jettisoning mammon.

I think there is another option available, and as a way into it we can recall The Parable of the Dishonest Manager, whose apparent problematic nature I noted in chapter 1. It is worth quoting the parable at length:

> Then Jesus said to the disciples, There was a rich man who had a manager, and charges were brought to him that this man was squandering his property. So he summoned him and said to him, "What is this that I hear about you? Give me an account of your management, because you cannot be my manager any longer." Then the manager said to himself, "What will I do, now that my master is taking the position away from me? I am not strong enough to dig, and I am ashamed to beg. I have decided what to do so that, when I am dismissed as manager, people may welcome me into their homes." So, summoning his master's debtors one by one, he asked the first, "How much do you owe my master?" He answered, "A hundred jugs of olive oil." He said to him, "Take your bill, sit down quickly, and make it fifty." Then he asked another, "And how much do you owe?" He replied, "A hundred containers of wheat." He said to him, "Take your bill and make it eighty." And his master commended the dishonest manager because he had acted shrewdly; for the children of this age are more shrewd in dealing with their own generation than are the children of light. And I tell you, make friends for yourselves by means of dishonest wealth so that when it is gone, they may welcome you into the eternal homes.

> Whoever is faithful in a very little is faithful also in much; and whoever is dishonest in a very little is dishonest also in much. If then you have not been faithful with the dishonest wealth, who will entrust to you the true riches? And if you have not been faithful with what belongs to another, who will give you what is your own? (Luke 16:1–12)

On its surface, the parable appears to contradict the disjunction between God and mammon, which occurs immediately after: "No slave can serve two masters; for a slave will either hate the one and love the other, or be devoted to the one and despise the other. You cannot serve God and wealth [mammon]" (Luke 16:13). The preceding parable seems to assume the opposite, that is, that one can indeed serve God and mammon. Indeed, not only can but it seems that we should, in that the parable recommends the shrewd use of wealth as a means and marker of faithfulness. So understood, the parable would limit the scope of the disjunction between God and mammon, rendering it relative rather than absolute; such a reading would, moreover, determine the problem of mammon in terms of individual desire rather than in mammon itself.

Such a reading depends on reading the disjunction in light of the parable rather than the other way around. If one gives hermeneutical priority to the parable, then the metaphorizing reading that results and reduces the decision between God and mammon to a matter of individual desire makes sense. Doing so, however, limits the scope of the disjunction in advance, and thus we should begin from the other direction. The disjunction should not be read in light of the parable but the parable in light of the disjunction, since the division between God and mammon is the conclusion to what precedes it.

Doing so, we see that one of the ways in which the choice between God and mammon manifests itself in actual practice is through the calculated use of money and wealth to undermine mammon from within. This is exactly what the dishonest manager does, in the form of debt relief or forgiveness. The manager's actions certainly benefit his master, who commends the dishonest manager for collecting on the debts owed to him. But the plan is even more beneficial to the manager and the debtors themselves. The dishonest manager does not initially negotiate a better deal with his master's debtors to win back the favor of his master, to prove to him that he can manage his affairs properly and that he is not ultimately a squanderer of wealth. Rather, the point of his actions, as he expresses it, is to set himself up with his master's debtors, to win favor with them in the hopes of offsetting what appears as his impending impoverishment. The relationship that he establishes with the debtors is, in a way, self-serving, although it is interesting to note that the parable doesn't impugn the manager's motivations but, rather, praises him. The plan also has obvious benefits for the debtors themselves, who through the manager's negotiations see what is likely their perpetual indebtedness disappear, in basically one stroke. The benefits to the master are, in this sense, a side-effect of the manager's debt-relief scheme, rather than its main goal.

In a way, we might say that the dishonest manager fulfills the conditions set down in The Lord's Prayer, which I mentioned in the previous chapter in connection to Jesus' program of debt forgiveness. In Matthew, Jesus recommends that his followers pray simply and materially, avoiding empty phrases and drawing attention to themselves:

> Our Father in heaven,
>   Hallowed be your name.
>   Your kingdom come.
>   Your will be done,
>   on earth as it is in heaven.
>   Give us this day our daily bread.
>   And forgive us our debts,
>   as we have also forgiven our debtors.
>   And do not bring us to the time of trial,
>   But rescue us from the evil one. (Matt 6:9–13).

Read in light of Jesus' model prayer, the manager's debt relief plan, which is a direct embodiment of "forgive us our debts, as we forgive our debtors," shifts the sense of his actions away from mammon and toward God. Given the discussion of the relationship between money, debt, and the state in the previous chapter, the manager's actions can be read as not merely beneficent but subversive as well, even if they are limited in scope. The actions undermine the sense of debt itself, which Jesus labels in the parable as "dishonest wealth." The manager, in effect, uses wealth against wealth, undercutting it from within.

One could argue that this is what charity does, which would bring us right back into a more benign, traditional interpretation of the disjunction between God and mammon. Clement of Alexandria, for instance, would likely have no problem with the notion of the wealthy giving or providing relief out of their abundance. For him, along with the mainstream of the theological tradition, such charity should be the point of wealth: wealth provides opportunities for the wealthy to use it well, to give to those in need. The difference in this case, however, is that charity assumes possession: one gives out of what is ostensibly one's own. Although the dishonest manager is in charge of his master's wealth, it is not really his to do with it whatever he pleases, which is why he can be accused of squandering it in the first place. Moreover, charity does not challenge the conditions in and for which it occurs but, rather, assumes those very conditions. Charity, in this sense, although individually satisfying and, at least theologically speaking, sacramentally significant, fails to get outside of a particular social logic, a logic that assumes the uneven distribution of wealth. The dishonest manager, I am claiming, challenges that logic.

That may not appear to be the case on the surface. Devin Singh, for instance, suggests that we should be cautious in setting God and mammon in opposition, both in theory and in practice, since it tends toward oversimplification and, moreover, ideological blindness with respect to certain structural elements that may be in play. Singh acknowledges that the opposition is, in many ways, attractive, especially since it appears to set theology and philosophy of religion on easy footing with regard to a critique of capitalism. Nevertheless, it fails to note the various ways in which God and money or, more specifically, theological language and monetization, are mutually implicated with each other historically and conceptually. Citing numerous studies that link the development of Greek philosophy and a monetary economy and arguing that Christian theology inherits this legacy, Singh notes, for instance, that even Jesus is not immune from such implication. Although Jesus certainly, at times, sets God and money in opposition, "the scriptural texts are more complex, as Jesus and the kingdom are favorably compared with lost coins and treasure, and faithful discipleship is likened to shrewd financial stewardship, for instance."[40] Failure to take account of such ambivalence and ambiguity, Singh argues, limits the critical potential of theological and philosophical discourse to analyze "wider political forms of sovereignty and the theopolitical visions that nourish them."[41]

Singh raises an important point, here, and I agree with him that much work needs to be done on the mutual implication of theological language and conceptuality and monetization. But it is important to emphasize that the use of the monetary language does not necessarily result in the type of mutual implication that Singh rightly wants to analyze and criticize, at least on the whole. Jesus does use numerous monetary metaphors which, on the surface, would seem to introduce an amount of ambivalence into his otherwise stated opposition to mammon. This is a fair point, and there is no point in arguing otherwise. It is important, however, to pay attention to what is being accomplished in that ambivalence. Although there is certainly

40. Singh, "Monetized Philosophy," 149.
41. Singh, "Monetized Philosophy," 150.

room to criticize Jesus in regard to his position and use of language, it is often the case that his use of monetary language undercuts its normal sense.

Alain Badiou's understanding of how subjects construct truth procedures based eventual ruptures in situations is helpful here. For Badiou, the production of new truths in sociohistorical contexts ("situations" or "worlds," as he calls them) depends upon a rupture with the status quo, with what passes for normal. This rupture, or event, breaks with the way in which its situation or world is organized and governed, including the knowledge and practices that institutions and individuals take for granted. An event, in other words, contains within itself the potential to pry open and, consequently, explode the ideological mechanisms that lay claim to reality. But only the potential, for the logic of an eventual irruption in a specific context has to be painstakingly constructed and adhered to in order for some novelty to emerge and subsequently establish itself. The process, that is, requires fidelity to the event, which may produce a new truth, constituted through the construction of a body of theoretical knowledge, language, and practices.

Badiou often describes the event, along with the consequences drawn from it, in stark terms: it is, he says variously, a "radical novelty" or something "absolutely new," a "pure beginning" or "absolute beginning," "a pure cut in becoming," an "exception" to what there is.[42] Badiou gives numerous examples throughout his writings of such eventual sequences, many of which determine his own philosophy, including the revolutionary political sequences associated with the French, Russian, and Chinese revolutions, mathematical sequences such as Cantor's theory of transfinite numbers, and Saint Paul's articulation of a nascent Christianity.[43] Although Badiou has often been criticized for describing the disjunction that an event instantiates in a situation or world in quasi-miraculous terms, a closer reading shows that the production of truth from an event is more subtle. Although the event certainly constitutes a break in and with the situation in which it occurs, subjects of the event must use to a certain extent the resources of that situation to construct a novel procedure. It is impossible to do otherwise, without lapsing into some sort of discourse of private illumination.

---

42. Badiou, *Saint Paul*, 33, 43, 49; Badiou, *Deleuze*, 90; Badiou, *Logics of Worlds*, 384, 360.

43. For the latter, see Badiou, *Saint Paul*. Technically speaking, however, Christianity for Badiou only contains the formal elements of a truth procedure and is not an effective truth procedure; although the role of religion in Badiou's philosophy is a complicated one, he is decidedly anti-religion, and limits truth to art, science, politics, and love. For a discussion of the role that theology and religion plays in his thought, see Phelps, *Alain Badiou*.

Specifically, a new truth procedure draws on the language circulating in the situation without, however, fully coinciding with its established sense. Lenin, for instance, uses the terms "party," "revolution," and "politics"; Cantor "ordinals" and "cardinals"; and Saint Paul "faith," "charity," "sacrifice," and "salvation."[44] The use of established language does not merely repeat its sense but, rather, filters it through the event itself. In so doing, that use shifts the sense of language in an anticipatory manner. Badiou thus says that the meaning of these terms "will have been presented in a *new* situation."[45]

We see such creative use of established language for the production of novelty, I think, in Stefano Harney and Fred Moten's essay "Debt and Credit," found in their *The Undercommons*. Harney and Moten use financial language, specifically the language of credit and debt, to propose another understanding of debt, one that has nothing to do with economic and moral exchange and calculation and, indeed, turns these against themselves. Harney and Moten refer to this other debt as "bad debt," and they conceive of it as completely detached from credit.

Credit, for Harney and Moten, is one-sided and, because of this, asocial. Credit gives only to receive more in return and, because of this, always keeps track and, if necessary, tracks down. When debt is tied to credit, the best that one can hope for if things go wrong is some form of forgiveness; forgiveness, however, is just another way to take account and make accounts, to restore, restructure, and rehabilitate for the purpose of extending more credit. Bad debt, in contrast, is mutual and, thus, social; it "runs in every direction, scatters, escapes, seeks refuge."[46] Bad debt does not forgive, but forgets and, in this sense, can sound very much like the so-called gift, made popular through the work of Marcel Mauss and deemed "impossible" by Derrida.[47] Harney and Moten, for instance, note that what they mean by "bad debt" can be felt in "the way someone saves the best stuff just to give it to you and then its gone, given, a debt. They don't want nothing. You have got to accept it, you have got to accept that. You're in debt but you can't give credit because they won't hold it. . . . Credit keeps track. Debt forgets."[48] Far from recapitulating normal economic logic, then, Moten and Harney's twisting of economic language and conceptuality, here in regard to credit and debt, constitutes instead a "fugitive public."

---

44. Badiou, *Being and Event*, 397.
45. Badiou, *Being and Event*, 398.
46. Harney and Moten, *Undercommons*, 61.
47. See Derrida, *Given Time*.
48. Harney and Moten, *Undercommons*, 62.

Such repurposing of economic language and logic for the purposes of exposing and overturning the latter can also be found in the initiatives undertaken by Strike Debt and its recent offshoot, the Debt Collective, both of which, as their names imply, focus on debt forgiveness and resistance.[49] Emerging out of Occupy Wall Street, Strike Debt's first significant actions in relation to debt occurred through its Rolling Jubilee campaign. Funded primarily through donations, in 2012 Strike Debt began to buy up millions of dollars of delinquent health care debt for pennies on the dollar on the secondary debt market. Instead of seeking to collect on those debts, as predatory debt collectors hoping to turn a quick profit do, Strike Debt simply forgave them. In 2014, Strike Debt began to do the same with certain types of student loan debt. All told, the Rolling Jubilee campaign forgave almost $32 million in healthcare and student loan debt.

Recognizing that the Rolling Jubilee campaign did not represent a long-term solution to the problem of debt, Strike Debt recently formed the Debt Collective, the goal of which is to move from forgiveness to organized resistance. Its first major campaign concerns student loan debt, specifically the debt owed by former and current students of the now-defunct for-profit Corinthian Colleges, Inc. Citing Corinthian Colleges, Inc.'s predatory practices, false promises, and ultimate dissolution and supported legally and financially by the Debt Collective, the Corinthian strike team, as they are called, have attempted to translate their refusal to repay their student loans into direct political action, calling on the Department of Education to cancel their debt, which they claim is illegitimate. The Debt Collective also hopes, however, that the campaign will be the impetus of a more widespread resistance to student loan debt, specifically as it relates to rising costs in higher education.

All of which is to say, the use of economic language, metaphor, and conceptuality does not necessarily indicate an irretrievable entanglement with economic logic. Singh is certainly correct to note the problems that attend to such use throughout the biblical, theological, and ecclesiastical traditions, and it is certainly the case that, in many instances, the latter have replicated problematic social relationships and forms of sovereignty.[50] Nevertheless, it is also the case that economic language, metaphor, and conceptuality can be used against itself, which is implied in Badiou's theory of

---

49. For Strike Debt, see http://strikedebt.org/; for the Debt Collective, see https://debtcollective.org/. For scholarly treatments of the movement, see "Against the Day" in the special issue of the *South Atlantic Quarterly*.

50. Anselm's articulation of the human condition as one of indebtedness in particular comes to mind. See my "Overcoming Resistance," 264–82.

evental truth, seen in Moten and Harney's articulation of bad debt, and put into practice with Strike Debt and the Debt Collective.

We also, I think, see something similar in much of Jesus' teachings and actions. Yes, Jesus freely draws on various monetary and economic concepts in his speech and actions, and often uses these to describe the kingdom of God or heaven in contradistinction to the social and political realities of his day. Nevertheless, the use of such language and concepts does not in and of itself entangle Jesus' speech and actions in the underlying logic, at least across the board. One has to look at how Jesus uses these notions and what they entail, generally speaking, in terms of a critique and possible alternative to existing arrangements.

That is not to say that Jesus is always entirely successful in this endeavor. The argument that I am making is not a theological argument, one that would assume the absolute inviolability of Jesus' claims simply because of the dogmatic identification of him as the Son of God. Indeed, at times, Jesus does appear to recapitulate and transpose the logic of the practices that he ostensibly, and at other times, opposes. Such would seem to be the case, for instance, with The Parable of the Ten Pounds.

> As they were listening to this, he went on to tell a parable, because he was near Jerusalem, and because they supposed that the kingdom of God was to appear immediately. So he said, "A nobleman went to a distant country to get royal power for himself and then return. He summoned ten of his slaves, and gave them ten pounds, and said to them, 'Do business with these until I come back.' But the citizens of his country hated him and sent a delegation after him, saying, 'We do not want this man to rule over us.' When he returned, having received royal power, he ordered these slaves, to whom he had given the money, to be summoned so that he might find out what they had gained by trading. The first came forward and said, 'Lord, your pound has made ten more pounds.' He said to him, 'Well done, good slave! Because you have been trustworthy in a very small thing, take charge of ten cities.' Then the second came, saying, 'Lord, your pound has made five pounds.' He said to him, 'And you, rule over five cities.' Then the other came, saying, 'Lord, here is your pound. I wrapped it up in a piece of cloth, for I was afraid of you, because you are a harsh man; you take what you did not deposit, and reap what you did not sow.' He said to him, 'I will judge you by your own words, you wicked slave! You knew, did you, that I was a harsh man, taking what I did not deposit and reaping what I did not sow? Why then did you not put my money into the bank? Then when I returned, I could have collected it with

interest.' He said to the bystanders, 'Take the pound from him and give it to the one who has ten pounds.' (And they said to him, 'Lord, he has ten pounds!') 'I tell you, to all those who have, more will be given; but from those who have nothing, even what they have will be taken away. But as for these enemies of mine who did not want me to be king over them—bring them here and slaughter them in my presence.'" (Luke 19:11-27)

The parable is correlative to The Parable of the Talents.

> For it is as if a man, going on a journey, summoned his slaves and entrusted his property to them; to one he gave five talents, to another two, to another one, to each according to his ability. Then he went away. The one who had received the five talents went off at once and traded with them, and made five more talents. In the same way, the one who had the two talents made two more talents. But the one who had received the one talent went off and dug a hole in the ground and hid his master's money. After a long time the master of those slaves came and settled accounts with them. Then the one who had received the five talents came forward, bringing five more talents, saying, "Master, you handed over to me five talents; see, I have made five more talents." His master said to him, "Well done, good and trustworthy slave; you have been trustworthy in a few things, I will put you in charge of many things; enter into the joy of your master." And the one with the two talents also came forward, saying, "Master, you handed over to me two talents; see, I have made two more talents." His master said to him, "Well done, good and trustworthy slave; you have been trustworthy in a few things, I will put you in charge of many things; enter into the joy of your master." Then the one who had received the one talent also came forward, saying, "Master, I knew that you were a harsh man, reaping where you did not sow, and gathering where you did not scatter seed; so I was afraid, and I went and hid your talent in the ground. Here you have what is yours." But his master replied, "You wicked and lazy slave! You knew, did you, that I reap where I did not sow, and gather where I did not scatter? Then you ought to have invested my money with the bankers, and on my return I would have received what was my own with interest. So take the talent from him, and give it to the one with the ten talents. For to all those who have, more will be given, and they will have an abundance; but from those who have nothing, even what they have will be taken away. As for this

worthless slave, throw him into the outer darkness, where there will be weeping and gnashing of teeth." (Matt 25:14–30)

Both versions of this parable seemingly clash with other aspects of Jesus' teachings, at least on the surface. For instance, we are told that success and general abundance (the "more" in Matt 25:29 and Luke 19:26), whether in this world or the next, depends on the shrewd use of wealth. Jesus' claim that more will be given to those who already have and who, the parable suggests, make good use of what they have, are praised. Elsewhere, most notably in the Sermon on the Mount/Plain, the reverse is the case: "woe to you who are rich, for you have received your consolation" (Luke 6:24). Indeed, whereas here the slave who hides his talent in the ground out of fear of his master is condemned, elsewhere similar actions are understood as signals of faithfulness and trust in the kingdom of God. Recall, for instance, that the "kingdom of heaven is like a treasure hidden in a field, which someone found and hid; then in his joy he goes and sells all that he has and buys that field" (Matt 13:44). All of which is to say, it would appear that, in the case of the Parable of the Ten Pounds and the Parable of the Ten Talents, Jesus somewhat unthinkingly repeats an economic logic that is elsewhere criticized, even condemned.

However, even through such repetition, we see a twisting of economic logic or, better put, a certain use of it that undermines the otherwise stable relationships within the parables. It is important, in this sense, to emphasize who is using the logic present, and for what. When Jesus criticizes wealth, money, and the logic that underpins their circulation and accumulation, it is often directed against those who have wealth and money, those who maintain a dominant position in social and economic exchanges in terms of differentiating wealth. Jesus' critique of wealth is, in a sense, asymmetrical, but that asymmetry is necessary, precisely because those who lack wealth cannot depend on the generosity of the wealthy with any reliability.

The rich ruler, for instance, is told to sell all that he has because he has much. In the Parable of the Ten Pounds and the Parable of the Ten Talents, in contrast, the characters who engage in the logic of exchange do so at the behest of their master, at least in part; they are not, in other words, in the position of someone like the rich ruler, who controls his own wealth. The servants in the parables, however, use that necessity for their own benefit, bettering their position and, in effect, achieving some amount of autonomy through exchange. The master thus praises their actions and rewards the servants, while condemning and punishing the one who merely sits on what was given to him. To quote again from the Parable of the Dishonest

Manager, "make friends for yourself by means of dishonest wealth so that when it is done, they may welcome you into the eternal homes" (Luke 16:9).

How, then, do we square this reading of wealth, which recommends its shrewd use by those who need to use it shrewdly, with Jesus' own lack, which he also commands of his immediate disciples, who certainly are not rich by any means? Understanding the two together requires understanding the point of the disjunction between God and mammon. I have emphasized repeatedly that the disjunction is absolute, but to say that it is absolute is not to say that it is simplistic or pure, in that it needs to be expressed in dogmatic terms. Jesus certainly opposes God to mammon, but the opposition is meant for us; it is not, in other words, meant as a lifeless abstraction. It is similar, in this sense, to Jesus' claim about the Sabbath, which also falls under the disjunction: "The sabbath was made for humankind, and not humankind for the sabbath" (Mark 2:27). The point is that something like the sabbath is designed for the benefit of humankind, both individually and as a whole. It should not be understood as a mere legal prescription, the strict following of which undermines its sense.

The same can be said for the distinction between God and mammon. Jesus is, I have argued, anti-money, anti-work, and anti-family, but this is because he views such institutions, as in place then but also now, as working against the benefit of humankind as a whole. Opposing God to these understood qua mammon, then, simultaneously serves as a means of denunciation and critique but also suggestion, in the form of fashioning an alternative. That alternative, however, is meant for human beings and the world as a whole, including its non-human beings, meaning that its expression should be beneficial rather than deleterious. This should not be understood in a liberal sense, where well-being is read in terms of respect for the individual as the freedom to pursue economic interests and advantage. As mentioned above, Jesus' stance in this respect is asymmetrical or, to use a term drawn from the work of liberation theologians, preferential. Jesus weights the "good news" toward the poor, the oppressed, the marginalized, and any sociopolitical system that ignores the asymmetry involved is, by default, on the side of mammon. Charity, as I have emphasized, does not so much rub against mammon but, rather, participates in its logic, in the sense that it functions as an ethical supplement. As Leonardo and Clodovis Boff put it, charitable actions in the form of aid and reformism represent "the 'Band-Aid' or 'corn-plaster' approach to social ills. But however perceptive they become and however well-intentioned—and successful—aid remains a strategy for helping the poor, but treating them as (collective) object of charity, not as subjects of their own liberation. The poor are seen simply as those who have nothing. There is a failure to see that the poor are oppressed and made poor *by others*."[51]

The point of the disjunction between God and mammon, then, is to conjure and instantiate an alternative to mammon, but it is this end that remains important, rather than a set of clearly identified means. This is not to say that the achievement of an alternative is left up to a calculated utilitarianism, which often goes hand in hand with mammon. It is rather to say that the end—God and God's kingdom, as Jesus names them—exists for human beings, rather than human beings for the end. Because of this, although the distinction between God and mammon is absolute, it may be achieved variously, but how it is achieved also depends on the subject position of the one acting and the fundamental asymmetry that governs the distinction. In the case of the dishonest manager, for instance, he undermines mammon from within, via debt negotiation and forgiveness, but it is his position with respect to mammon—as manager, he is simultaneously included and excluded with respect to it—that makes his actions possible. His actions can, in this respect, be classified as shrewd use of dishonest wealth but also in terms of Jesus' request of his disciples: "See, I am sending you out like sheep into the midst of wolves; so be wise as serpents and innocent as doves" (Matt 10:16).

---

51. Boff and Boff, *Introducing Liberation Theology*, 4.

Bibliography

Agamben, Giorgio. *The Time that Remains: A Commentary of the Letter to the Romans.* Translated by Patricia Daley. Stanford: Stanford University Press, 2005.
Althusser, Louis. "Contradiction and Overdetermination." In *For Marx*, translated by Ben Brewster. London: Verso, 2006.
Anderson, Gary A. *Charity: The Place of the Poor in the Biblical Tradition.* New Haven: Yale University Press, 2013.
———. *Sin: A History.* New Haven: Yale University Press, 2009.
Anselm of Canterbury. *The Major Works.* Edited by Brian Davies. Oxford: Oxford University Press, 2008.
Arendt, Hannah. *The Human Condition.* Chicago: University of Chicago Press, 1998.
Aristotle. *Politics.* In *The Basic Works of Aristotle*, edited by Richard McKeon. New York: Random House, 2001.
Athanasius. *The Life of Antony.* In *Athanasius: The Life of Antony and the Letter to Marcellinus,* edited by Robert C. Gregg. Mahwah, NJ: Paulist, 1979.
Augustine of Hippo. *Confessions.* Translated by R. S. Pine-Coffin. London: Penguin, 1961.
———. *On the Sermon on the Mount.* In vol. 6 *Nicene and Post-Nicene Fathers*, edited by Philip Schaff. Buffalo, NY: Christian Literature Publishing, 1888.
———. *Sermons,* III/5. Translated by Edmund Hill. New Rochelle, NY: New City Press, 1990.
Badiou, Alain. *Being and Event.* Translated by Oliver Feltham. London: Continuum, 2007.
———. *Deleuze: The Clamor of Being.* Translated by Louise Burchill. Minneapolis: University of Minnesota Press, 1999.
———. *In Praise of Love.* Translated by Peter Bush. New York: New Press, 2012.
———. *Logics of Worlds.* Translated by Alberto Toscano. London: Bloomsbury Academic, 2009.
———. *Saint Paul: The Foundation of Universalism.* Translated by Ray Brassier. Stanford: Stanford University Press, 2005.
Bataille, Georges. *The Accursed Share.* Vol. 1. Translated by Robert Hurley. Brooklyn, NY: Zone Books, 1989.
———. *Theory of Religion.* New York: Zone Books, 1992.
Bell, Daniel M., Jr. *The Economy of Desire.* Grand Rapids: Baker Academic, 2012.
Berardi, Franco. *The Soul at Work: From Alienation to Autonomy.* Los Angeles: Semiotext(e), 2009.

Black, Bob. "The Abolition of Work." Primitivism.com. http://www.primitivism.com/abolition.htm.

Boer, Roland. *The Sacred Economy of Ancient Israel*. Louisville: Westminster John Knox, 2015.

Boff, Leonardo, and Clodovis Boff. *Introducing Liberation Theology*. Translated by Paul Burns. Maryknoll, NY: Orbis, 1987.

Bonhoeffer, Dietrich. *The Cost of Discipleship*. Translated by R. H. Fuller. New York: Touchstone, 1995.

Boring, Eugene. *Matthew*. In *The New Interpreter's Bible*, edited by Leander Keck. Nashville: Abingdon, 1995.

Brown, Raymond. *The Gospel According to John I–XII*. Anchor Bible. Garden City, NY: Doubleday, 1966.

Brown, Wendy. *Undoing the Demos: Neoliberalism's Stealth Revolution*. New York: Zone Books, 2015.

Brueggemann, Walter. *Sabbath as Resistance: Saying No to the Culture of Now*. Louisville: Westminster John Knox, 2014.

Buber, Martin. *I and Thou*. Translated by Walter Kaufmann. New York: Touchstone, 1970.

Calvin, John. *Calvin's Commentaries*. Vol. 1, *Genesis, Part I*. Translated by John King. http://www.sacred-texts.com/chr/calvin/cc01/cc01008.htm.

The Catechism of the Catholic Church. http://www.vatican.va/archive/ccc_css/archive/catechism/p2s2c3a7.htm.

Cavanaugh, William T. *Being Consumed: Economics and Christian Desire*. Grand Rapids, MI: Eerdmans, 2008.

Certeau, Michel de. *The Practice of Everyday Life*. Translated by Steven Rendall. Chicago: University of Chicago Press, 1984.

Clement of Alexandria. "Who Is the Rich Man Who Shall Be Saved?" In vol. 2 of *Ante-Nicece Fathers*, edited by Alexander Roberts, James Donaldson, and A. Cleveland Coxe. Buffalo, NY: Christian Literature Publishing, 1885. http://www.newadvent.org/fathers/0207.htm.

Connolly, William E. *The Fragility of Things: Self-Organizing Processes, Neoliberal Fantasies, and Democratic Activism*. Durham, NC: Duke University Press, 2013.

Cosdon, Darrell. *A Theology of Work: Work and the New Creation*. Eugene, OR: Wipf & Stock, 2006.

Cox, Harvey. *The Feast of Fools*. Cambridge: Harvard University Press, 1969.

Crary, Jonathan. *24/7: Late Capitalism and the Ends of Sleep*. London: Verso, 2014.

Danker, Frederick William, ed. *A Greek-English Lexicon of the New Testament and Other Early Christian Literature*. Chicago: University of Chicago Press.

Davies, Glyn. *A History of Money: From Ancient Times to the Present Day*. Cardiff: University of Wales Press, 2002.

Davis, Mark. "The Politics of Just Wages—Matthew 20:1–16." *Political Theology Today*, September 15, 2014. https://politicaltheology.com/the-politics-of-just-wages-matthew-201-16/.

Deleuze, Gilles, and Feliz Guattari. *Anti-Oedipus*. Translated by Brian Massumi. Minneapolis: University of Minnesota Press, 1994.

Derrida, Jacques. "From a Restricted to General Economy: A Hegelianism without Reserve." In *Writing and Difference*, translated by Alan Bass, 317–50. Chicago: University of Chicago Press, 1978.

———. *The Gift of Death*. Chicago: University of Chicago Press, 1995.
———. *Given Time: I. Counterfeit Money*. Chicago: University of Chicago Press, 1994.
———. *Spectres of Marx*. London: Routledge, 2006.
Dolgopolski, Sergey. *What Is Talmud? The Art of Disagreement*. New York: Fordham University Press, 2009.
Eagleton, Terry. *Terry Eagleton Presents Jesus Christ—The Gospels*. London: Verso, 2007.
Edelman, Lee. *No Future: Queer Theory and the Death Drive*. Durham: Duke University Press, 2004.
Ehrenreich, Barbara. *Dancing in the Streets: A History of Collective Joy*. New York: Holt Paperbacks, 2007.
Evans, Dylan. *An Introductory Dictionary of Lacanian Psychoanalysis*. London: Routledge, 1996.
Federici, Sylvia. *Wages against Housework*. Bristol, UK: Falling Wall, 1975.
Feuerbach, Ludwig. *The Essence of Christianity*. Translated by George Eliot. Amherst, NY: Prometheus, 1989.
Fink, Bruce. "Analysand and Analyst in the Global Economy, or Why Anyone in Their Right Mind Would Pay for an Analysis." *New Formations* 72 (2011) 20–32.
Florida, Richard. *The Rise of the Creative Class—Revisited: Revised and Expanded*. New York: Basic Books, 2014.
Foucault, Michel. *The History of Sexuality*. Vol. 1. Translated by Robert Hurley. New York: Vintage, 1990.
Freud, Sigmund. *Civilization and Its Discontents*. Translated by Joan Riviere. Mineola, NY: Dover, 1994.
Gay, Craig M. *Cash Values: Money and the Erosion of Meaning in Today's Society*. Grand Rapids, MI: Eerdmans, 2003.
Gonzalez, Justo L. *Faith & Wealth: A History of Early Christian Ideas on the Origin, Significance, and Use of Money*. New York: Harper & Row, 1990.
Goodchild, Philip. *Capitalism and Religion: The Price of Piety*. London: Routledge, 2002.
———. *Theology of Money*. Durham: Duke University Press, 2009.
———, ed. *On Philosophy as a Spiritual Exercise*. New York: Palgrave Macmillan, 2013.
Gorz, Andre. *Critique of Economic Reason*. London: Verso, 2011.
Graeber, David. *Debt: The First 5000 Years*. Brooklyn, NY: Melville House, 2014.
———. "On the Phenomenon of Bullshit Jobs." *Strike!*, August 17, 2013.
Gulli, Bruno. *Labor of Fire*. Philadelphia: Temple University Press, 2005.
———. *The Ontology of Labor between Economy and Culture*. Philadelphia: Temple University Press, 2005.
Guthrie, Stewart. *Faces in the Clouds: A New Theory of Religion*. New York: Oxford University Press, 1993.
Hadot, Pierre. *Philosophy as a Way of Life*. Edited by Arnold Davidson. Oxford: Wiley-Blackwell, 1995.
———. *What Is Ancient Philosophy?* Translated by Michael Chase. Cambridge, MA: Harvard Belnap, 2004.
Hanson, R. P. C. *Allegory & Event*. Louisville: Westminster John Knox, 2003.
Hardt, Michael, and Antonio Negri. *Commonwealth*. Cambridge, MA: Belknap, 2009.
Harney, Stefano, and Fred Moten. *The Undercommons: Fugitive Planning and Black Study*. New York: Minor Compositions, 2013.
Hartigan, John, Jr. *Aesop's Anthropology: A Multispecies Approach*. Minneapolis: University of Minnesota Press, 2016.

Hauerwas, Stanley. *Character and the Christian Life: A Study in Theological Ethics*. South Bend: University of Notre Dame Press, 1994.

———. *A Community of Character: Toward a Constructive Christian Social Ethic*. South Bend: University of Notre Dame Press, 1991.

———. *Vision and Virtue: Essays in Christian Ethical Reflection*. South Bend: University of Notre Dame Press, 1986.

Hauerwas, Stanley, and Will Willimon. *Resident Aliens*. Nashville: Abingdon, 2014.

Heidegger, Martin. *Being and Time*. Translated by Joan Stambaugh. New York: SUNY Press, 2010.

Hénaff, Marcel. *The Price of Truth: Gift, Money, and Philosophy*. Translated by Jean-Louise Morhange. Stanford: Stanford University Press, 2010.

Hendren, John. "Obama: Wall Street 'Arrogance and Greed' Won't be Tolerated." *ABC News*, January 31, 2009. http://abcnews.go.com/Politics/CEOProfiles/story?id=6778419.

Henry, Michel. *Words of Christ*. Translated by Christina M. Gschwandtner. Grand Rapids, MI: Eerdmans, 2012.

Herzog, William R., II. *Parables as Subversive Speech*. Louisville: Westminster John Knox, 1994.

Hudson, Michael. "The Lost Tradition of Biblical Debt Cancellations." 1993. http://michael-hudson.com/wp-content/uploads/2010/03/HudsonLostTradition.pdf

Hudson, Michael, and Marc Van De Mieroop. *Debt and Economic Renewal in the Ancient Near East*. Bethedsa, MD: Capital Decisions Ltd., 2002.

Ingham, Geoffrey. *The Nature of Money*. Cambridge, UK: Polity, 2004.

Irenaeus of Lyons. *Against Heresies*. London: Routledge, 2004.

Jensen, David H. *Responsive Labor: A Theology of Work*. Louisville: Westminster John Knox Press, 2006.

John Paul II. *Laborem exercens*. http://www.catholic-pages.com/documents/laborem_exercens.pdf.

Jones, Campbell. *Can the Market Speak?* Winchester, UK: Zero Books, 2013.

Joris, Pierre. "Michel Serres on Gay Marriage." Nomadics (blog), February 8, 2013. http://www.pierrejoris.com/blog/?p=9866.

Joseph, Miranda. *Debt to Society: Accounting for Life Under Capitalism*. Minneapolis: University of Minnesota Press, 2014.

Karatani, Kojin. *The Structure of World History*. Translated by Michael K. Bourdaghs. Duke: Duke University Press, 2014.

Kittel, Gerhard, ed. *A Theological Dictionary of the New Testament [TDNT]*. Vol. IV. Translated by Geoffrey Bromiley. Grand Rapids: Eerdmans, 1977.

Konings, Martijn. *The Emotional Logic of Capitalism*. Stanford: Stanford University Press, 2015.

Lacan, Jacques. *The Ego in Freud's Theory and in the Technique of Psychoanalysis: The Seminar of Jacques Lacan, Book II*. Translated by Sylvana Tomaselli. New York: W. W. Norton & Company, 1991.

———. *The Ethics of Psychoanalysis: The Seminar of Jacques Lacan, Book VII*. Translated by Dennis Porter. New York: W. W. Norton & Company, 1992.

———. *The Four Fundamental Concepts of Psychoanalysis: The Seminar of Jacques Lacan, Book XI*. Translated by Alan Sheridan. New York: W. W. Norton & Company, 1981.

Lafargue, Paul. *The Right to Be Lazy*. Translated by Charles Kerr. Floating Press, 2012.

Lazzarato, Maurizio. *Governing by Debt*. Translated by Joshua David Jordan. Los Angeles: Semiotext(e), 2015.
———. *The Making of the Indebted Man*. Translated by Joshua David Jordan. Los Angeles: Semiotext(e), 2012.
———. *Signs and Machines: Capitalism and the Production of Subjectivity*. Translated by Joshua David Jordan. Los Angeles: Semiotext(e), 2014.
Le Goff, Jacques. *Your Money or Your Life*. Translated by Patricia Ranum. New York: Zone Books, 1990.
Lehr, Valerie. *Queer Family Values: Rethinking the Myth of the Nuclear Family*. Philadelphia: Temple University Press, 1999.
Leo XIII. *Rerum Novarum*. http://w2.vatican.va/content/leo-xiii/en/encyclicals/documents/hf_l-xiii_enc_15051891_rerum-novarum.html
Lordon, Frédéric. *Willing Slaves of Capital: Spinoza and Marx on Desire*. London: Verso, 2014.
de Lubac, Henri. *Medieval Exegesis*. Volume I. Grand Rapids: Eerdmans, 1998.
Marazzi, Christian. *The Violence of Financial Capitalism*. Los Angeles: Semiotext(e), 2011.
Marx, Karl. *Capital: Volume I*. Translated by Ben Fowkes. London: Penguin, 1992.
———. *Economic and Philosophic Manuscripts of 1844*. Translated by Martin Milligan. New York: International Publishers, 1964.
Massumi, Brian. *The Power at the End of the Economy*. Durham: Duke University Press, 2014.
Mauss, Marcel. *The Gift: The Form and Reason for Exchange in Archaic Societies*. Translated by W. D. Halls. New York: W. W. Norton & Company, 2000.
McGowan, Todd. *Enjoying What We Don't Have: The Political Project of Psychoanalysis*. Lincoln: University of Nebraska Press, 2013.
Metzger, Bruce M. *Breaking the Code: Understanding the Book of Revelation*. Nashville: Abingdon, 1993.
Milbank, John. *Theology and Social Theory*. Oxford: Blackwell, 1990.
Milton, John. *Paradise Lost*. Edited by Gordon Teskey. New York: W. W. Norton & Company, 2005.
Miranda, Jose P. *Communism in the Bible*. Translated by Robert Barr. Eugene, OR: Wipf & Stock, 2004.
Moore, Jason W. *Capitalism in the Web of Life*. London: Verso, 2015.
Myles, Robert. *The Homelessness of Jesus*. Sheffield: Sheffield Phoenix Press, 2014.
Nietzsche, Friedrich. *The Anti-Christ*. In *The Portable Nietzsche*, edited and translated by Walter Kaufmann. New York: Penguin, 1982.
Oakman, Douglas. *Jesus, Debt, and the Lord's Prayer: First Century Debt and Jesus' Intentions*. Eugene, OR: Cascade, 2014.
Phelps, Hollis. *Alain Badiou: Between Theology and Anti-theology*. London: Routledge, 2013.
———. "Overcoming Resistance: Neoliberalism, Atonement, and the Logic of Debt." *Political Theology* 17.3 (2016) 264–82.
Polk, Sam. "For the Love of Money." *The New York Times*, January 18, 2014. http://www.nytimes.com/2014/01/19/opinion/sunday/for-the-love-of-money.html?_r=3.
Polyani, Karl. *The Great Transformation: The Political and Economic Origins of Our Time*. Boston: Beacon, 2001.

Radford Reuther, Rosemary. *Christianity and the Making of the Modern Family.* Boston: Beacon, 2000.

Raferty, Andrew. "Ax Hovers Over Food Stamp Program as Costs Grow." *NBC News*, May 19, 2013. http://www.nbcnews.com/feature/in-plain-sight/ax-hovers-over-food-stamp-program-costs-grow-v18307642.

Robbins, Jeffrey, W. "The Politics of Paul." *Journal for Cultural and Religious Theory* 6.2 (Spring 2005) 89–94.

Sandford. Michael J. "Luxury Communist Jesus: Ideology, the Work Ethic, and the Antiwork Politics of Jesus." *Postscripts* 7.2 (2012) 245–55.

Schweitzer, Albert. *The Quest of the Historical Jesus.* London: Dover, 2005.

Scorcese, Martin, dir. *The Wolf of Wall Street.* Paramount: Los Angeles, 2013.

Seaford, Richard. *Money and the Early Greek Mind: Homer, Philosophy, Tragedy.* Cambridge: Cambridge University Press, 2004.

Serres, Michel. *The Natural Contract.* Ann Arbor: University of Michigan Press, 1995.

———. *The Parasite.* Translated by Lawrence R. Schehr. Minneapolis: University of Minnesota Press, 2007.

Shell, Marc. *Money, Language, and Thought: Literary and Philosophic Economies from the Medieval to the Modern Era.* Berkeley: University of California Press, 1982.

Singh, Devin. "Monetized Philosophy and Theological Money: Uneasy Linkages and the Future of a Discourse." In *The Future of Continental Philosophy of Religion*, edited by Clayton Crockett, B. Keith Putt, and Jeffrey W. Robbins, 140–53. Bloomington: Indiana University Press, 2014.

Smith, Adam. *The Wealth of Nations.* New York: Modern Library, 1994.

Smith, Jeremy Adam. *The Daddy Shift: How Stay-At-Home Dads, Breadwinning Moms, and Shared Parenting Are Transforming the American Family.* New York: Beacon, 2009.

South Atlantic Quarterly 112.4 (Fall 2013).

Stein, Stephen J. *The Shaker Experience in America: A History of the United Society of Believers.* New Haven: Yale University Press, 1994.

Sundararajan, Arun. *The Sharing Economy: The End of Employment and the Rise of Crowd-Based Capitalism.* Cambridge: MIT Press, 2016.

Sundeen, Mark. *The Man Who Quit Money.* New York: Riverhead, 2012.

Sung, Jung Mo. *Desire, Market, and Religion.* London: SCM Press, 2007.

Taylor, Mark C. *After God.* Chicago: University of Chicago Press, 2009.

———. *Confidence Games: Money and Market in a World Without Redemption.* Chicago: University of Chicago Press, 2004.

Thoburn, Nicholas. *Deleuze, Marx and Politics.* London: Routledge, 2014.

Tiessen, Matthew. "Infinite Debt and the Mechanics of Dispossession." In *Revisiting Normativity with Deleuze*, edited by Rosi Braidotti and Patricia Pisters, 115–30. London: Continuum, 2013.

Tillich, Paul. *Dynamics of Faith.* New York: Harper & Row, 1957.

———. *Systematic Theology.* Vol. 1. Chicago: University of Chicago Press, 1973.

Tucker, Robert C., ed. *The Marx-Engels Reader.* New York: W. W. Norton & Co., 1978.

Vogl, Joseph. *The Specter of Capital.* Stanford: Stanford University Press, 2014.

Volf, Miroslav. *Work in the Spirit: Toward a Theology of Work.* Eugene, OR: Wipf & Stock, 2001.

Weber, Max. *The Protestant Ethic and the Spirit of Capitalism.* Translated by Stephen Kalberg. Oxford: Oxford University Press, 2010.

Weeks, Kathi. *The Problem with Work: Feminism, Marxism, Antiwork Politics, and Postwork Imaginaries*. Durham: Duke University Press, 2011.
Wilson-Hartgrove, Jonathan. *New Monasticism: What It Has to Say to Today's Church*. Grand Rapids, MI: Brazos, 2010.
Witherington, Ben, III. *Work: A Kingdom Perspective on Labor*. Grand Rapids: Eerdmans, 2011.
Yuran, Norm. *What Money Wants: An Economy of Desire*. Stanford: Stanford University Press, 2014.
Žižek, Slavoj. *The Parallax View*. Cambridge: MIT Press, 2006.
———. *The Plague of Fantasies*. London: Verso, 1997.
———. *The Sublime Object of Ideology*. London: Verso, 1989.
———. *Violence: Six Sideways Reflections*. New York: Picador, 2008.

Index

2007–08 financial crisis, 31, 66
666, as mark of the beast, 75

accumulation, of wealth, 11, 48, 52,
    112, 127, 135–40, 147, 151
adoption, 119
Abraham, biblical patriarch, 25
Agamben, Giorgio, 2
Alcoholics Anonymous, 31
alienation, 29, 88–90, 109
allegory, as method of exegesis, 33
altruism, 111, 116
analysand-analyst relationship, 60
Anderson, Gary A., 28–30, 142
Anthony the Great, 123
Arendt, Hanna, 82–83
Aristotle, 20–22, 47, 49
Athanasius, 123
Augustine of Hippo, 15, 28

Badiou, Alain, 3–5, 7, 116–17, 135,
    147, 157–58
barter, as economic practice, 47–49,
    58–59, 62–63, 68
Bataille, Georges, 103, 132–33,
    148–49
Belfort, Jordan, 31
belief, 6, 29, 34–37, 41, 51
Bell Jr., Daniel M., 125
Berardi, Franco, 91
biopower, 54
Black, Bob, 95
Boff, Clodovis, 163–64
Boff, Leonardo, 163–64
Brown, Raymond, 130

Brueggemann, Walter, 105–6
Buber, Martin, 59

Caesar, Nero, 75
Cavanaugh, William T., 26, 28
class struggle, 90
Clement of Alexandria, 26–28, 33,
    127, 155
Charity, 26, 28–30, 41, 57, 60, 73, 100,
    112, 115, 121, 140–43, 150–52,
    156, 158, 163
commodity fetishism, 34
commodity theory of money, 10, 46,
    58, 62, 68
competition, 14, 23, 56, 63–64, 94,
    106, 147
consumption, 11, 48, 81, 93–94, 106,
    126–29, 133, 135–40, 149–51
credit, 10, 57–58, 62–69, 121, 141–42,
    158
creditor-debtor relationship, 66–67
creditworthiness, 65
cynicism, as a type of consciousness,
    34–35, 51

Dasein, 64
death, 25, 40, 46, 56, 64, 77, 81, 93, 95,
    103, 119, 142, 145, 147
death of God, 44–46
debt cancellation, 71
debt forgiveness, 24, 155, 159
Deleuze, Gilles, 7, 61
Derrida, Jacques, 58, 148–49
deterritorialization, 61

Index

differentiating wealth, 10, 56–57, 67, 69, 81–84, 93, 112, 120, 140, 147, 150, 162
division of labor, 111
drug addiction, 31

Eagleton, Terry, 1–2
Eden, garden of, 107, 110
Edelman, Lee, 112
empty gesture, 40–41
eschatology, 30, 132, 134
eternal life, 25, 33, 35–37, 42, 77, 82, 98, 113, 138, 142, 146
Eucharist, the, 144, 146
exchange-value, 48–49

fantasy, 40
Feuerbach, Ludwig, 50
Federici, Sylvia, 84–85
freeloader, Jesus as, 104
Freud, Sigmund, 115–16
Fink, Bruce, 60
forced choice, 39–40, 74, 81

general economy, 131–33, 147–49, 152
gift economies, 59–60, 107, 145, 147, 151, 157–58
gig economy, 92
Goodchild, Philip, 10, 18–20, 43–45, 47, 63–65, 68, 129
Google, 93
Gorz, Andre, 93–94
grace, 29, 31, 39, 109, 112, 127, 135, 140, 144–45
Graeber, David, 59, 85
greed, 15, 31, 37, 47, 147
Guattari, Felix, 7, 61
guilt, 67, 76, 128
Gulli, Bruno, 83

Hardt, Michael, 110–12
Harney, Stefano, 158
Heidegger, Martin, 64
Hénaff, Marcel, 19
Henry, Michel, 118, 120
Herzog, William, 100
heteronormativity, 111–12

homelessness, 96
hospitality 114, 140
housework, as unpaid labor, 84–85
Hudson, Michael, 70–71
hypocrisy, 35–37, 40, 73

ideology, 9, 34–35, 40, 96, 100, 106
idolatry, 34
indebted subject, 66–67
individualism, 61, 111, 145
inequality, 22, 48, 56–57, 69
Ingham, Geoffrey, 58–59, 62–67

John Paul II, 86–87
jouissance, 60, 116
Jubilee, year of, 70–73, 152, 159
Judas, 76–77, 95, 150
Judge, Mike, 91

Kingdom of God, 6, 25–26, 32–33, 35, 39, 82, 95, 98, 101, 113, 121, 132, 134, 143–44, 149, 152, 160, 162

Lacan, Jacques, 39–40, 115–16, 59–60
labor power, 84
LaFargue, Paul, 107
Last Supper, the, 144, 146
Lord's Prayer, the 155
Lazzarato, Maurizio, 66–68
le Goff, Jacques, 21–22
Leo XIII, 86

Manna, 137–38
Mardi Gras, 125
Marx, Karl, 2, 10, 47–51, 53–55, 57, 68, 88–91, 136, 152
Mauss, Marcel, 158
McGowan, Todd, 158
Milton, John, 16
Miranda, Jose P., 56–57, 74–76, 120
monasticism, 41, 61, 123–25, 140
money-form, 49
money of account, 58, 62–63, 67
Moses, 25, 35, 37, 127
Moten, Fred, 158, 160
Myles, Robert, 96

Negri, Antonio, 110–12

Index

neoliberalism, 54–55, 59, 66, 69
Nietzsche, Friedrich, 10, 44, 46, 122–23
nostalgia, 45, 135

Occupy Wallstreet, 159
Office Space, 91
Obama, Barack, 31

Paradise Lost, 16
Parasitism, 124, 140–41, 145, 147
Passover, 77, 79, 131
Paul, the apostle, 2–3, 5, 54, 74, 87, 95, 103–4, 117, 125, 134, 145, 158
Polanyi, Karl, 45
poll tax, in Roman Empire, 74
potlatch, 148
promise, in relation to money, 62–65
preferential option for the poor, 120
prophets, biblical, 25, 35, 37, 78
Protestant work ethic, 99

redistribution of wealth, 70, 150
reversal of values, 25, 56, 99, 123, 143
resurrection, 3, 25, 87, 135

sabbath, 69–70, 105–7, 138, 163
sacrifice, 75, 84, 94, 97, 109, 158
scarcity, myth of, 75, 84, 94, 97, 109, 147–50

Serres, Michel, 119, 124, 140–42, 145
sin, 21, 28–29, 78, 107, 127, 136
Singh, Devin, 156
Socrates, 19
soft asceticism, 128–29
Sophists, the, 19–20
Strike Debt, 159–60
surplus value, 84, 136
symbiosis, 145, 147

taxation, 67–68, 74
Thomas of Chobham, 22
Tillich, Paul, 31–32
trust, in relation to money, 58–59, 63, 65, 67, 143

ultimate concern, money as, 31–33, 53, 103
unemployment, 100
use-value, 20, 48–50
usury, 21–22

wage relationship, 83–86, 94, 98, 102
wage stagnation, 94
Weber, Max, 99

Zealots, the, 1
Žižek, Slavoj, 34–35, 40, 46, 51–52, 92, 127–28, 136

www.ingramcontent.com/pod-product-compliance
Lightning Source LLC
Chambersburg PA
CBHW020851160426
43192CB00007B/883